# GLOBAL PERSPECTIVES ON INCOME TAXATION LAW

GLOBAL PERSPECTIVES ON INCOME TAXATION LAW

# GLOBAL PERSPECTIVES ON INCOME TAXATION LAW

Reuven S. Avi-Yonah, Nicola Sartori,
and Omri Marian

OXFORD
UNIVERSITY PRESS

Oxford University Press, Inc., publishes works that further
Oxford University's objective of excellence
in research, scholarship, and education.

Oxford   New York

Auckland   Cape Town   Dar es Salaam   Hong Kong   Karachi
Kuala Lumpur   Madrid   Melbourne   Mexico City   Nairobi
New Delhi   Shanghai   Taipei   Toronto

With offices in
Argentina   Austria   Brazil   Chile   Czech Republic   France   Greece
Guatemala   Hungary   Italy   Japan   Poland   Portugal   Singapore
South Korea   Switzerland   Thailand   Turkey   Ukraine   Vietnam





Published by Oxford University Press, Inc.
198 Madison Avenue, New York, New York 10016
http://www.oup.com





**Library of Congress Cataloging-in-Publication Data**

Avi-Yonah, Reuven S. (Reuven Shlomo), 1957-
    Global perspectives on income taxation law / Reuven Avi-Yonah, Nicola Sartori,
Omri Marian.
        p. cm.
    Includes bibliographical references and index.
    ISBN 978-0-19-532136-4 (pbk. : alk. paper)
1.   Income tax—Law and legislation.
I. Sartori, Nicola. II. Marian, Omri. III. Title.
    K4505.A94 2011
    343.05'2—dc22        2010044231



Printing number: 9 8 7 6 5 4 3 2 1



Printed in the United States of America
on acid-free paper

Reuven
*—To Orli, my inspiration*

Omri
*—To Taly, Yonatan, and Alma*

Nicola
*—To my wife, Paola*

# Contents

# Preface

Herodotus 1.1: I, Herodotus of Halicarnassus, am here setting forth my history, that time may not draw the color from what man has brought into being, nor those great and wonderful deeds manifested by both Greeks and Barbarians fail of their report . . .

Thucydides 1.22: The absence of romance in my history will, I fear, detract somewhat from its interest; but if it be judged useful by those inquirers who desire an exact knowledge of the past as an aid to the interpretation of the future, which in the course of human things must resemble if it does not reflect it, I shall be content. In fine, I have written my work, not as an essay which is to win the applause of the moment, but as a possession for all time.

Comparative legal studies, like historical studies, have always been a battle ground between culturalists and functionalists. Culturalists take their inspiration from Herodotus: they focus on what is unique and distinctive about each (legal) culture, and value each one equally as different manifestations of the same shared humanity. Functionalists are inspired by Thucydides: they are interested in formulating general rules that will apply "for all time" and seek to emphasize commonalities and unifying themes.

It has been our good fortune to form a team in which one author has culturalist preferences, another is a confirmed functionalist, while the third can see the benefits of both approaches and is unable to decide which is better. The advantage for the student is that the book is written from both perspectives, and she is left free to make up her own mind.

Nevertheless, while all the three authors read and approved the whole book, for the sole purpose of giving appropriate credit to each author, it should be specified that Reuven Avi-Yonah coordinated and supervised the research work and wrote chapter 3. Chapter 2 was jointly written by Reuven Avi-Yonah and Omri Marian. Nicola Sartori wrote chapters 4, 5, 6 and 7. Omri Marian wrote chapters 1 (except for the discussion in comparative economics, which was written by Nicola Sartori) and 8. Chapter 9 was jointly written by Reuven Avi-Yonah and Nicola Sartori. Every author is fully responsible for the whole book.

Challenge: with this information, after reading the book, can you guess who among the authors is the culturalist, who is the functionalist, and who is the ambivalent one?

We would like to thank the many colleagues and students who helped with the book. Kyle Logue and Jim Hines provided helpful comments in the early stages, as well as research assistance. Special thanks are due to Yossi Edrey, Ehab Farah and Victor Thuronyi for reviewing the entire manuscript. Michael Mendelevich, Tianlong Hu and Karen Sheppard helped with information relating to Russia, China, India and Brazil. Pushpa Giri at Oxford University Press provided invaluable editorial support.

# Foreword

During the last two decades, comparative law has experienced an impressive revival in the wake of the globalization processes triggered by the end of the cold war, especially in Europe and the United States. At the same time, comparative tax law has begun to develop into a sub-discipline in its own right, albeit a small and highly specialized one. A growing number of books and articles by various authors have created an increasingly substantial literature in this field. None of these works, however, are designed for student consumption. The present book fills this gap.

It thus fits the recent salutary trend to produce teaching materials that introduce comparative and international perspectives into core domestic law courses. These materials proffer the traditionally recognized benefits of comparative law: a broader perspective on law, a critical look from the outside back at one's own legal system, an understanding of the historical and social contingency of law, recognition of convergence of laws, tolerance for remaining differences, etc.

The present book, however, pursues an additional and more specific goal: it provides comparative material in order to add value to what the students learn. In particular, it makes students look beyond their own domestic tax rules to have them focus on the underlying policy issues and the alternative options to resolve them. This pedagogy pays off in two ways. First, it extends the shelf-life of student knowledge. Tax rules are so fast-changing that studying them in and of themselves makes little sense—mastering them today may mean little tomorrow; the underlying policy issues and the options to resolve them, however, endure, at least in the medium term. Second, mastery of domestic rules alone is of little help when tax questions transcend national boundaries, as they increasingly do.

By contrast, understanding the fundamental policy concerns facilitates access to foreign tax regimes because other jurisdictions often face the same problems, although they will often respond to them differently. There is a broader message in this approach: the faster law changes, and the more legal work turns transnational, the less sense it makes for teaching to focus on domestic legal rules as such. Tax law is just an extreme example of this phenomenon and many, if not most, other areas of law, are closely on its heels in these regards.

The team of authors for the present volume in Oxford's *Global Perspectives* series is ideally situated for this project because of its internationality and diversity. The authors hail not only from different countries, they are also steeped in a common law (United States), civil law (Italy), and mixed (Israel) legal culture, and while they are focusing mainly on Western jurisdictions, they do look to other parts of the world as well, especially to China, Japan, and Russia. They also pursue different approaches to comparative studies with some leaning more in the direction of functionalism and economic analysis, others feeling more grounded in a cultural or critical approach. The result of their cooperation is a book broad in scope and rich in viewpoints.

Mathias Reimann
Professor of Law,
University of Michigan Law School
Editor-in-Chief,
*American Journal of Comparative Law*

# Introduction

## I. WHAT IS THIS BOOK ABOUT?

The idea of this book is rather straightforward. It is intended to cover
the standard topics taught in a basic income tax course from a comparative perspective. It does not seek to explore in depth any particular
country's approach to income taxation.

Instead, the book will follow the usual order of topics covered in a
typical basic tax course as taught in most U.S. law schools, and for each
topic, it will highlight possible alternatives or policy choices. The book
will frequently consider the U.S. approach as a benchmark and compare it with approaches used in other countries that form an interesting
contrast (or a telling similarity).

Admittedly, and even without the additional burden of a comparative perspective, tax classes are probably amongst the least (if not *the*
least) popular classes in the eyes of law students in both American and
European law schools.

This is hardly surprising because taxation is usually not as self-
explanatory and logically grasped as other fields of law. Rather, at least
at first glance, tax is an overly complex and highly technical field, which
is controlled by its own unique legal language. It is sometimes difficult
to understand, always demanding, and occasionally boring.

If this were not enough, along comes this book to burden tax law students with comparative tax issues. It is hard enough for any student to
master the local tax materials in her tax classes—why should she trouble
herself with comparative tax materials that are not, by any means, less
difficult? This introduction is aimed at answering this question.

## II. WHY SHOULD WE CARE ABOUT COMPARATIVE TAXATION?

Comparative tax studies can probably serve multiple purposes. Many
commentators have suggested comparative taxation as an instrument
to advance, inter alia, successful tax reforms,[1] cultural understanding,[2]

---

[1] *See* e.g., Victor Thuronyi, Tax Law Design and Drafting (International
Monetary Fund 1996); Victor Thuronyi, Tax Law Design and Drafting
(International Monetary Fund 1998); Victor Thuronyi, Comparative Tax
Law (Kluwer 2003).

[2] *See,* e.g., Michael A. Livingston, *Law, Culture, and Anthropology: On the Hopes
and Limits of Comparative Taxation*, 18 Can. J. L. & Jurisprudence 119 (2005);

democratic values,[3] legal harmonization,[4] and a better understanding of domestic tax laws.

We could have easily filled the coming pages with the usual clichés about the necessity of studying foreign legal materials in our very globalized world, where the laws of multiple jurisdictions frequently interact, and legal ideas freely flow across national and, sometimes, cultural boundaries. As much as these clichés are true, they have probably become a matter of common knowledge by now, and there is little sense of repeating them here.[5]

We do, however, want to suggest some points to consider, which we believe make the comparative study of taxation unique in this regard and even more specifically so in the context of tax teaching.

First, unlike many other areas of law—where comparative perspectives have become ingrained both in scholarship and in academic teaching—most law schools in the world have yet to adopt any meaningful comparative perspective in their core tax colloquia.

The first person to address the desirability of adopting a comparative perspective for tax teaching in American law schools was John Chommie, who recommended, as early as 1957, adding comparative tax seminars to law school colloquia.[6] Since then, unique seminars and elective courses in comparative taxation have indeed dotted law schools' syllabi throughout the country. Nevertheless, core tax classes remain strictly inward looking. Due to the unique nature of tax law, this situation might seriously cripple students. The "inward-looking approach" that currently dominates tax education prevents its subjects (the students) from getting a grasp of alternative policy choices, which may have been adopted elsewhere and are frequently considered in the context of contemplated reforms in the United States (or elsewhere).

What we are essentially offering here is a general approach to comparative tax studies that goes beyond the view of comparative taxation as an autonomous field of legal studies. We realize, of course, the

---

Michael A. Livingston, *From Milan to Mumbai, Changing in Tel-Aviv: Reflections of Progressive Taxation and "Progressive" Politics in a Globalized but Still Local World*, 54 Am. J. Comp. L. 555 (2006).

[3] William Barker, *Expanding the Study of Comparative Tax Law to Promote Democratic Policy: The Example of the Move to Capital Gains Taxation in Post-Apartheid South Africa*, 109 Penn. St. L. Rev. 703 (2005).

[4] Carlo Garbarino, *An Evolutionary and Structural Approach to Comparative Taxation: Methods and Agenda for Research*, 57 Am. J. Comp. L. 677 (2009).

[5] Others had already done so, and we could not possibly do any better job than they did. For a pioneering work on tax and globalization, *see* Vito Tanzi, Taxation in an Integrating World (The Brookings Institution 1995).

[6] John C. Chommie, *A Proposed Seminar in Comparative Taxation*, 9 J. Legal Educ. 502 (1957).

importance of courses and research specifically dedicated to a comparative perspective.

Our (admittedly not original)[7] suggestion is to use a comparative approach to complement core tax colloquia. In this sense, we believe that it is more useful to read this book one chapter at a time, rather than sweep through it. It is intended that the student will turn to each relevant chapter of this book once she has concluded the study of the respective chapter in her basic tax class. We hope that such an approach will stimulate students to question possible alternatives to the routinely taught domestic perspective, and in the process, sharpen their understanding of the rationale of domestic tax policy.

These issues are of real importance, first and foremost, because one of the defining characteristics of tax laws is that they are constantly changing at an amazingly rapid pace. For example, in the United States alone, the entire tax code (I.R.C.) was completely revamped twice over the past 60 years (in 1954 and in 1986), and major reforms in specific areas take place on an almost yearly basis (some important examples include reforms in the areas of partnership taxation, business entities classification, taxation of financial derivatives, and the tax treatment of passive investment losses). Other countries surveyed in this book have also been subject to a wave of major tax reforms starting in the early 1980s and lasting through this very day. In fact, after the drafting of this book has already been completed, and during the editing process, several major reforms in United States tax law have completely reshaped major areas of the federal tax environment. Most notably, in March 2010, President Barak Obama signed into law the Patient Protection and Affordable Care Act, which included some far reaching tax reforms, such as the implementation of 3.8% federal "health tax", imposition of special tax on "excess benefits" for employer-sponsored health plans, the codification of the economic-substance doctrine and many other important changes. Only a few days earlier, the Hiring Incentives to Restore Employment Act was also signed into law. This act introduced a new set of comprehensive reporting requirements applicable to financial institutions doing business in the United States, and subjected U.S. persons with foreign financial assets to an equally elaborate set of reporting requirements.

The readers will have to excuse us for failing to include (and discuss) some of these new legislations. But given the unique nature of tax law

---

[7] *See* Mathias Reimann, *The End of Comparative Law as an Autonomous Subject,* 11 Tul. Eur. & Civ. L. F. 49 (1996); Hugh J. Ault and Mary Ann Glendon, *The Importance of Comparative Law in Legal Education: United States Goals and Methods of Legal Comparison,* 27 J. Legal Educ. 599 (1975).

being subject to rapid changes, no tax book would ever be complete if the authors had to wait for tax law to take concrete shape.

When this is the case, there is little sense in studying tax rules in a strictly local approach. Much of the law might become substantially less relevant by the student's graduation time. Policy choices, however, always remain in the background and are always relevant. Unlike areas of private law such as torts and contracts, where common principles have a long-established history in our legal system (and thus are unlikely to dramatically change), tax law is a new creation that is still in its experimental phase. In other words, the comparative study of tax law is not strictly theoretically oriented, as may be the case in other "policy" classes. Rather, it is a study of what may indeed become a reality in the foreseeable future.

To summarize this point, there is much benefit in studying tax policy because it will constantly and inevitably remain relevant. The actual tax laws, on the other hand, are short lived. Tax policy is best understood through researching its implementation in practice. Because there is only so much policy being "implemented" locally at any given time, we must look elsewhere.

Second, the research of alternative policy choices in other countries can facilitate the understanding of one's own local policy considerations. A current example may help to illustrate this point. Any American student graduating from a basic tax class might believe that the granting of generous deductions for health-care expenses is an obvious policy choice, not realizing that the United States is probably the only country in the world awarding its citizens with such a generous deducting scheme. These deductions and their relationship to the recently enacted health-care reform legislation can be better understood by examining the interrelations between health-care tax subsidies and state-supported health-care systems (or the lack thereof) abroad. American and European tax students are not inclined (and were probably never encouraged during their basic tax classes) to look for alternative tax policy choices that may be available, tested, and proven (or disproven) in other tax jurisdictions.[8]

When comparing two significantly different policy choices, the underlying cultural or political differences of the countries at stake emerge. This may allow us to understand why despite them being inherently conflicting; they can both be regarded as correct policy choices. This can also help us in understanding how policy choices

---

[8] For an analysis of the interrelations between the tax system and healthcare see, Amy Monahan, *The Complex Relationship between Taxes and Health Insurance* (January 4, 2010). Minnesota Legal Studies Research Paper No. 10-01. Available at SSRN: http://ssrn.com/abstract=1531322 ; Leonard E. Burman et al., Tax Incentives for Health Insurance (The Urban Institute 2003).

similar in nature can nevertheless operate differently. Or, this can expose how things that appear to be different in theory or in form are almost identical in practice and substance.

In essence, examining comparative policy choices is necessary not only to reveal the weaknesses of any local tax system but also to understand its areas of strength. The idea is that by looking at other tax solutions (which may or may not differ from those adopted in the local jurisdiction under consideration and which may or may not been successful), we can reflect efficiently on and better understand our own tax system. We hope that by using such comparisons, a tax student who is unfamiliar with foreign tax systems will nevertheless be able to uncover some hidden possibilities and will be encouraged to question some of the premises underlying domestic tax policy.

Third, turning back to the usual clichés, an outward-looking approach is also practically unavoidable in the current environment of tax practice. Tax, by its very nature, is an international field of practice. We doubt that any future lawyer working in the tax group of any leading law firm will find herself dealing exclusively with domestic tax issues. We truly believe that in today's environment, a student graduating from law school with the intent of becoming a tax lawyer should, at the minimum, understand some basic notions of foreign taxation.

Of course, we do not intend to transform the readers of this book into foreign tax experts. Rather, our intention is to give the prospective tax attorney some basic concepts that are frequently used in actual tax practice but only seldom used in core tax classes. For example, terms such as "GmbH" or "S.a.r.l" are unlikely to be mentioned in an individual tax class at a U.S. law school but would probably be addressed almost daily in any tax group of an American firm with American clients doing business Europe.

1

# Some Theoretical Aspects of "Comparative Taxation"

## I. WHAT IS COMPARATIVE TAXATION?

As surprising as it may seem, even amid voluminous scholarly writings in comparative tax law, tax comparatists usually neglect to define what it is, exactly, they deal with. We have no intention of launching such a scholarly effort here (and this is certainly not the main purpose of this book), but we would like to suggest two possible answers to the question presented in the subtitle above.

Possibly and obviously, "comparative taxation" could be seen as a form of scholarly method of research and teaching. To assert such an argument is also to argue that whatever this method is, it holds its own unique characteristics, processes, techniques, and modes of evaluation. We cautiously assert that to date, no such method can be identified. Rather, legal tax comparatists have usually adopted well-defined comparative methods that are used in general comparative legal studies. Given the wide array of methods available for legal comparison (some of which are briefly surveyed below); there is probably no need to invent a unique method of comparing tax rules.

But "comparative taxation" can also represent a unique body on knowledge. However, this is not immediately apparent. To explain this assertion, we must start by pointing to the obvious: any process of tax comparison will involve, at some point, the juxtaposition of tax laws of several jurisdictions. However, the mere juxtaposition is not, by itself, "new knowledge." Simply looking at the tax treatment of punitive damage awards in the **United States** and in **Germany,** for example, and noting the similarities or differences between them does not tell us a whole lot. These tax laws are already "there." By "comparative tax knowledge," we mean, rather, the new insights and conclusions that can only be reached by way of comparison. An example may illustrate this point.

In a book titled *Tax Law Design and Drafting*, Victor Thuronyi pioneered what may be referred to as the taxonomy of legal "tax families."[1]

---

[1] Victor Thuronyi, Tax Law Design and Drafting, xxiii–xxxv (International Monetary Fund 1996 ); Victor Thuronyi, Tax Law Design and Drafting (International Monetary Fund 1998 ) ; Victor Thuronyi, Comparative Tax Law, 23–44 (Kluwer 2003).

Even though the classification of legal families is a long-established concept in general comparative law, such a comprehensive classification was new to tax laws when introduced by Thuronyi. According to Thuronyi, such classification plays an important role, as it provides "assistance to those seeking to understand the tax law of different countries, whether for the purpose of comparative study or as part of tax practice."[2] Specifically, such a classification is most helpful in generating "relevant questions."[3] The concept of classification is regarded by its proponents as an essential part of the process of comparison,[4] as it suggests which jurisdiction might be "successfully compared" with others. Of course, any such typology may be criticized or completely rejected. But it is obvious that such typology could not have been produced without the comparison of multiple tax jurisdictions and hence certainly qualifies as "comparative tax knowledge." In other words, it is an insight that could not have been achieved absent the process of comparing tax rules.

In the following text, we will try to attach this meaning to the term "comparative taxation."


## II. SOME POSSIBLE APPROACHES TO THE STUDY OF COMPARATIVE TAX LAW


One of the main problems with the comparative study of law is that there are probably as many approaches to it as there are comparative scholars. Although over the past three decades or so, legal comparatists have fiercely debated what approaches should be deemed appropriate when conducting a comparative study of law, they have failed to produce any coherent outcome.[5] This is not surprising, since this academic discussion is strictly embedded in the ideological and political stances of its participants. Since ideologies are many times irreconcilable, the same fate may apply to the methodological offshoots of such ideologies.

Some legal comparatists did try to sketch a so-called objective blueprint for comparative research. Professor W. J. Kamba, for example, portrayed legal comparison as a three-phase process.[6] The first phase is the *descriptive phase*, in which the comparatist is expected to describe

---

[2] THURNOYI, COMPARATIVE TAX LAW, *supra* note 1, at 23–24.

[3] *Id.* at 8.

[4] John C. Reitz, *How to Do Comparative Law*, 46 AM. J. COMP. L. 617, 622 (1998).

[5] *See, e.g.,* Mathias Reimann, *The Progress and Failure of Comparative Law in the Second Half of the Twentieth Century*, 50 AM. J. COMP. L. 671 (2002).

[6] Walter J. Kamba, *Comparative Law: A Theoretical Framework*, 23 INT'L COMP. L.Q. 485 (1974).

the "*norms, concepts and institutions of the systems concerned.*"[7] The second phase is the *identification phase,* in which the researcher indentifies the differences and similarities among the systems studied. The third phase is the *explanatory phase,* in which the reasons for convergences and divergences are explained. However, even if we accept such a generalized scheme, it is obvious that once executed, it must be filled with some real contents. One must choose which jurisdictions to compare, what laws to compare, which legal and nonlegal texts to read, and so on. In other words, we are thrown back into the realm of subjective choices, which, by definition, are ideologically affected.

Obviously then, we cannot possibly point to a single approach that can be regarded as superior to others. Indeed, given that these approaches represent different ideological views, we would probably not be able to reach an agreement among ourselves as to the most promising method of comparative tax research. Hence, any reader of this book would clearly identify some shifts in the focal points of the discussion, a result of our theoretical agreements and disagreements. Thus, a shift from a functional discussion to a discussion in comparative economics, with side trips to cultural comparativism, should be viewed as an invitation to consider multiple possibilities of analysis, rather than to suggest a "proper" one in each case.

However, this unsolved debate did successfully emphasize the pivotal points of ideological differences. Some "schools of thought" can be clearly identified, each of which has its own basic assumptions and purposes and each of which has its own idea as to how comparison should be executed. In this respect, the key debates revolve around three basic questions: the first is the purpose of comparative legal studies; the second is the objects of comparatives studies, namely which jurisdictions and which laws should be compared; and the third addresses the techniques of actual comparison. The intent here is not to overburden the reader with theoretical aspects of research but rather to briefly survey some of the possible ways by which one might approach a comparative study in the context of tax laws.[8]

Unavoidably, such a short summary tends to generalize and ignores some important nuances. Hence, it does not by any means intend to prescribe in details any technique that should be followed when conducting a comparative study in tax law. But it can still clearly illustrate where the key ideological (and consequently methodological) differences lie. These approaches can thus serve as "ideological rallying points" from which a comparative debate can be launched. We will survey four possible approaches to the comparative study of

---

[7] *Id.* at 511.

[8] For a more elaborative survey, *see* Omri Y. Marian, *The Discursive Failure in Comparative Tax Law,* 58 Am. J. Comp. L. 415 (2010).

tax law: functional, cultural, critical, and economical. It is important to note that each of the approaches described below is full of sub-schools and inner conflicts. Also, none of the scholars mentioned can be purely regarded as adopting a particular approach. Most tax comparatists embody in their writings assumptions and arguments that absorb their vitality from multiple methods and from various traditions. Thus, the reader is encouraged to consider these views openly, rather than completely embrace or reject any of them.

## A. The functional approach to comparative tax studies

The functional approach to comparative law has a long-established tradition and is probably the most widely adopted. Comparative legal functionalism rests on the assumption that "the legal system of every society faces essentially the same problems, and solves these problems by quite different means, though very often with similar results."[9] In other words, functionalists see the convergence of legal systems as an inevitable and desirable phenomenon. If legal problems and legal outcomes are the same, unifying the laws (the means to solve these similar problems and to reach the similar outcomes) would save a lot of headache. In their view, legal terminological heterogeneity is only a façade that covers the real similarities that may be unobservable at a first glance. A tax comparatist's job would be to uncover these similarities in the context of tax laws.

The premises of functionalism, as well as the view that tax laws are converging, are widely adopted among international and comparative tax scholars. Such commentators repeatedly point out the remarkable degree of similarity in the tax laws of different jurisdictions, which have started quite far apart.[10] More importantly, a comparative tax functionalist would typically see convergence not only as an easily observed phenomenon but also as a desirable process from a normative perspective. In the functionalist view, there is little sense in adopting different legal rules that are aimed at dealing with similar social problems and to achieve similar results. Thus, when tax functionalists execute their comparative research, they might do so with the purpose of the *harmonization* of tax laws in mind.

---

[9] KONRAD ZWEIGERT & HEIN KOTZ, AN INTRODUCTION TO COMPARATIVE LAW 34 (Oxford University Press 3d ed. 1998).

[10] *See, e.g.,* Carlo Garbarino, An Evolutionary and Structural Approach to Comparative Taxation: Methods and Agenda for Research , 57 AM. J. COMP. L. 677 (2009). REUVEN AVI-YONAH, INTERNATIONAL TAX AS INTERNATIONAL LAW: AN ANALYSIS OF THE INTERNATIONAL TAX REGIME (Cambridge University Press 2007); Yariv Brauner, *An International Tax Regime in Crystallization,* 56 TAX L. REV. 259 (2003).

Garbarino's functionalist approach is a good example.[11] He refers to the European Common Consolidated Corporate Tax Base Project (CCCTB), among others. In 2001, the European Commission "identified corporate taxation across the European Union as one major obstacle to the achievement of a common market."[12] To address this problem, the European Commission launched a project with the aim of mitigating this obstacle by eliminating, as efficiently as possible, double taxation of European corporate groups doing business in multi-European jurisdictions. One of the possible approaches for such a project is to apply an all-European comprehensive solution. Indeed, by late 2004, a CCCTB working group began discussions with the prospects of replacing "national tax systems by a common tax base."[13] Garbarino specifically uses the CCCTB example of comparative tax research to show that through a comparative study of tax laws, we can "reveal the existence of an EU common model of tax consolidation on which agreement can be reached through reinforced cooperation at EU level."[14] In other words, such research should bring about tax harmonization.

Such a purpose would have significant implications for choosing which jurisdictions and tax laws to compare. Since functionalists are looking at "similar" social problems, they only compare things that are indeed "comparable." This means comparing jurisdictions which are "at the same evolutionary stage"[15] and are thus likely to face similar social problems. In addition, in order for the comparative process to be effective, one must also compare those tax laws and institutions which essentially fulfill the same social functions.

Assuming that a tax comparatist adopts such an approach, the tax family classification discussed above becomes an essential tool in selecting the objects of comparison. This is so since classification provides us with an a priori template of "comparable" jurisdictions and "comparable" rules. For example, Thuronyi's classification leads him to suggest a "rule of thumb" for the selection of jurisdictions that are "representatives" of a larger family or tradition. He suggests **Germany, France**, the **United States,** and the **United Kingdom** as natural choices of tax comparison.[16] According to Thuronyi, these countries can be regarded as "leaders in influencing the tax laws of other countries."[17]

---

[11]  *See* Garbarino, *id.*

[12]  Michael Lang et. al., *Preface, in* Common Consolidated Corporate Tax Base 5, 5 (Michael Lang et. al. eds., 2008).

[13]  Michel Aujean, *The CCCTB Project and the Future of European Taxation, in* Common Consolidated Corporate Tax Base 11, 32 (Michael Lang et. al. eds., 2008).

[14]  Garbarino, *supra* note 10, at 709.

[15]  Clive M. Schmitthoff, *The Science of Comparative Law*, 7 Cambridge L.J. 94, 96 (1941).

[16]  Thuronyi, Comparative Tax Law, *supra* note 1, at 9.

[17]  *Id.*

The functionalist premises suggest that a comparative legal researcher should start by identifying a particular practical problem and question the way in which it is solved in each of the jurisdictions compared (the "problem-solving approach").

Another possible way to address such assumptions is to take an institutional view, namely, to ask which institutions in the countries compared perform the same problem-solving functions ("the institutional approach"). Two comparative methods are worth mentioning here.

The first is the comparison of legal transplants. According to this approach, most legal systems are built upon the borrowing of legal models of other systems. In that sense, transplantation is the main source of legal development and evolution.[18] In the tax context, Garbarino argued that the "pervasiveness of tax transplants challenges the idea that tax law is exclusively a local response to social demands felt by a specific national community."[19] In other words, an effective comparative tax study might be conducted by identifying the tax rules that successfully circulate among various jurisdictions and are being similarly implemented.

A derivative of the transplants approach is the "common core" approach to comparative research. Given that legal rules are borrowed and re-borrowed in the multinational context, it is not unreasonable to assume that models that successfully address common problems will survive, while those unable to do so will disappear. Over time, this may create a "common core" of tax rules that may be shared by many jurisdictions. Comparative tax researchers are sometimes specifically aiming at exposing this core.

A good example for a common core-style project in the tax arena can be found in the book that is regarded as canonic by many, authored by Hugh Ault and Brian Arnold.[20] Their book states its functional orientation at the outset by saying that "the purpose of this book is to compare different solutions adopted by nine industrialized countries to common problems of income tax design."[21] Ault and Arnold approached local specialists in many jurisdictions, who were requested to provide accounts of their home tax systems. Ault and Arnold later synthesized the country reports into a form of general analysis that categorizes the findings into an easily read classification. Their work is primarily oriented to reveal the "many communalities"[22] among the systems compared, thus providing us with a form of tax common core.

---

[18] ALAN WATSON, LEGAL TRANSPLANTS: AN APPROACH TO COMPARATIVE LAW (1974).

[19] Garbarino, *supra* note 10, at 696.

[20] HUGH J. AULT & BRIAN J. ARNOLD, COMPARATIVE INCOME TAXATION: A STRUCTURAL ANALYSIS (University Press of Virginia 2004).

[21] *Id.* at xix.

[22] Miranda Stewart, *The "Aha" Experience: Comparative Income Tax Systems*, 19 TAX NOTES INT'L 1323, 1327 (1999).

## B. Comparative tax law as a study of cultural differences

Cultural comparatists reject the functional assumptions of similarities of social problems and legal solutions. Rather, cultural comparatists assume that law is part of a broader cultural phenomenon. Each culture contains elements such as values, traditions, and beliefs, which give each culture its uniqueness. This "differentiation of cultures" entails, according to such an approach, that the laws (which are embedded in these cultures) are also necessarily different.[23] Thus, it is not surprising that cultural comparatists also reject harmonization projects, since they call—by definition—for the annulment of cultural identity as expressed in the unique laws of a given society. Writings in comparative legal culture have long celebrated (or urged that we should celebrate) the virtue of "difference," since difference "satisfies the need for self-transcendence."[24] Even if harmonization was somehow desirable, cultural comparatists perceive it as an unattainable goal, since cultural and political differences are irreconcilable.[25]

Rather, according to this approach, comparative analysis should be aimed at *understanding* the cultural; social; political; and ultimately, the legal identities of "the other." In turn, such "understanding" should serve us better when reflecting on our own legal rules and cultural identity. In a sense, cultural comparison is a hermeneutic process; a culture cannot successfully reflect on its own law without the process of comparison and cannot reflect on the process of comparison without questioning its own law.

Such a cultural "difference-oriented" stance is clearly visible in the writings of several comparative tax commentators.[26] Michael Livingston, for example, defines "tax culture" as "the body of beliefs and practices that are shared by tax practitioners and policy makers in a given society and thus provide the background or context in which

---

[23] *See* Roger Cotterrell, *Comparative Law and Legal Culture, in* THE OXFORD HANDBOOK OF COMPARATIVE LAW 709 (Mathias Reimann & Reinhard Zimmerman eds., 2006).

[24] Pierre Legrand, *The Same and the Different, in* COMPARATIVE LEGAL STUDIES: TRADITIONS AND TRANSITIONS 240, 280 (Pierre Legrand & Roderick Munday eds., 2003).

[25] Pierre Legrand, *European Legal Systems Are Not Converging*, 45 Int'l & Comp. L.Q. 52, 61–62 (1996); Julie Roin, *Taxation without Coordination*, 31 J. LEGAL STUD. 61 (2002) (In the tax context).

[26] *See, e.g.*, Michael A. Livingston, *Law, Culture, and Anthropology: On the Hopes and Limits of Comparative Taxation*, 18 CAN. J. L. & JURISPRUDENCE 119 (2005); Michael A. Livingston, *From Milan to Mumbai, Changing in Tel-Aviv: Reflections of Progressive Taxation and "Progressive" Politics in a Globalized but Still Local World*, 54 AM. J. COMP. L. 555 (2006); ANN MUMFORD, TAXING CULTURE: TOWARDS A THEORY OF TAX COLLECTION LAW 1 (Ashgate 2002); Assaf Likhovski, *The Duke and the Lady: Helvering V. Gregory and the History of Tax Avoidance Adjudication*, 25 CARDOZO L. REV. 953 (2004).

substantive tax decisions are made."[27] The comparison of such cultures is specifically useful when comparing jurisdictions that are different in their social and cultural background, thus exposing themes of taxation that are affected by local considerations even amid globalization.

On the other hand, it is also helpful to examine arguably "similar" jurisdictions, particularly to show that any similarity might be a superficial one and that the underlying cultural traditions, which are by definition different, significantly affect the execution of such so-called "similar" policy choices, even when the jurisdictions compared face similar problems.

According to the same logic, cultural tax comparatists would probably be very careful in asserting that legal transplantation points to a process of convergence. Rather, the assumption here would be that as the borrowed rule crosses the national border, it undergoes a significant modification that is intended to assure its acceptance in its new local environment.[28] Such alteration might be so heavily influenced by local considerations that the ultimate outcome is a completely different animal than the original rule. Thus, two rules that originated in the same place and tradition will produce two completely different outcomes, even though their titles may still remain similar. For example, Assaf Likhovsky studied the transplantation of British income tax laws in Mandatory Palestine and concluded that in order to survive the transplantation, the original tax rules had to be significantly altered so as to take into account the unique multicultural society of Mandatory Palestine.[29]

Similarly, cultural tax comparatists would probably have a hard time accepting the idea that there is such thing as "common core" tax principles. Rather, their idea is to identify "tax cultures" and by doing so, point to *real differences* in policy choices. It is not exactly clear how one should approach this process of defining tax cultures, but some ideas have been brought forward in this respect. For example, according to Livingston, a tax comparatist must assume a priori that tax cultures are different. He also notes that tax culture does not necessarily correlate with a society's general culture.[30] It is certainly possible, according to Livingston, that political or sociological culture would favor different or even contradicting values to those advanced by the tax culture. Livingston also asserts that narrow and localized factors play a more important role than "broad cultural norms which are often subject to misleading or over stated stereotypes."[31] These arguments

---

[27] *See* Michael A. Livingston, *From Milan to Mumbai, supra* note 26, at 560.

[28] *See, e.g.,* Anthony C. Infanti, *The Ethics of Tax Cloning,* 6 FLA. TAX. REV. 251 (2003); Mark D. West, *The Puzzling Divergence of Corporate Law: Evidence and Explanations from Japan and The United States,* 150 U. PA. L. REV. 527 (2001).

[29] Assaf Likhovski, *Is Tax Law Culturally Specific? Lessons from the History of Income Tax Law in Mandatory Palestine,* 11 THEORETICAL INQ. L. 725 (2010).

[30] *See* Livingston, *The Hopes and Limits of Comparative Taxation, supra* note 26.

[31] *Id.* at 132.

suggest that tax cultures are best understood as a general category from which narrow indicators can be subsumed and easily compared. Such indicators might be the education and training of tax elites; the relationship between lawyers, economists, and other tax professionals; the nature of tax administration; the attitudes toward tax compliance and evasion; and the unwritten traditions that govern the making and implementation of tax policy in the country in question.[32]

## C. The critical approach to comparative tax studies

At the most general level, critical studies in comparative law are aimed at exposing the pretentious apolitical nature of so-called mainstream discourse in comparative law and to suggest alternative discursive agendas. Critical scholars of comparative law often see mainstream comparative law as a hegemonial-ideological project aimed at either assimilation or inclusion of other traditions, a process culminating in projects of harmonization.[33] Such scholars argue that comparative legal studies should be a "liberating project," releasing us from the cognitive cage of abstract relativist dichotomies (such as common law/civil law, Western/Oriental, self/other), which are wrongly perceived to be "objective."[34]

In the tax arena, critical comparisons can be easily associated with Infanti. For example, Infanti explains his choice of comparative tax studies as a tool of tax reform by noting that "[t]he ensuing debate over how to reform the ailing U.S. international tax regime has largely been shaped by the traditional concerns of efficiency, fairness, and simplicity."[35] He further notes that "[t]he traditional focus on these concerns may stem from the fact that they lend themselves to the theoretical analysis preferred by commentators."[36] Professor Anthony Infanti suggests that tax reform debates should shift their perspective. He believes that placing the reform debate in a comparative perspective is needed in order to liberate current discussion from its own "parochial" view.[37] By doing so, Infanti expresses a true critical stand, aiming at exposing the true nature of current "mainstream" tax policy debate and to suggest an alternative agenda.

---

[32] *See* Livingston, *From Milan to Mumbai, supra* note 26, at 557.

[33] Anne Peters & Heiner Schwenke, *Comparative Law Beyond Post Modernism,* 49 INT'L & COMP. L. Q. 800, 822–24 (2000).

[34] Gunter Frankenberg, *Critical Comparisons: Re-thinking Comparative Law,* 26 HARV. INT'L. L.J. 411, 444–45 (1985).

[35] Anthony C. Infanti, *Spontaneous Tax Coordination: On Adopting a Comparative Approach to Reforming the U.S. International Tax Regime,* 35 VAND. J. TRANSNAT'L L. 1105, 1113 (2002).

[36] *Id.* at 1119.

[37] *Id.* at 1119–20.

To do so, one must step out of the usual choices of objects and jurisdictions to compare. One must specifically "free herself" from the commonly selected issues of tax comparison in order to expose what the common paradigmatic discourse prefers to avoid. Indeed, Infanti explained his choice to compare the tax treatment of contributions made by domestic taxpayers to foreign nonprofit organizations for its marginality, specifically "because it was not a topic about which academics studying international tax normally write."[38] Part of his purpose in doing so, he continues, "was to try to move the international tax discourse beyond the usual subjects."[39]

Frankenberg portrays the actual process of critical legal comparison as a three-stage process.[40] Critical study should start, according to Frankenberg, where other studies end: the conceptualization of complicated social phenomena into abstract terms, which can be easily fitted with a legal framework. Then, the critical comparative scholar is asked to deconstruct the process of legal decision making, questioning, and exposing the political interests underlying the process. Once we are in clear view of the abstract "objective" legal framework on the one hand, and the underlying political interests on the other, the third step is to reintroduce the legal process, showing how its discourse "ignores, marginalizes or transforms."[41] Namely, the third step shows how interests shape legal understanding and create the abstract concepts with which we started.

## D. Comparative tax study as an exercise in economic analysis

Comparative Law and Economics (CLE) is sometime categorized as an approach of its own right, but it may also be viewed as an offshoot of functionalism, taking a more self-aware ideological turn: efficiency.[42] Instead of simply asking which laws or institutions fulfill which functions, it asks which do so in the most efficient way.

CLE starts with an assumption that "there is a competitive market for the supply of law."[43] Legal transplants, from an economic point of view, are actually a competitive circulation of legal models, a process in

---

[38] Anthony C. Infanti, *A Tax Crit Identity Crisis? Or Tax Expenditure Analysis, Deconstruction, and the Rethinking of a Collective Identity*, 25 WHITTIER L. REV. 707, 796 (2005).

[39] *Id.* at 796–97.

[40] Gunter Frankenberg, *Critical Comparisons: Re-thinking Comparative Law*, 26 HARV. INT'L. L. J. 411, 450–52 (1985).

[41] *Id.* at 452.

[42] *See* UGO MATTEI, COMPARATIVE LAW AND ECONOMICS (Michigan University Press 1997).

[43] Raffaele Caterina, *Comparative Law and Economics*, *in* ELGAR ENCYCLOPEDIA OF COMPARATIVE LAW 161 (Jan M. Smits ed., 2006).

which only successful (or efficient) models survive, hence leading to convergence.[44]

From a methodological point of view, CLE "seeks to begin the comparison from a 'neutral scale' that can be validated by observable data: economic efficiency."[45] In essence, CLE research is aimed at comparative inquires into the deviations of different jurisdiction from an economically efficient benchmark: a so-called "model legal institution."[46] From that perspective, CLE can be either "problem-solving oriented"[47] (asking how we can solve a common problem in the most efficient way) or "institutional oriented" (asking which existing institution is the most efficient).

At least one legal tax comparatist adopted a similar approach. Barker asserted that a comparative tax analysis should seek to measure how tax systems deviate from a well-known benchmark: the Haig-Simons model.[48] Under Barker's approach, this model has to be used as a reference point for the identification of similarities and differences among tax systems.

Yet, unlike the traditional approach to law and economics, Barker sees comparative law and economics as aimed at distributive justice rather than efficiency. Such an assertion has an important implication with respect of the choice of laws to be compared: if we seek tax benchmarks of distributive justice, we should probably study tax laws that deviate from the Haig-Simons formula by way of actual "distribution." Barker provides some examples of significant tax laws that should be regarded creating "exemptions and tax preferences" rules,[49] namely those which affect economic distribution. For example, with respect to the taxation of service income, he includes deferred compensation arrangements, the tax preferential treatment of health and other insurance, and fringe benefits. With respect to the taxation of capital gains, he notes the inclusion of interest and dividend income, the deduction of interest payments, rules for capital cost recovery, the deductibility of current versus capital expenditures, timing of income and deduction, and the deduction of net operating losses.

---

[44] *Id.* at 161–62.

[45] Oliver Brand, *Conceptual Comparisons: Towards a Coherent Methodology of Comparative Legal Studies*, 32 Brooklyn J. Int'l L. 405, 421 (2007).

[46] Mattei, *supra* note 42 at 182; Ugo Mattei & Fabrizio Caffagi, *Comparative Law and Economics*, *in* The New Palgrave Dictionary of Economics and Law 346, 347 (P. Newman ed., 1998).

[47] The language of this approach is the one mainly adopted in this book.

[48] William Barker, *Expanding the Study of Comparative Tax Law to Promote Democratic Policy: The Example of the Move to Capital Gains Taxation in Post-Apartheid South Africa*, 109 Penn. St. L. Rev. 703, 712–714 (2005).

[49] *Id.* at 715–16.

## 1. The economic principles of taxation: efficiency, equity, and simplicity

As noted above, this book is intended to serve as a supplement to the basic tax class. Thus, many times this book stops exactly in the juxtaposition of tax rules and only briefly compares them using the economic principles of taxation. Therefore, even if the book is not a scholarly effort to produce "comparative tax law knowledge," it follows, to a certain extent, a comparative law and economics perspective in a problem-solving-oriented manner. This is why it is worth offering a few words about the three general economic principles of taxation: efficiency, equity, and simplicity.[50] However, this mode of explanatory analysis is primarily technical. Namely, it does not seek to advance a particular normative choice but rather to use economic analysis as a handy tool to illustrate differences and similarities. Particularly, even though each of the terms explained below is in essence an economic term, each represents a completely different (usually competing) ideological choice that may be exemplified using economic language but can probably be explained only by looking at social, cultural, and historical perspectives. To summarize, the "economics" underlying this book are not really "comparative" economics in that they do not advance a particular policy choice. Similarly to Barker, we occasionally adopt an economic technique, but we do not necessarily advance an efficient (or any other, for that matter) outcome in particular in this book.

1. *Efficiency*–The concept of efficiency is the one which is usually associated with comparative economics, i.e., the comparative search for the most efficient solution. The concept of efficiency moves from the invisible hand theorem by Adam Smith: under certain conditions, an *unfettered free-market economy* will be *efficient* and will move on its own, like if it was an invisible hand.

*Unfettered economy* means that there is no government interference or a minimal government intervention (i.e., government should not intervene).

*Free-market economy* means that there is perfect competition. The conditions in order to have perfect competition (i.e., the conditions needed for the invisible hand theorem to work) are the following:

- Small agents: each agent has to be small enough so not to single-handedly affect the economic market. For example, no matter how many pops one buys, it will not affect the prices (this brings in the assumption that we cannot have monopoly, otherwise prices would be affected). In other words, each participant needs only to

---

[50] For an in-depth analysis of these three principles, see JOEL SLEMROD & JON BAKIJA, TAXING OURSELVES. A CITIZEN'S GUIDE TO THE DEBATE OVER TAXES (The MIT Press 2008).

know about his or her own preferences and constraints. There is no need to manage a huge amount of information like in a planned economy;

- Rational agents: each agent has to be a rational one: rational agents are agents who try to maximize their profits;
- No public goods[51] or externalities: the theorem works only when there are not public goods, because the free market economy would not be able to produce public goods in an efficient way. There is an externality when actions of one individual or firm affect other individuals or firms, other than through the price system; and
- Perfect information: buyers are well informed about prices and quality of what they may purchase. In fact, imperfect information leads to adverse selection (which is information asymmetries between buyers and sellers) and moral hazard (which is every situation in which a person does not bear the full adverse consequences of his actions).

However, in the real economy, the above-mentioned conditions are not met. In fact, we could always identify market failure, government failure, and people failure.

There is market failure because there are monopolies (and therefore there are not only small agents), public goods, externalities, and imperfect information (adverse selection and moral hazard).

There is government failure because unfettered economies do not exist; since governments do intervene and interfere (tax policy would probably qualify as one of the most significant forms of government interventions).

Finally, there is people failure because very often, people do not make choices that are in their own interest. This field is also known as behavioral economics.[52] For example, it has been proven that people are susceptible to framing (the same person in the same situation may choose differently depending on how the situation is framed).

The concept of (Pareto) *efficiency* is that "no one can be made better off without making someone else worse off. In other words, resources are not wasted."

Let's assume we have two kinds of people in the economy. They only differ in their ability to sell their services; that is why we have highs and lows. The more resources one has, the higher her well-being is. The theorem of the invisible hand assumes that the unfettered free market economy will always be on the frontier (the utility possibility frontier or UPF). The assumption is that when we are on the utility

---

[51] A public good is a good that if it is consumed by one person does not diminish its availability to anyone else.

[52] *See* BEHAVIORAL PUBLIC FINANCE (E.J. McCaffery & J. Slemrod eds., 2006).

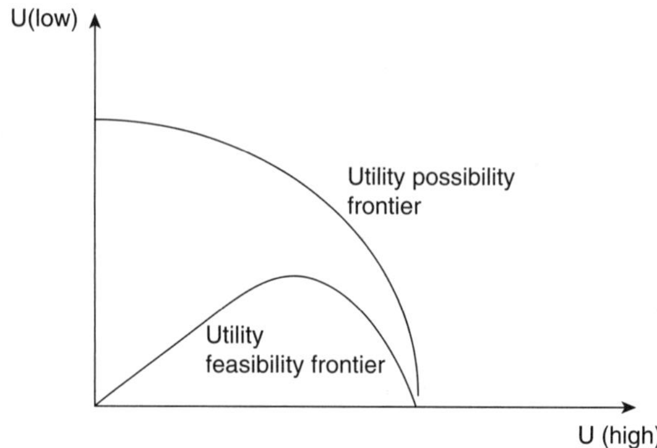


possibility frontier, no resources are wasted or, in other words, no one can be made better off without making someone else worse off.

Every point inside the curve means that there is a waste of resources, because, theoretically, it is still possible to reach a point where both parties are better off.

It is noteworthy that the theorem does not tell anything about fairness. Therefore, saying that an economy operates efficiently says nothing about the distribution of well-being among the citizens. This means that an efficient economy is not necessarily a fair one. The distribution may be deemed to be inequitable, although the grounds for making such a judgment are ethical rather than economic.

However, the concept of efficiency is fundamental in analyzing or comparing different tax systems. Most taxes have efficiency costs because they distort taxpayers' decisions. For example, income taxes make leisure more attractive. Generally, for a given amount of tax revenue collected, efficiency cost is higher the greater is the behavioral response to taxes. For example, a tax on food is not necessarily inefficient because it would raise revenue without causing major behavioral responses (besides the ethical problems that may arise). Similarly, a tax on skies is not inefficient because it would reduce leisure and would therefore induce people (at least theoretically) to spend more time working. Efficient taxes are those that correct negative externalities or create positive ones.

Regarding progressive income tax systems, these are inevitably accompanied with a waste of resources. This is because the more progressive the income tax system is, the more influenced the behaviors are, which in turns involves a waste of resources. According to the invisible hand theorem, the only neutral tax is the lump sum tax, which does not grant any redistribution of wealth.

2. *Equity*–The *vertical equity* principle states that the wealthier a person, the more taxes she should pay. In a progressive income tax system, a taxpayer's tax liability, as a fraction of income, rises when

higher income is Produced. In a proportional income tax system, all taxpayers are subject to a "flat rate" tax at the same percentage of their income, regardless of the amount of income. In a regressive income tax system, as the income increases, the tax percentage decreases.

Vertical equity could be introduced in our analysis using one of two principles.

The first is the so-called "benefit principle": the tax burden is proportionate to the benefits received by the taxpayers. According to this principle, taxes are seen as a charge for the services provided by the government. However, the benefit principle precludes redistribution policies, and valuation issues for public goods may also emerge.

The second is the "ability to pay" principle, according to which, as a taxpayer's well-being increases, so does her ability to pay. However, this principle provides only vague guidance for progressivity and ignores the expenditure side of the government budget. Theoretically speaking, this may be a well-established principle, yet it seems too abstract to actually be implemented. Yet, in many European countries, the "ability to pay" principle is a constitutional one.

Another way to deal with vertical equity is to analyze the trade-off between equity and efficiency. Refer to the diagram of the utility possibility frontier. The efficiency costs of redistributing via progressive tax and transfer policies are represented by the "utility feasibility frontier" that lies within the utility possibility frontier. The more the UFF lies within the UPF, the greater is the efficiency cost of progressivity. This, in turn, depends on the behavioral response to such policies.

The principle of *horizontal equity* is also fundamental for analyzing and comparing different tax systems. According to this principle, individuals (or families?) at the same level of well-being should have the same tax burden.

Finally, the principle of *intergenerational equity* has also to be considered: first, because a tax policy that may seem not equal in a year-period horizon could be considered equal in a lifetime horizon or the other way around; second, because certain tax policies may create tensions between different generations.

3. *Simplicity*–Simplicity is not really an independent criterion (and for that matter, not a strictly an economical one, though it carries with it economic implications), because unnecessary complexities waste resources (inefficiency) cause a capricious assignment of tax burden (inequity).

Simplicity is usually measured by looking at compliance and administrative costs.

*Compliance costs* measure the time and money spent by taxpayers to comply with the tax system. They represent the time and resources expended by taxpayers to interact with the income tax system. These costs include the value of individuals' time spent learning the tax law, maintaining records for tax purposes, completing and filing tax forms, and responding to any correspondence from the tax administration (including tax audits). Compliance costs also include amounts paid to others to conduct any of these tasks on behalf of an individual or a business.[53] If compliance costs are too high, taxpayers may have an advantage not to comply with the tax system (therefore reducing compliance costs) if the risk of detection and the other costs are relatively low.

*Administrative costs*[54] measure the time and money spent by the government to implement the tax system.

We are left with the fact that the simplest tax system may not be the fairest. The fairest tax system might have efficiency costs. The most efficient system is probably not the fairest.

## E. What to expect next

From here, what to do with the information supplied in this book is for the reader to choose. The examples to follow are the start, not the end, and are intended to ignite modes of thinking that are not usually applied in basic tax classes. The foreign examples will be based primarily on the foreign countries covered in depth in Hugh Ault and Brian Arnold's *Comparative Income Taxation: A Structural Analysis*, namely, Australia, Canada, France, Germany, Japan, The Netherlands, Sweden, and the United Kingdom. Italian and Israeli tax systems, for obvious reasons, will also be addressed. We will also use examples from developing countries in order to emphasis the policy choices made by countries with less familiar social and political backgrounds and in which the income tax system plays different roles in economics and politics. This is why occasional examples will also be drawn from the tax law of other countries other than those mentioned above.

The organization of the book is designed to help the tax student follow the book in parallel with the regular tax casebook that he or she is using. Since most U.S. tax casebooks follow a basic pattern (income, deductions, the taxable unit, timing, capital gains, and so on), the book will follow the same order. A critical comparatist will probably be quick to note this construction and may even criticize us for trying to manipulate foreign tax systems to accommodate the "mainstream" American discourse. Point taken. We invite, by all means, critical tax comparatists to bring forward a critical analysis on the construction of comparative tax discourse around these usual focal points. This would be a much-needed (and long overdue) contribution the comparative tax discourse.

---

[53] Slemrod & Bakija, *supra* note 50.
[54] *See* The President's Advisory Panel on Federal Tax Reform, Simple, Fair, and Pro-Growth: Proposals to Fix America's Tax System (Government Printing Office 2005).

# 2

# Taxable Income

This chapter addresses the starting point of any income tax: the definition of income as the base of the tax (the subject matter on which the tax is imposed).

First, we discuss the two main concepts of taxable income, source concept and accretion concept, and the two main ways used by countries with income taxes to define the tax base, by exclusion (a "global" definition of income) or by inclusion (a "schedular" definition).

The chapter then reviews some of the major problems of defining income in the U.S. income tax system and juxtaposes the U.S. solutions against those used by other countries.

Finally, we discuss the realization requirement, which has been described as the "Achilles' heel" of the income tax.[1]

## I. TAXABLE INCOME DEFINITION: GLOBAL vs. SCHEDULAR AND SOURCE vs. ACCRETION

The definition of taxable income can be based upon either the accretion concept or the source concept.[2]

The *accretion* concept derives from the so-called "Haig/Simons" definition of income, under which a person's annual income is the value of what she could consume in that year while keeping her wealth constant. Equivalently, it is equal to actual consumption plus the change

---

[1] William D. Andrews, *The Achilles Heel of the Comprehensive Income Tax, in* NEW DIRECTIONS IN FEDERAL TAX POLICY FOR THE 1980s, at 278, 280–85 (Charles E. Walker & Mark A. Bloomfield eds., 1983).

[2] VICTOR THURONYI, COMPARATIVE TAX LAW 233 (Kluwer 2003) distinguishes between accretion, source, and trust concept. *See also* Paul Hahn Wueller, *Concepts of Taxable Income I,* 53 POLIT. SCI. Q., 1938, 83; KEVIN HOLMES, THE CONCEPT OF INCOME. A MULTI-DISCIPLINARY ANALYSIS (Amsterdam: IBFD, 2001).

in wealth.[3] This concept has been adopted in the **United States,**[4] where any realized accession of wealth is income unless it is specifically excluded.

The *source* concept of income has been developed by the Italian economists De Viti De Marco and Quarta, and it has been adopted by **Italy** and many other civil law countries.[5] It has also been adopted by certain common law countries such as the **United Kingdom.** The source concept of income provides that a certain item is income only when it derives from a specific source, most likely an economic one.

Another important distinction exists with regard to the definitional structure of taxable income. Any tax system can define taxable income in a global way (e.g., **United States**) or in a schedular way (e.g., **Italy**). Taxable income is defined in a global way when any item of income is included in taxable income unless specifically excluded. Taxable income is defined in a schedular way when an item of income is not taxable income unless specifically included in a specific schedule.

One may think that income tax systems that define taxable income in a global way would follow the accretion concept (as is the case in the **United States** and **Brazil**), while a tax system that defines taxable income in a schedular way would rather prefer the source concept (as is the case in **France, Germany, Italy, Spain,** and the **United Kingdom**). The logic works as follows: in a schedular system, income is taxable only if there is a specific "scheduled" source for such income. On the other hand, global systems will not look for a specific source for the income. All that matters is the accumulation of income (the source of which does not matter). Hence, "accretion" is the key concept here. As much as we would have liked to end this description now, the source/ schedule vs. accretion/global distinction is much generalized, many times misleading. In fact, both **Australia** and **Canada** define income in

---

[3] *See* ROBERT M. HAIG, THE CONCEPT OF INCOME—ECONOMIC AND LEGAL ASPECTS, THE FEDERAL INCOME TAX 59 (Columbia University Press 1921); HENRY C. SIMONS, PERSONAL INCOME TAXATION: THE DEFINITION OF INCOME AS A PROBLEM OF FISCAL POLICY 5 (Chicago University Press 1938).

[4] For a comparison between the U.S. and the Italian way to define taxable income and for a comparison of the different concepts of income, *see* Nicola Sartori, *La nozione di reddito d'impresa negli Stati Uniti d'America: profili di diritto comparato,* RIVISTA DI DIRITTO FINANZIARIO E SCIENZA DELLE FINANZE 587, part I, (2007).

[5] *See* ORONZO QUARTA, COMMENTO ALLA LEGGE SULLA IMPOSTA DI RICCHEZZA MOBILE 111, vol. I (Società Editrice Libraria 1902); ORONZO QUARTA, OSSERVAZIONI SUL CONCETTO DI REDDITO IN FINANZA (Italgrafica 1932), also published in *Opere giuridiche* (F. Forte e C. Longobardi eds.,1962); ANTONIO DE VITI DE MARCO, PRINCIPI DI ECONOMIA FINANZIARIA 192 (Einaudi 1939).

a global way yet adopt a source concept of taxable income.[6] **Japan** defines income in a schedular way yet adopts an accretion concept of taxable income.

It is worth noting that there are no countries that define income in either a purely global or purely schedular way, and there are none that have adopted a pure source or accretion concept: this is because, as we will show, there has been a considerable convergence process in these matters. Nevertheless, every income tax system will necessarily address these two issues (definitional structure and the concept of taxable income).

In the **United States**, the Code[7] defines the base of the tax imposed by Section 1 by reference to "gross income." Gross income is defined in circular fashion in § 61 as "all income from whatever source derived." Since 1955, this language has been interpreted by the U.S. Supreme Court as applying to all "accessions to wealth, clearly realized, and over which the taxpayers have complete dominion."[8] This means that the United States employs a "global," or all-encompassing, definition of income based on the accretion concept: any accession to wealth is presumed to be income unless Congress specifically *excludes* it.[9]

In **Brazil,** taxable income is legally defined as the product from capital or labor (or a combination of both), and any increase in the net worth of the taxpayer (*proventos de qualquer natureza*), which may not be a product of capital or labor.[10] For purposes of defining taxable income, the name given to the revenue or income, its location, legal status or nationality of the source, its origin, or how it is perceived, are irrelevant.[11]

Other countries begin their definition of the tax base differently. In the **United Kingdom,** as well as in many other countries (e.g., **China, France, Germany, Italy, Japan**), income is only subject to tax if it is listed in a particular schedule, and each type of taxable income has its own schedule (which may also include a separate rate or a different taxing mechanism such as withholding vs. tax return filing). Thus, there is a schedule for wages, for dividends, for interest, and so on. This system

---

[6] This is because the Australian and Canadian systems were originally schedular systems in which each schedule represented a different source of income.

[7] All references to the "Sections," "Code," and "Regulations" are to the U.S. Internal Revenue Code of 1986, as amended, and to the U.S. Treasury Regulations promulgated thereunder.

[8] Commissioner v. Glenshaw Glass Co., 348 U.S. 426 (1955).

[9] Internal Revenue Code § 61 states: "Except as otherwise provided in this subtitle, gross income means all income from whatever source derived. . . ."

[10] See Article 43 of the National Tax Code (Law No. 5,172, Oct. 25, 1966—hereinafter "NTC")

[11] See Article 43, § 1°, of the NTC.

is therefore called "schedular," and under it, no item of income is taxable unless the policy maker specifically *includes* it in the tax base. In addition, deductions are applied to specific schedules, and losses cannot be carried over from one schedule to another, unless specifically permitted by the policy maker.

What difference does it make if a tax system is global or schedular? The difference is at the margin, for those items of income that are not enumerated.

In the U.S. system, Code § 61 states that gross income includes, but is not limited to, a long list of enumerated items.[12] This means that if an item does not appear on the list, it is still taxable if it meets the criteria set out in *Glenshaw Glass*.[13] Such definition is based on the accretion concept. For example, the Supreme Court held that punitive damages for antitrust violations were taxable even though they did not have a "source" in any activity of the taxpayer.

In a schedular system, on the other hand, items of income that are not enumerated in a schedule are simply not taxable.

For example, in **Italy,** the realized capital gain on the private sale of a piece of art is not taxable, since it is not listed under any particular "schedule".

In the **United Kingdom,** as well as in other commonwealth countries, capital gains were not taxable until a separate tax was enacted to reach them.[14]

Interestingly, tax historians[15] have shown that even the **U.S.** system was originally conceived as being more similar to a schedular system, based on the source concept. The references to "sources" of income in Code § 61 (which dates back to the original Revenue Act of 1913) was understood at the time as referring to a series of particular sources from which income flowed. Therefore, if income had no source, it could not be taxed (just as if it was not included in a schedule). Thus, in 1920, the Supreme Court held that "income may be defined as the gain derived from labor, from capital, or from both combined."[16] This definition

---

[12] (1) Compensation for services, including fees, commissions, fringe benefits, and similar items; (2) Gross income derived from business; (3) Gains derived from dealings in property; (4) Interest; (5) Rents; (6) Royalties; (7) Dividends; (8) Alimony and separate maintenance payments; (9) Annuities; (10) Income from life insurance and endowment contracts; (11) Pensions; (12) Income from discharge of indebtedness; (13) Distributive share of partnership gross income; (14) Income in respect of a decedent; and (15) Income from an interest in an estate or trust. Most of the categories enumerated as examples in Code § 61 have their own schedule in tax systems.

[13] See footnote n. 8.

[14] *See* Chapter 6.

[15] Steven A. Bank, *Mergers, Taxes, and Historical Realism*, 75 Tul. L. Rev. 1 (2000).

[16] Eisner v. Macomber, 252 U.S. 189 (1920).

embodied a schedular notion of income as deriving from one of these three possible sources and was interpreted (correctly) as implying that gains that did not derive from these three sources should not be taxed. However, by 1955, the time that *Glenshaw Glass*[17] was decided, the Court had moved from this schedular idea toward a more global notion of the concept of income. This has been the U.S. definition ever since.

In the sections below, we will offer examples of items of income in which the differences between global and schedular systems—and source and accretion concepts—manifest themselves.

However, as many commentators have noted, over time, there has been considerable convergence between the global and schedular approaches, as well as between source and accretion concepts.

As Eric Zolt[18] has shown, the **U.S.** system contains significant schedular elements, and the definition of income every so often follows the source concept. For example, from the beginning, capital gains have been subject to a separate rate structure from the outset. This has persisted despite the 1986 attempt to abolish the capital gain preference. Similarly, capital losses are treated separately from other losses, and certain types of deductions, such as investment interest and passive activity losses, are also segregated from other losses and deductions.

In schedular systems, as we will discuss below in greater detail, the adoption of catch-all "miscellaneous income" schedules and the possibility of moving losses from one schedule to another have led to the inclusion of most items of income that are subject to tax in the **U.S.** system. This has created a partial convergence of schedular systems toward global systems.

In **Italy,** for example, there are six schedules of income, one of which is the "other income" schedule. This schedule is not a residual category, but it includes many items of income that are not includable in the other schedules.

In **Israel,** the Income Tax Ordinance counts nine schedules of income. However, eight of them refer to particular sources of income, and the ninth lists "income from any other source." This is a good example for a schedular system adopting a global approach.

**China** also offers a good example of a schedular system that converged toward a global one. The Chinese individual income tax system is still essentially schedular. There are many taxable items of individual income tax,[19] including wages and salaries; income derived by individual industrial and commercial households from production or business

---

[17] *See* footnote n. 8.

[18] Eric M. Zolt, *The Uneasy Case For Uniform Taxation*, 16 Va. Tax Rev. 39 (1996).

[19] *See Regulations for the Implementation of the Individual Income Tax Law of the People's Republic of China, available at* http://www.chinatax.gov.cn/n6669073/n6669088/6888494.html (last visited on November 19, 2009).

operation, income from contracted or leased operation of enterprises or institutions, remuneration from personal services, author's remuneration, royalties, interests, dividends, bonuses, income from lease of property, income from transfer of property, contingent income, and other income specified as taxable by China's Ministry of Finance. To a certain extent, the possibility for the Chinese Ministry of Finance to specify if an item of income becomes taxable makes the Chinese income tax system similar to a global system. In fact, new items of income can be rapidly (but not immediately) added as taxable items of income.

The reverse (global systems converging toward schedular ones) is also true. For example, the **United States** follows a global approach, but there are so many excluded items of income in the U.S. Code that it is possible to say that the system partially converged toward a schedular system. The most obvious example is the different treatment of labor (i.e., "ordinary") income as compared to capital gains. Both are, in essence, "income" but are taxed differently, each under it own "schedule," each defined according to the source from which it is derived.

Despite this considerable convergence, there are still differences at the margin between global and schedular systems, and there persists some tendency to tax items in the former that are excluded in the latter. New forms of income arise over time as the economy changes (e.g., income from derivative financial instruments). When courts confront the question of whether such new items should be taxed, their decision to tax depends on whether the system they operate in is global or schedular. This example illustrates a broader phenomenon that underlies the whole topic of comparative taxation and gives it some of its appeal.

It is also important to note that "source" remains highly relevant even in global systems due to the international nature of business transactions. In an international transaction, even where only "global" systems are involved, source will define which jurisdiction gets the priority in taxation and will also affect the classification on the transaction for tax purposes (for example, as an interest or a dividend payment).

At least from a functional perspective, the design problems facing an income tax are, to a significant extent, identical across jurisdictions. Therefore, it is not surprising to find a degree of convergence that makes all income tax systems look alike, even without any showing of conscious borrowing (although that exists as well in some areas, such as international tax). However, jurisdictions also differ in their underlying history and legal culture, and thus it is understandable that convergence will never be complete.[20] In fact, the widespread phenomenon of

---

[20] This is generally true for all comparative legal studies, as suggested by studies on the convergence or divergence of the common and civil law traditions. Mathias Reimann, *The Progress and Failure of Comparative Law in the Second Half of the Twentieth Century*, 50 AM. J. COMP. L. 671 (2002).

cross-border tax arbitrage depends on the persistence of differences between the tax rules of different countries, even if they all attempt to tax income. In essence, tax arbitrage refers to the exploitation by taxpayers of the differences among tax systems to lower their overall tax liability.


## II. TAXATION OF FRINGE BENEFITS

No income tax system can focus exclusively on cash compensation paid to employees without raising significant efficiency and fairness issues. If only cash compensation is taxed, workers would tend to ask for non-cash compensation. A negative twofold result follows: workers would receive noncash fringe benefits instead of other items upon which they place greater value, which is inefficient; also, workers with similar incomes would be taxed differently depending on whether they received income in cash or in other form, which is unfair.

Different countries have responded to this issue in different ways, depending on the fringe benefits involved.

As a general matter, in most systems (the **United States** included), fringe benefits are included in income. Specifically, they are included in the employee's income and usually deductible for the employer.[21] From a *fairness* perspective, this is probably the best solution because horizontal equity requires that similarly situated taxpayers be treated alike.

Despite this general concept, in most (if not all) tax systems, some fringes are excluded (which again raises fairness questions with respect to these specific fringes). This is one area in which the global vs. schedular issue matters: under schedular systems, fringes must be specifically included or they are not taxable, while in the **United States** and other global systems, all fringes are taxable unless specifically excluded (I.R.C. § 132; § 119). These marginal differences are discussed below with reference to specific fringes.

Admittedly, taxing noncash fringe benefits is difficult. There is the issue of valuation, which is frequently difficult to perform; especially when the items are restricted (the value in such a case is obviously less than fair market value, but by how much?). The general valuation rules of the law apply to the valuation of the benefits in kind. The valuation process becomes even more complicated in countries that do not have a set of detailed rules for performing valuations. Another issue with

---

[21] As it will be shown, the Australian tax system constitutes an exception on this regard.

fringe benefits is that the business and personal aspects of a fringe benefit, such as use of a company car, may be difficult to separate.

Before commencing in analyzing the various ways in which different tax systems approach the problems presented by fringe benefits, one notable exception to the general rule (i.e., that fringe benefits are taxable to the employer) must be emphasized: the **Australian** tax system, which applies a comprehensive system of surrogate taxation with respect to fringe benefits. In general, under Australian law, any benefit provided by an employer to an employee with respect to the employment is included in the *employer's* income.[22]

The major advantage of this approach is administrative simplification: the problem of valuation is shifted from employee to employer, and it is much easier to audit employers than employees because of their limited numbers. The major disadvantage is that the wrong person is taxed, and there is always the concern as to whether the tax is passed onto employees in the form of lower wages (which depends on market conditions). In general, Australian economists have concluded that it took awhile for the new fringe benefit tax to be reflected in wages.

As noted, however, in most other countries, fringe benefits are taxed to employees, and the main challenge is dealing with the administrative and valuation difficulties raised by this method. In most countries, the value of fringe benefits is measured through a comparison to fair market value or retail prices.

For example, in **Russia,** the law requires only that goods and services be valued at the market price of similar goods and services, increased by the appropriate amount of value-added tax (VAT) and excise duties. However, the fair market value of many fringes is hard to establish, especially in the case of fringes provided for the use of multiple employees (such as company retreats).

If one does not adopt the Australian approach of shifting the burden to the well-informed (and better regulated) employer, one might try to take the valuation difficulties head-on by trying to prescribe statutory rules for valuation.

For example, in **Brazil,** benefits in kind are fully taxable and valued at their cost to the employer or at market value,[23] except those which are specifically exempted, such as food and transportation vouchers, and uniforms or special clothing for work, freely provided by the employer, or the difference between the price charged and the market value of the goods.

---

[22] See *Fringe Benefit Tax: A guide to employers and tax professionals,* published by the Australian Tax Office (2006), at http://www.ato.gov.au/content/downloads/N1054.PDF; HUGH J. AULT AND BRIAN J. ARNOLD, COMPARATIVE INCOME TAXATION: A STRUCTURAL ANALYSIS 174–176 (Kluwer 2004).

[23] IBDF. Latin-American Taxation: Brazil. http://ip-online.ibfd.org/la/.

The **Canadian** system prescribes a complex and comprehensive set of rules to value the benefits of employer-provided automobiles.[24]

Under **Chinese** tax law, if the benefit received is in the form of physical asset (car, dwelling, etc.), the amount of taxable income is calculated according to the price specified in the purchase documentation or as determined by tax authorities. The taxable value of the benefits may be incorporated into the taxation of employees' wages on an average monthly basis of the employees' required service period. The payment of income tax by an employer on behalf of an employee is also regarded as a taxable remuneration. The employee is taxed on the grossed-up amount.[25]

A *middle way* to deal with the valuation problem is to simply attach a standard value to certain fringes ("valuation tables") and include it in the employee's income. This method is applied in **Italy**[26] for company-provided cars and in the **United States,**[27] **the United Kingdom, Sweden,** and **Germany** for fringes such as company cars, meals, and lodging. A similar approach is taken in **Israel:** each year the Tax Authority publishes a "value of use" table which specifies the amount to be added to employees' income for each type of vehicle provided by the employer.

The valuation problem may lead countries to omit hard-to-value or small fringes for simplicity reasons,[28] but excluding fringes altogether leads to a violation of horizontal equity. Suppose, for example, that A gets taxable income of 10,000 and an excluded fringe of 1000, while B gets 11,000 in taxable income and buys the fringe with after-tax money. Assuming a flat tax rate of 30 percent, A is left with 7000 cash (10,000 taxable income taxed at a 30 percent rate) plus the fringe at hand, while B remains with 6700 cash (11,000 taxable income taxed at the 30 percent rate minus the 1000 spent to purchase the fringe) plus the fringe.

The valuation problem can also lead to a violation of vertical equity, for example, by a nontaxed fringe given only to senior, highly paid employees.

---

[24] AULT & ARNOLD, *supra* note 22, at 173. The **French** system is similar.

[25] IBDF. Asia-Pacific Taxation: China. http://www.ibfd.org/portal/Product_tiap.html.

[26] FRANCESCO TESAURO, ISTITUZIONI DI DIRITTO TRIBUTARIO. PARTE SPECIALE 67 (Utet 2008). What the author underlines as fringe benefits are generally taxed in Italy for two main reasons: anti-avoidance purposes and efficiency (improve the productivity of employees or to develop faithful employees).

[27] AULT & ARNOLD, *supra* note 22, at 172–74; Treas. Reg. 1.61-21; 1.132-1–8; *see* KBS p. 51.

[28] Both administrative and compliance costs would be lower.

Possible solutions to the fairness issues include the U.S. method of limiting the exclusion for highly paid employees.[29]

The **French** system uses certain coefficients to value the benefit included, depending on the employee's income level. Thus, if a certain fringe benefit is given to both low-income and high-income taxpayers, the low-income taxpayer will include less in her income than her high-paid counterpart.

The fact that most countries generally include noncash benefits in income provokes the following intriguing comparative questions: What are the exceptions? How broad is the exclusion? And specifically, what kind of benefits escapes taxation? Are fringes of different character excluded in different countries? A few examples are worth mentioning.

A major fringe in some countries is health-care expenses or insurance paid by the employer. In the United States, these are excluded or deferred to a certain extent by the employee and immediately deductible to the employer.[30]

However, in other countries with developed health-care systems, such as Sweden, this fringe is included in income (or not included but also not deductible to the employer).[31]

This contrast is understandable given the different background conditions (weak health care outside the employment context in the **United States,** strong in **Sweden**) and provides a striking example as to how different political contexts (private versus state-supported health care) create variations in tax rules.

Such differences can provide us with a methodological rallying point from which to launch a comparative discussion. A functional approach would start by questioning what the social function is, which the above-discussed laws are intended to fulfill. Presumably, the theoretical discussion would go that countries wish to maintain the health of their citizens. From a comparative perspective, such research would try to evaluate whether the best way to achieve this goal is to give tax preferences or to grant free state-sponsored health care. On the other hand, the cultural perspective would not address it as a question of functional efficiency but rather as a question of cultural societal difference. It would try to identify the societal values that have grown state-sponsored health-care systems in one place and health-related tax subsidies in another. It may well be, according to such an approach, that both solutions are right, each in its localized context. Finally, a critical approach would try to expose which political or sectorial interests are advanced by each approach and to explain how other interests are

---

[29]  *See* Code § 132(j).

[30]  Code § 106(a), § 162(a).

[31]  AULT & ARNOLD, *supra* note 22, at 172.

marginalized in the process. Namely, who are the beneficiaries of each system, and how did they affect the creation of such systems? For example, who would be on the "receiving side" of a privately held health care system, and what arguments does such a party make when reforms are considered?

Another context-dependent example involves certain working conditions related to fringes. It is plausible to argue that a tax system reflects different cultural and social values by the benefits it chooses to exclude. For example, one may compare the benefits excluded by Code §132 in the United States to the benefits excluded in other countries.

In **Germany,** social policy dictates that cash payments for birth of a child, extra pay for overtime work on holidays, and "happy work force" payments are all excluded, while in **Japan,** length of service gifts are excluded.[32] No similar excluded fringes can be found in the **United States.**

In **China,** wages and salaries do not include allowances and subsidies paid by employers in accordance with state regulations.

## III. IMPUTED INCOME FROM OWNER-OCCUPIED HOUSING

We must start by tackling the very basic definition of income imputation, since such concept is almost completely neglected in the U.S. Code. Imputed income is income that a taxpayer derives from providing goods or services to herself. For example, when a person lives in her own house, she is providing the value of housing to herself, and at the same time saving the amount she would otherwise have to pay as rent. When she tends her own garden, she earns as imputed income what she would otherwise have to pay a gardener. Under the Haig/Simons definition of income, imputed income should be taxed, since it clearly represents a wealth accretion.

Nevertheless, most countries do not tax most forms of imputed income, primarily because to do so would be both administratively difficult (because of valuation issues) and politically unpopular.[33] However, in many countries, there has been some attempt to tax imputed income because omitting it altogether would create a harsh distinction between, for example, homeowners and renters.

---

[32] AULT & ARNOLD, *supra* note 22, at 171.

[33] Administrative difficulty is, in essence, a functional argument, while political impropriety is a cultural-comparative one.

The **United States, Canada, Brazil,** and **China** never seriously considered taxing the imputed income of owner-occupied homes.

A simple example can clarify the consequences of not taxing imputed income: Assume A and B both have 100k of after-tax money. A buys a house for 100k and then lives there. At the end of the year, A sells the house to a third party for 103k. B invests the 100k in bonds which pay 8k a year but also rents a practically identical house to A's house for 5k a year. Both earn 50k a year.

| At the end of year 1: | | |
| --- | --- | --- |
| | **A** | **B** |
| Taxed investment yields: | 3 (house appreciation) | 8 (interest) |
| Nontaxed imputation: | 5 (rent saved) | 0 |
| Salary earned: | 50k | 50k |
| Taxable income: | 53k | 58k |
| Nondeductible rent paid: | 0 | (5) |

Clearly, B is taxed more heavily than A, even though—from a pure financial perspective—they are in the same situation. In other words, refraining from taxing A's imputed income clearly creates an unbalance in horizontal equity. This scenario represents a policy choice to encourage home ownership over residential leasing.

Two straightforward solutions to bring A and B to equality would be to either (1) include as income the imputed rent saved by A, comparing his income to B's 58, or (2) deduct the rent paid by B, thus comparing his taxable income to A's 53. The first would simply rebalance the equities while the latter would represent a shift in policy choices toward inducing residential leasing rather than ownership.

There are various reasons why imputed income from owner-occupied housing is not taxed in the United States.

*Valuation difficulties*—Since in many countries, houses are being valued for other purposes such as property and estate taxes,[34] one may think that valuation difficulty is not a sufficient reason to exclude imputed income from tax. However, many countries have taxed imputation in the past but abandoned it at least partially due to administrative reasons. For example, in 1987, **Germany** tried and abandoned a tax on the imputed value of homes, finding that rental valuation was seldom accurate and often undervalued. Since interest and maintenance costs were deductible against imputed rent, losses were generated

---

[34] It is certainly arguable that from a financial perspective, the very levy of property taxes is a crude form of imputation.

by taxpayers, which were used to offset other income.[35] **Australia** and **France** abandoned a tax on the imputed value of homes for similar reasons. Similarly, **Israel** abolished the taxation of imputed income from home ownership in 1963. So it seems that valuation plays at least a partial role in the justification for nontaxation of imputed income, but given the ubiquity of valuing housing, it cannot be a complete explanation.

*Political (and historical) considerations*—Given the fact that valuation difficulties alone do not justify nontaxation, other simple explanations come to mind: imputed income was never taxed, so why tax it now? Indeed, one could easily imagine the political outcry which would arise if imputed income taxation were presented suddenly in **Canada** or the **United States**. But this is not a good tax policy argument.

*Freedom of choice*—Another justification is that B could simply buy a house, just as A did; if B did not have the money to purchase a house, he could borrow it and be in the same position, given the deductibility of mortgage interests. However, again, this rationale is not tax related. Even if fairness is not a problem under this argument, we may encourage investment in housing.

Under such circumstances, where it can be plausibly argued that there is no good justification from a pure tax perspective for nontaxation of imputed income, it is not surprising that other countries have found various ways to tax imputed income from owner-occupied houses. This thus diminishes, at least to a certain extent, the negative results in the example described above. As we shall see, the solutions were partly affected by policy considerations. Methods of taxation of imputed income include the direct taxation and the indirect taxation of imputed income.

*Direct taxation of imputed income*—In many European countries, tax is levied on the ownership of residential homes.

In **Italy**, *"reddito fondiario,"* the imputed income from the ownership of land and buildings, is taxable, with an exception for the first residential house, according to Art. 26, Presidential Law Degree n. 917/1986 (*"Testo Unico delle Imposte sui Redditi"* or *"TUIR"*). The amount of imputed income is based on a cadastral system. In the case of rented property, the taxable income is the greater of the imputed income or the actual rental income. The taxable income so determined has to be summed up to the amount of income emerging from the other categories of income and will be subject to individual income tax (IRPEF).

In **Belgium,** "all real estate is assigned a notional rental income, known as 'cadastral' income, which is determined by estimating the potential annual rental income of the property at a given date.

---

[35]  AULT & ARNOLD, *supra* note 22, at 181.

A property tax of 30% to 50% (depending on the location of the property) of the cadastral income is payable . . . annually by all property owners."[36]

Consider this method with respect to the above example, in which the notional income is 5k:

|  | A | B |
| --- | --- | --- |
| Taxed investment yields: | 3 (house appreciation) | 8 (interest) |
| Taxed imputation: | 5 (notional income) | 0 |
| None deductible rent paid: | 0 | (5) |
| Salary earned: | 50k | 50k |
| Taxable income: | 58k | 58k |

Generally, the **Belgian** system adopts a straightforward approach in comparing A's and B's statuses (although B would still have less after tax money since his rent is paid out of after-tax money). Interest on loans is deductible if the loans were taken for the purpose of acquiring a residential home.

Other systems tax the imputed income with reference to standard values. **Sweden** uses the home value rather than calculating the notional value of rent. Home owners are taxed at a nominal rate of 1 percent of 75 percent of the home value. Going back to our initial example, where A had 53k of taxable income, and B had 58k, if both A and B are in a 20 percent tax bracket, B would pay 11.6k in taxes, while A (if it wasn't for the imputed income tax) would only pay 10.6k. Under the Swedish system, A still owes taxes of imputed income of an amount equals to (1 percent)*(75 percent)*($100k) = 750, bringing his total tax paid to 11.35k, substantially reducing the inequality with B.

Although the general notion that imputed income taxation is directed at equalizing the status of renters to the preferable status of home owners, imputed income taxation may be triggered by the exact opposite consideration.

In **The Netherlands,** the taxation of imputed income was presented in order to induce home ownership in a country of renters.[37] While imputed

---

[36] Deloitte, *Real Estate Guide—Belgium, available at* http://www.deloitte.com/dtt/article/0,1002,sid%253D5214%2526cid%253D104818,00.html.
[37] AULT & ARNOLD, *supra* note 22, at 182.

income is taxed, the valuation of imputed rent is set at deliberately low values and may be offset by mortgage interest, thus generating a loss which may be used to shelter other income. Going back to our example, let's assume now that A and B both borrowed 100k, at an annual interest of 5 percent. A used his proceeds to buy his house, and B used it to invest in a bond. Also assume the notional (low) imputed rent is only 2.5 percent. Under the Dutch system, the results are as follows:

|  | A | B |
|---|---|---|
| Taxed investment yields: | 3 (house appreciation) | 8 (interest) |
| Taxed imputation: | 2.5 (notional income) | 0 |
| None deductible rent paid: | 0 | (5) |
| Deductible mortgage interest: | 5 | 0 |
| Salary earned: | 50k | 50k |
| Taxable income: | 50.5k | 58k |

Thus, the Dutch system is heavily aimed at inducing borrowing for home purchase.

*Indirect taxation of imputed income*—In **Japan**, the general rule is that home owning imputation is not taxed. However, Japan's unique system of depreciation gives an economic effect as if it does. Home owners must adjust the basis in their homes as if they took depreciation deductions, but, actually, they are not allowed to utilize any of the deduction on a yearly basis. It cannot be used to shield income from other sources. The sole purpose of the deductions is to decrease the basis in the house. The effect is that the value of imputation is taxed but deferred until disposition. Going back to our example, let's assume that A deducted 5k of the adjusted basis of the house.

|  | A | B |
|---|---|---|
| Taxed investment yields: | 8 (3k house appreciation+ 5k deduction recapture) | 8 (interest) |
| Nontaxed imputation: | 5 (rent saved) | 0 |
| Nondeductible rent paid: | 0 | (5) |
| Salary earned: | 50k | 50k |
| Taxable income: | 58k | 58k |

Although at a first glance the system might look fair, consider what happens if A (as expected) does not sell his house after one year but rather after five years. So, at the end of year 5:

|  | A | B |
| --- | --- | --- |
| Taxed investment yields: | 41 (16k[38] house appreciation + 25k deduction) | 8 (interest) |
| Nontaxed imputation: | 5(rent saved) | 0 |
| Nondeductible rent paid: | 0 | (5) |
| Salary earned: | 50k | 50k |
| Taxable income: | 91k | 58k |

This form of concentrating the entire taxation at once creates a "lock-in effect" that makes people less inclined to move. This is a particular policy choice for which comparables are hard to find.

In summary, there seem to be no good tax policy reasons behind the **U.S.** approach of ignoring imputed income from housing, and there are various ways of actually taxing such income. It is obvious that the choice not to tax imputed income is not tax driven and that the tax system is being used to advance (as in many other cases) nontax goals. Nevertheless, it seems unlikely that the **United States** tax system will change in this regard, given the likely political outcry. Even the mortgage interest deduction, which is less defensible, has survived reform efforts.

## IV. WINDFALLS

Under **U.S.** tax law, windfalls (e.g., a $20 bill found on the street) are taxable income under the general concept of accretion of wealth and taxing all income "from whatever source derived."

Similarly, under **Brazilian** law, taxable income also includes any increase in the taxpayer's net wealth that is not a product of labor or capital, or a combination of the two.

These solutions are compatible with the accretion concept of income. However, from a comparative perspective, this straightforward treatment (adopted by both the United States and Brazil) of windfalls is quite unique.

In most other systems, windfalls are excluded from income. This is understandable for schedular systems since windfalls typically fall outside the schedules. But windfalls tend to be excluded even in global tax systems that define taxable income as any item of income with a source. In fact, windfalls do not have a "source."[39]

---

[38] Taking into account 3 percent appreciation a year.

[39] This is similar to the U.S. treatment before *Glenshaw Glass*.

In **Canada, Australia,** and the **United Kingdom**, common law countries that historically began as schedular tax systems, personal windfalls are not included in taxable income. The justification for such exclusion is based on the notion that if economic gain is to be defined as "income," it must have a "source":

> Over forty years after Glenshaw Glass, the Supreme Court of Canada has recently confirmed in a number of cases that accretions to wealth such as windfalls that lack a source do not have the character of income for tax purposes. Indeed, the concept of income adopted by the U.S. Supreme Court in Glenshaw Glass explains the different organization of material found in basic Canadian tax texts compared to their American counterparts. In Canada we are familiar with texts and casebooks that divide the discussion of income into the traditional sources of employment, property, business, and capital gains; basic American texts are much more likely to discuss the characteristics of a global concept of gross income and then discuss separately deductions and the recognition of gains and losses.[40]

Indeed, **Canadian** cases such as *Queen vs. Cranswick* (40 N.R. 296) employ a strict approach, according to which "income from a source will be that which is typically earned by it or which typically flows from it as the expected return." Obviously, windfalls do not typically produce income nor expected return.[41]

It is likely that this quest for source reflects the fact that the systems derived from the United Kingdom were originally schedular systems, in which each schedule represented a different source of income. Thus, although schedular and global systems have converged in many aspects, and previously, schedular countries have adopted global regimes, the origins of each system can still be perceived in the treatment of items such as windfalls.

---

[40] Kim Brooks, *Book Review: Tax Stories: An In-Depth Look at Ten Leading Federal Income Tax Cases Paul L. Caron, Ed. New York: Foundation Press, 2003*, 28 Queen L. J. 705 (2003).

[41] In the *Carnswick* case, the respondent owned shares in a Canadian corporation, which the majority of its shares were owned by a U.S. company. Pursuant to a plan of acquisition of the Canadian corporation by a third party, and in order to please dissenting shareholders of the Canadian corporation (including the plaintiff), the U.S. parent company offered to buy the shares of the Canadian corporation or, as an alternative, to pay the minority shareholders $3.35 per share. The plaintiff elected to keep his shares and received $2,144 from the U.S. company. The issue was whether this amount was income in the respondent's hands. The Federal Court of Appeal held that it wasn't, that since the payment "was of an unusual and unexpected kind, one could not set out to earn as income from shares, and it was from a source to which the respondent had no reason to look for income from his shares." In the United States, such a payment would clearly be income.

Another interesting example with this respect is the **Israeli** system. Even though windfalls are generally excludable under Israeli law, the Income Tax Ordinance particularly addresses so-called "random business income" and prescribes that it is taxable if it is of "the nature of trade." Israeli courts have struggled quite a bit over the years to define "the nature of trade," but it is quite clear that income such as the one described in the Canadian *Carnswick* case *would have been* taxable in Israel. Israeli courts developed a series of characteristics that, when present, will tend to cause the windfalls to be includable. Generally, any income that is derived from the investment of either human or monetary capital, made with the anticipation of making profits while taking risk that is economic in nature, will be taxable. Thus, compensation paid for a plaintiff, for example, as a result of a successful class action, was ruled to be includable in income.[42] Since in *Carnswick*, the taxpayer derived the income as a result of equity investment in a corporation, she would have been taxable in **Israel.** In **Israel,** probably, only literal windfalls (such as money found on the street), which had almost no chance of reoccurring, may escape taxation.

The idea stemming from this comparison is that even in systems in which windfalls are not taxed, there may be a spectrum of opinions as to what exactly "windfalls" are from an income taxation perspective.

As noted above, in a schedular system, one must point to a specific schedule in which windfall is included, in order to make it income. Attaching a windfall to an identifiable "schedule" is indeed a task for the creative and inspired. The result is that in most schedular systems, windfalls aren't taxed unless they can be classified under a specific schedule (**The Netherlands**), or if the windfall was derived in a business setting (**Germany**) such as money found in the business premises, or if the windfalls are listed in the other income category (**Italy**).[43]

One unique schedular system that found a way to tax windfalls is the **Japanese** system, in which windfall income is taxed under the schedule of "occasional income." Such a broad residual category moves the Japanese system further toward a global regime, since almost any non-scheduled item can fall into the residual schedule. This phenomenon indicates that some degree of convergence can indeed be found between global and schedular regimes.


## V. DAMAGE AWARDS[44]


This subchapter addresses two basic issues: (1) taxation of damage awards for personal injury, which presents the general issue of

---

[42] ITA 1109/04 *Keren Haim v. Dan District Assessment Officer* (PM, 11/19/2006).

[43] For instance, lottery wins are listed and therefore taxable, while money found in the street is not listed and therefore is not taxable.

[44] *See generally* THE WEB GUIDE BOOK FOR PERSONAL INJURY COMPENSATION IN

distinguishing true compensation from taxable income; and (2) the "damage awards" that receive favorable treatment—only compensation for physical injuries or also nonphysical injuries.

## A. Taxation of damage awards

The general question of taxation of damage awards revolves around two issues: (1) the general treatment of damage awards (are damage awards includable?) and (2) the case of deferred damage compensation.

### 1. The treatment of damage awards

Under **U.S.** Code § 104 and the U.S. case law, compensatory damage awards are excluded from income, while punitive damages are included. Arguably, from a pure tax perspective, the policy embedded in Code § 104 seems to be incorrect. Code § 104 excludes *all* (nonpunitive) damage awards (we will deal with the definition of damage awards later). Such a broad exclusion is not compatible with basic income tax principles. Namely, such awards usually represent, at least in part, compensation for lost income that otherwise would have been taxable. One might argue that at least the portion of the award attributable to "otherwise earned income" should be taxed. On the other hand, social values may support the current policy.[45]

Similarly, under **Brazilian** law, the following payments related to damage awards are exempt from income tax[46]: compensation for injury, disability, or death or an asset damaged or destroyed as a result of an accident, until the limit of judicial condemnation, except for payment of continuing obligation in relation to the accident; and compensation for accidents at work. The following are also not taxable: compensation for repairing damaged property due to termination of contract, payments made to civil servants as an incentive to adhere to voluntary employment termination programs,[47] compensation paid and the notice for dismissal

---

EUROPE, published by the *Pan-European Organization of Personal Injury Lawyers*, and available on its Web site at http://www.peopil.com/pdf/ WebGuideBook1.pdf?id=978%0F%22uctname=Personal. [Hereinafter: THE GUIDE] An extended hard-cover version of THE GUIDE was also published as by Kluwer Publishing under the title PERSONAL INJURY COMPENSATION IN EUROPE: A COMPARATIVE GUIDE TO COMPENSATION PAYABLE IN EUROPEAN COUNTRIES TO VICTIMS OF ACCIDENTS (M. Bona & P. Mead eds., 2003).

[45] For a comprehensive discussion on tax policy considerations with respect to damage awards *see* Douglas A. Kahn, *Compensatory and Punitive Damages For A Personal Injury: To Tax Or Not To Tax?*, 2 FLA. TAX REV. 327 (1994).

[46] Art. 39 (IX) Brazilian Income Tax Law. https://www.planalto.gov.br/ ccivil_03/decreto/D3000.htm.

[47] Although the law states that only payments made by state-owned companies to its employees are tax exempt, the courts has extended that right to employees that adhere to employment termination programs carried out by

or termination of employment contract, and compensation received for settlement of loss or theft on insured goods.

On the other hand, in several tax systems, the portion of the award representing loss of income is taxed as ordinary income.

For example, according to the **Italian** system, damage awards are taxable to the extent that they compensate for the loss of taxable income and are included in the same category of income that they compensate for. On the other hand, damage awards that compensate patrimonial losses (*damnus emergens*) are not taxable.[48]

**Belgium** has adopted a similar approach: "Under Belgian law . . . [The] part of the personal injury award which replaces any loss of income is taxed. Generally, loss of future earnings is calculated on the basis of net wages . . . Personal injury awards for pecuniary losses are taxed in the same manner as the income they replace."[49]

**Israel** takes also a similar approach. The Supreme Court clearly stated that damage awards are only taxable as long as they compensate for the loss of otherwise taxable income[50] (note that any excess compensation may still be taxed, as we have seen, as income with the nature of trade).

The **Dutch** system is somewhere in between a total exemption of damage awards and the taxation of all awards replacing lost earnings. "When calculating loss of earnings, the starting point is the net income of the victim, after deduction of tax, social insurance and pension contributions. Where the net loss is known, the influence of taxation is minimal."[51]

Consider the following example: A was injured and was awarded damages by a court order. Due to his injuries, he was absent from work for a month, a period in which he would have earned 10,000 Euros. His tax rate is 50 percent, which would have left him with 5000 Euros net income for that month. Assume A received $20,000 in damage awards—how much (if any) is taxable under the **U.S., Italian, Belgian** and the **Dutch** systems? In the **United States,** under § 104, the entire amount is excludable. Under the **Italian** and **Belgian** systems, $10,000 is includable since it represents lost income. Under the **Dutch** system, only $5000, the net loss after tax, is taxable. The idea behind the **Dutch** system is

---

companies. The rationale is that the employee is giving up his right and, therefore, the payment is not an accession to wealth (or income for that matter), but a simple reimbursement of the employee's net worth.

[48] Article 6, paragraph 2, TUIR.

[49] THE GUIDE, *supra* note 44, at p.13.

[50] CA 171/67 The Assessment Officer of Large Businesses v. Gordon 21 P.D. 186 (1967).

[51] THE GUIDE, *supra* note 44, at p.74.

still to tax awards given in lieu of lost earnings, but in a favorable way, reflecting the type of social values underlying the **U.S.** approach.

## 2. The issue of deferred damage compensation

An interesting issue, which may exemplify the difference between different tax systems, arises in cases where damages are paid in the form of an annuity. Periodic payments resemble periodic income and thus are more "suspect" of being "pure" income rather than damage restoration. § 104(a)(2) of the U.S. I.R.C. actually induces periodic payments by excluding the entire periodic amount (even though such payments may include an interest component). Thus, a periodic payment may be even more favorable for the taxpayer than a single payment.

In **Germany,** however, the concept of taxing damages replacing lost income extends to deferred payments as well, but the application of the tax is narrower. Under the German tax system, "annuities for damages will only be subject to income tax where they are paid as compensation for other taxable income." The German system further provides that "Annuities covering additional expenditure . . . are therefore not taxable pursuant to § 22 (1) Income Tax Act (EStG) as annuities or other recurrent payments **although from their outer appearance they are recurrent benefits. . . .** [T]hese principles will also apply to payments for pain and suffering. . . . "[52]

The **French** system goes beyond the German one to include any periodic payments for damage awards in income, as such payments reflect a periodic concept of income.[53] Indeed, it can be argued that periodic payments for damage are less likely "recovery of human capital," because if the payment is aimed at making a person "whole" again, one should expect that an injured person would prefer to be "whole" as soon as possible and not defer his recovery.

In **Brazil,** as mentioned above, compensation for injury, disability, or death, or an asset damaged or destroyed as a result of an accident (until the limit of judicial condemnation), is not taxable except for payment of continuing obligation in relation to the accident.

## B. Which "damages" receive favorable treatment? physical? mental? reputation?

Section 104 of the U.S. Code specifically states that only awards for physical damages are excluded from income. This is a result of a change made by Congress in 1997 (previously, all nonpunitive damages

---

[52] THE GUIDE, *supra* note 44, at p.44., emphasis added.
[53] AULT & ARNOLD, *supra* note 22, at 192.

were excluded). The issue was discussed in the much publicized *Murphy* case. In *Murphy*, a three-judge panel of the U.S. Court of Appeals for the DC circuit held that including damages for nonphysical injuries in income was unconstitutional because such damages were not "income" under the Sixteenth Amendment. The result in *Murphy* launched an intense debate over the question, with most academic commentators sharply criticizing the outcome of the case. This eventually led the DC Circuit Court, sitting *en banc*, to reverse the decision.[54]

Indeed, other systems (e.g., **Belgium**) allow for the exclusion of damages for nonphysical injuries. It can be argued that the **U.S.** system is generous on one hand (excluding even damages paid in lieu of lost income) and tight on the other hand (excluding only physical damages awards). Other systems balance it the other way: wide definitions for excludable damages (including damages for mental injuries) but a narrower scope of exclusion (only "punitive" damages excludable).

In general, the **European** approach (including damages in lieu of income and excluding nonphysical nonincome damages) seems more accurate from both tax and tort perspectives. The **U.S.** approach, as expressed in *Murphy*, is a distortion of tort principles, which in turn is a result of a prior distortion of tax principles. Two wrongs may offset each other a bit and give us a better result in the *aggregate*, but it does not make it right from a pure tax policy perspective (and gives us a wrong result in individual cases).


## VI. CANCELLATION OF INDEBTEDNESS

The discussion on income resulting from cancellation of indebtedness revolves around two focal points: whether discharge of indebtedness constitutes taxable income, and, provided that the answer is positive, what exceptions, if any, should be allowed in special cases (such as bankruptcy and insolvency).

### A. Inclusion of debt relief in gross income

When a taxpayer borrows, the loan proceeds are not treated as income because of the offsetting obligation to repay the debt. If the debt is cancelled, the offsetting obligation no longer exists, and the taxpayer

---

[54] *See, e.g.*, RUSSELL F. ROMOND, *Income, Taxes And The Constitution: Why The D.C. Circuit Court Of Appeals Got It Right In Murphy*, 12 FORDHAM J. CORP. & FIN. L. 587 (2007); ELISABETH A. ROSE, *Murphy's Mistakes: How The Circuit Court Should Analyze Section, 104(A)(2) Upon Rehearing*, 60 TAX LAW. 533 (2007); *But see* GREGORY L. GERMAIN, *Taxing Emotional Injury Recoveries: A Critical Analysis Of Murphy v. Internal Revenue Service*, 60 ARK. L. REV. 185 (2007).

realizes a net accretion to wealth. As stated by the U.S. Supreme Court in *Kirby Lumber*,[55] the result is realization of taxable income (see Code § 61(a)(12)).

However, as simple as the principle may seem, the mentioned tax problem is approached very differently by global and schedular income tax jurisdictions.

Most countries defining income based on the global model consider cancellation of indebtedness taxable income (similar to any other accretion of wealth), unless a specific exception applies.

Most countries defining taxable income based on the schedular model consider cancellation of indebtedness taxable income only if it is specifically included in a taxable schedule.[56]

Very broadly, it has been observed, with some exceptions, that in schedular systems, income from the cancellation of indebtedness is taxable only if the debt is related to the production of business income. On the contrary, cancellation of personal indebtedness (which is indebtedness unrelated to the production of business income) does not constitute taxable income. The principle behind this tax solution is similar to the principle guiding the tax treatment of windfalls. Since the taxpayer expectation at the time the loan is made is to repay the debt, debt relief can be seen as an unexpected "windfall." As long as this sort of windfall cannot be attributed to a specific schedule, it remains untaxed.

Although a relatively bright line can be drawn between schedular and global systems in this context, there are some exceptions. Notably, the tax systems of commonwealth countries (**Australia, United Kingdom, and Canada**) treat forgiveness of indebtedness along the same lines of the distinction between capital and ordinary gains. Cancellation of debt in the context of business income, such as accounts payable, will always be treated as ordinary business income. However, in the capital gains context, the cancellation is applied to reduce tax attributes (such as capital losses, carry-over basis, credits, etc.).

For example, in the **United Kingdom,** cancellation of indebtedness is taxed only in very specific cases, such as when the debtor and the borrower are related parties. Any other relief is not taxable, but it reduces tax attributes of the taxpayer. Even if the relief is in excess of the tax attributes, there is no taxable income.[57]

In **Canada,** only half of the relief is included in taxable income. This approach does not treat debt relief on investments as a realization event but also takes the necessary measures to prevent debt relief from

---

[55] United States v. Kirby Lumber Co., 284 US 1 (1931).

[56] AULT & ARNOLD, *supra* note 22, at 189.

[57] AULT & ARNOLD, *supra* note 22, at 190.

becoming a tax-evasion strategy (by deferring the tax to when the assets whose basis was reduced are sold).

## B. Exceptions to inclusion

Even though cancellation of indebtedness is taxed in most countries as a general rule, both schedular and global systems adopt exceptions when the taxpayer is bankrupt or insolvent. This is a good example of tax policy convergence.

In the **United States,** Code § 108 provides for attribute reductions in cases of bankruptcy or insolvency, similar to the treatment generally granted by the **United Kingdom** outside of the bankruptcy context. Indeed, most countries give some sort of relief to taxpayers in financial duress. Even if the extent of this relief may vary, generally the nontaxation of this debt relief is accompanied by a reduction of tax attributes.

The rationale for such easement is quite straightforward: if a taxpayer is unable to settle a debt due to financial hardship, he or she will not be able to pay the tax on any income derived from relief from the debt. If the aim of any relief from debt is to allow the borrower to "start over" and be financially rehabilitated, the rationale is that the tax system should not impede such attempts.

However, a remarkable exception is offered by the **French** system, under which any cancellation of business indebtedness is included in gross income, even if the taxpayer is insolvent.[58] It may well be argued that such an approach may hamper any attempt to recover a distressed business, but it may also serve as a powerful anti-avoidance tool.

# VII. GIFTS AND BEQUESTS

The treatment of gifts and inheritances, as we shall see, are places where redistributive ideologies and taxes are intertwined. Political ideologies and political cultures greatly affect taxes on gifts and bequests. The key tax issue involving gifts and bequests is who (if anyone) bears the tax appreciation of the gift or deducts the loss if a gift is depreciated relatively to the donor's basis.

There are at least three approaches to taxing gifts and bequests from an income tax perspective[59]: (1) no inclusion for the transferee and no deduction for the transferor, (2) inclusion for the transferee and

---

[58] AULT & ARNOLD, *supra* note 22, at 190.

[59] AULT & ARNOLD, *supra* note 22, at 183. We ignore estate taxes for this purpose, although they are obviously relevant from a broader social perspective.

deduction for the transferor (there is also the possibility here to treat the gift as a simple realization event in which the transferor would have to include any appreciation of the gift in his hands), (3) any combination of the first two that would not stand in line with pure tax theory but would encourage other ends or be more administratively feasible.

As in most systems, we shall deal separately with personal gifts and commercial gifts, since the issues raised by each are different.

## A. Personal gifts and bequests

In the **U.S.,** under Code § 102 and § 1015, gifts are not deductible and are excluded from income. Thus, gift appreciation is carried over and taxed to the donee, but losses are not carried over under Code § 1015. In the case of bequests, Code § 1014 provides for a stepped-up basis, and therefore the appreciation is not taxed to either transferor or transferee.

Some countries adopted systems similar to the U.S. one. For example, in **Brazil,** gifts and inheritances received by resident individuals are exempt from income tax.[60]

However, it should be noted that in a schedular system, the issue is raised a bit differently.[61] The issue of income inclusion would arise only if the receipt falls within a particular schedule.

Thus, in **The Netherlands,** for example, the carryover of tax attributes of the gift happens only if such a transaction would have been taxable had it not been a gift. Otherwise, this issue is simply ignored.

The **U.S.** system of no inclusion/no deduction can be justified by the argument that the appreciation will ultimately be taxed. The U.S. approach prevents the possibility of income shifting through "loss gifts" and does not create negative incentives for "real" gifts made out of pure affection. The Code § 1014 rule is based on the argument that it makes it administratively easy to determine basis, rather than looking for historic basis of the deceased. This is a "mixed" system, since appreciation would always be taxed while losses may be unusable for tax purposes. It is also inconsistent with Haig/Simons (which would include gifts and bequests in income).

---

[60] IBDF. Latin-American Taxation: Brazil. http://ip-online.ibfd.org/la/and Art 39 (XV) of Brazilian Tax Law. Regulations. Nevertheless, in order not to be subject to income tax, the beneficiary of the gift or inheritance must keep the historical value that the goods or rights inherited/donated had in the hand of the donor/deceased. If the beneficiary chooses to valuate the goods or rights received at market value, she will be subject to capital gains tax at the amount of the positive difference between the two amounts.

[61] AULT & ARNOLD, *supra* note 22, at 183.

The U.S. solution has also some disadvantages: the case of gifts raises administrative difficulties in determining the basis of the donor in a gift (if it has been a long time since the gift was transferred until the date of disposition by the transferee). Most obviously, it defers the tax by not treating the gift as realization, and in the case of bequests, it provides for exemption.

Thus, other systems adopted methods under which gifts, inheritance, or both are taxed. In this respect, countries choose different paths. In most commonwealth countries, gifts are treated as simple realization events. The tax burden, therefore, is laid at the doorstep of the donor.

In **Australia,** for example, any *inter vivos* gift is treated as a realization event. The donor is taken to have received the fair market value (FMV) of the gift and pays tax on the excess of the FMV over the basis.[62] Hence, no appreciation avoids taxation. As a corollary, the donee is attributed with a FMV basis in the gift.

The same method is implemented in the **United Kingdom**[63] and in **Canada.**[64] Inter vivos gifts are treated, albeit with some exceptions,[65] as realization events.

The rules are different for bequests. In **Australia,**[66] any capital gains or losses resulted from a transfer of property at death are generally ignored if the assets are transferred to a "beneficiary," which, according to Australian law, is "a person entitled to assets of a deceased estate. [This person] can be named as a beneficiary in a will or can be entitled to the assets as a result of the laws of intestacy (when a person dies without having made a will)."[67] Due to multiple legislative reforms, the calculation of basis in the hands of the recipient is complex, but the general rule is that the basis carries over. So, unlike the **United States,** no appreciation can avoid tax (even though it may well be deferred, in case of bequests, for a long time).

In **Canada,** however, transfers at deaths, just as *inter vivos* gifts, are treated as realization events. This is probably more "tax accurate," and the least favorable for wealthy families, and can also be understood as a means for redistribution of wealth achieving a higher level of vertical equity.

Other countries, particularly civil law countries, burden the recipient rather than the donor. For example, in **Russia,** there is no inheritance or

---

[62] Australian Taxation Office, GUIDE TO CAPITAL GAINS TAX 2007, 11 (2007).

[63] HM Revenue and Customs, CAPITAL GAINS MANUAL, CG12922, http://www.hmrc.gov.uk/manuals/CG1manual/CG12922.htm.

[64] Canada Revenue Agency, GIFT AND INCOME TAX, P113(E) Rev. 07, http://www.cra-arc.gc.ca/E/pub/tg/p113/p113-e.html.

[65] HM Revenue and Customs, CAPITAL GAINS MANUAL, CG12925, http://www.hmrc.gov.uk/manuals/CG1manual/CG12925.htm.

[66] Australian Taxation Office, GUIDE TO CAPITAL GAINS TAX 2007, 95–98 (2007).

[67] *Id.* at 95.

gift tax (provided that such inheritances are not awards payable to a taxpayer for inheritance of intellectual property held by the deceased such as copyrights[68]). However, gifts of immovable property, vehicles, and shares received from individuals other than close relatives (i.e., spouse, parent/child, grandparent/grandchild, or sibling) are subject to income tax under the general provisions. Gifts received from individual entrepreneurs and legal entities are exempt up to RUR 4000 per calendar year. The excess is taxed at the general rates of income tax (13 percent for residents and 30 percent for nonresidents).

Of course, for schedular income tax systems, this is true only if the transaction falls within a particular schedule. Otherwise, it is exempt. This is the case in **Italy,** where gifts are generally not taxable (for income tax purposes), unless appreciated assets are gifted within a business or from a business to a stockholder. In this case, gains are realized and recognized and are part of the business income schedule if certain requirements are met.

In **Germany,** for example, "[T]he gift tax supplements the inheritance tax. It is necessary so that inheritance tax for a future right to inherit cannot be avoided through gifts amongst the living. It therefore corresponds that gifts amongst the living are subjected to the same measures of taxation as acquisition through death."[69] Unlike the commonwealth countries, the tax is levied on the heirs. Every inter vivos gift is subject to a gift tax, payable by the recipient. Taxes are assessed based on the FMV of the gift or bequests,[70] net of any liabilities and expenses incurred in connection with the claim for the inheritance or gift. However, recipients are allowed certain exemptions (for example, 307,000 euros if the recipient is the spouse of the donor), and the tax is levied only on the excess over the exemptions.

**China** offers another example of a schedular system, where taxable items of individual income tax do not include gifts and inherences.

In **Israel,** gift transactions are exempt as long as the gift is made to the state of Israel or to a relative or when the gift is made "with good faith" with no expectation that the donee will curry favor in return. In most of such cases, the basis simply carries over to the donee.

---

[68] §217(18) RTC.

[69] German Ministry of Finance, The Tax Department, The Tax Information Center, Inheritance Tax/Gift Tax, *available at* http://www.steuerliches-nfocenter.de/en/003_menu_links/002_ISt/005_ertunab/054_SchenkErbSt/index.php.

[70] The EC's Taxes in Europe Data Base, Germany—Capital Tax—Inheritance and Gift Tax (updated 2007), *available at* http://ec.europa.eu/taxation_customs/taxinv/getcontents.do?mode=normal&kw1=gift&kw2=-&kw3=-&coll=VERITY_DE+-+Capital+tax+-+Inheritance+and+gift+tax.

Some countries simply ignore gifts or inheritance for tax purposes altogether. **Sweden** abolished both the inheritance and gift tax in 2004.[71] The only relevance for taxation is that basis is being carried over and that recipients step into the shoes of the donors. Thus, no country follows the **U.S.** system, which may itself be subject to change as the estate tax is scheduled for reform.

## B. Commercial gifts

In a commercial setting, the differences between countries' approaches to the taxation of gifts (for income tax purposes) are far less apparent. As a general rule, most countries adopt the inclusion/deduction rule, which make sense because in a business environment, gifts are rarely made out of affection, with no valuable consideration expected in return. Thus, most countries treat commercial gifts as a taxable transaction but may allow, in the case of small gifts, certain exemption for the recipients.

In the **United States,** Code § 274(b) is in line with the above principle. The disallowance of deductions makes it clear that one cannot treat a gift as both not included and deductible at the same time. This forces transfers to be either "real gifts" or "real business expenses."

As noted above, this policy is implemented in most countries. It is interesting though, from a cultural perspective, to note what kinds of exemptions/deductions are allowed for commercial gifts and what exactly constitutes a "gift" under local law.

For example, in the United States, Code § 102(c) completely rejects the notion that transfers in an employment relationship can be a "gift."

In **Germany** and **France,** however, gifts are still gifts (even between employer and employee) unless it is shown that the "gift" is directly related to a service rendered (and then it is treated as compensation). Compare Code 274(j) in this respect, which precludes deduction for achievement awards.

Most systems provide de minimis rules where small gifts are not includable for the employee (in the **United States,** it may be covered by Code § 132).

In **The Netherlands** or in **Italy,** small gifts given to employees on special occasions are exempted.

The de minimis amounts gifted to the employees may be even deducted by the employer, which creates double benefits that can be seen as a policy intended to encourage better labor relations (**Canada**—CAD 500; **Germany**—EUR 40).

---

[71] Swedish Tax Agency, Taxes in Sweden 11 (2006). In **Israel,** the taxation of inheritances was abolished even earlier—in 1981.

In the **United States,** Code § 274(b) allows de minimis deductions for gifts, made to someone other than employees, if the logo of the donor is shown on the gift. In other words, it is a small subsidy for public relations expenses.

As noted, in **Germany** and **Canada,** the small deduction is allowed only if gifts are made to employees. This is a consequence of the cultural and political differences in the approach to labour relations issues.

## VIII. THE REALIZATION REQUIREMENT

Realization has been described as the "Achilles' heel" of the income tax. It is no longer considered a constitutional requirement in the **United States,** and there are several accrual- or mark-to-market–based aspects of the U.S. tax system (e.g., the treatment of dealers in securities under Code § 475 and the elective mark-to-market regime for publicly traded PFICs under Code § 1296). Nevertheless, despite many suggestions to the contrary, the United States has remained largely a realization-based system. Moreover, compared to other countries, the scope of realization events in the United States has been limited to the actual sale or disposition of property, although the "realization trigger" has been lowered under the Supreme Court's decision in *Cottage Savings*[72] to include various deemed realizations (such as debt modifications).

In both common and civil law countries, while the income tax remains a transactional tax and incorporates a realization requirement, the scope of realization events tends to be broader than in the United States. For example, gifts are considered realization events for property in **Australia, Canada,** and The **Netherlands.** Death, which in the **United States** is not a realization event even though it gives rise to a step-up in basis under Code § 1014, is a realization event in **Canada** and **The Netherlands.**

Other realization events involve attempts to police the jurisdictional scope of the income tax. Emigration, which involves for most countries the cessation of personal jurisdiction to tax, is a realization event in **Israel, Australia, Canada,** and **Germany** (for substantial stock holdings). Withdrawal from a business, which involves the end of business level taxation, is a realization event in **Canada, France, Germany, Italy, The Netherlands,** and **Sweden.** Notably, the **United States** has recently (after many years of rejecting such proposals) adopted expatriation as a realization event for high net worth individuals (Code § 877A).

Nevertheless, despite the different scope of defining realization, it is noteworthy that mark-to-market—or accrual-based regimes are quite rare. For example, it has been argued that it would be relatively easy to

---

[72] Cottage Savings Association vs. Commissioner, 499 US 554 (1991).

adopt such a regime for the stock of publicly traded corporations because in that case, there are no liquidity or valuation concerns (the stock can easily be sold, and its value is established every day). Such a reform could enable countries to abandon the corporate income tax with its attendant complexities and inefficiencies. But no country we are familiar with has adopted this proposal, despite its congruence with the Haig/Simons ideal. It may be that political resistance to paying tax on "phantom income" (which may disappear with the next market downturn) is too entrenched. Realization, it seems, is here to stay.

3

# Deductions

An income tax is supposed to be levied on net income; therefore, it is supposed to allow the costs of generating income to be deducted from gross income. The problem is defining what these costs are and separating them from personal consumption expenses, which are not deductible.

In addition, most income tax systems allow deductions for certain types of personal expenses, either to encourage particular activities (e.g., deductions for charitable contributions or home mortgage interest) or to improve horizontal equity (e.g., deductions for medical expenses).

In this chapter, we will first discuss problems associated with business expenses and then move on to mixed (business/personal) expenses and pure personal expenses.

Before launching such a discussion, it is useful to note why the comparative study of tax deductions serves as an important tool in understanding tax policy choices: although we observed the variations in the definitions of "income" among jurisdictions in the previous chapter, most of these changes can be regarded as relatively marginal from a policy perspective. This is so since the observable differences are all, in a sense, various interpretations of the same policy concept that is widely adopted worldwide: the Haig/Simons concept (or accretion concept) for the definition of income, which is "the algebraic sum of (1) the market value of rights exercised in consumption and (2) the change in the value of the store of property rights between the beginning and end of the period in question."[1]

When jurisdictions start to deviate from this basic concept, policy divergences (or convergences—assuming the deviations are toward the same direction) become more clearly apparent and may provide us with interesting observations. We briefly discussed one such important form of deviation in the "exemptions" sections of the previous chapter. When different countries elect to exempt different gains that otherwise would clearly be captured by the Haig-Simons concept, it reflects a certain ideological choice that is intended to support certain groups of taxpayers. With respect to individual taxpayers, those groups are often the

---

[1] Henry C. Simons, Personal Income Taxation 206 (Chicago University Press 1938).

lessfortunate ones who, for example, suffered bodily injuries and received compensation in consideration.

A second way to deviate from the accretion of income concept is to tax income but give a "tax credit" in consideration for specific kinds of income. The issue of tax credits is not discussed at length in this book. A credit reduces the amount of taxes due dollar for dollar, while a deduction reduces the amount of income that is subject to tax. Therefore, the value of a deduction depends on the taxpayer's tax bracket, while a credit is invariable. Otherwise, in principle, any deduction can be converted into a credit and vice versa.

The third important factor that is used to "deviate" from the usual income concept is the deductions factor. Because deductions are regarded as the expenses burdened by the taxpayer in order to generate the income, the very definition of an expense as "deductible" represents a policy choice, sometimes ideological, that draws the line between personal, intimate activities and economic, profitable activities that add value to the community. In other words, taken to the extreme, a deduction is an indicator to policy consideration which differentiates the public from the private sphere.

The granting of tax deductions is also a favorite course of action by all jurisdictions that intend to induce specific activities and is thus a clear indicator for policy goals pursued by governments.

## I. BUSINESS EXPENSES

### A. Commuting, clothing, and other nondeductible expenses

#### 1. Commuting

Commuting to work has long been considered a nondeductible personal expense in the **United States** because the taxpayer chooses where he or she lives.

The same approach has been followed in the **United Kingdom,** where court cases have denied commuting expenses to taxpayers who worked both in the office and at home because the cost of travel was not "wholly and exclusively" business related.[2] In 2003, legislation was passed to clarify that while the costs of travel between two places of work is deductible, commuting from home, even when the taxpayer has a home office, is not deductible. Similar rules apply in **Canada** and in **Australia.**

However, in some continental European countries, a deduction for commuting costs is allowed on the theory that housing patterns are not

---

[2] HUGH J.AULT AND BRIAN J. ARNOLD, COMPARATIVE INCOME TAXATION: A STRUCTURAL ANALYSIS 208 (KLUWER 2004).

entirely under the taxpayer's control (to determine where he or she lives). In the frame of this chapter's exposition, there is recognition that the "private" choices made by a taxpayer (such as where to live) are not in effect solely derivatives of an individual's free will. Some governments, by allowing certain expenses, recognize that public factors sometime impede individual behavior and thus offer some relief.

For example, in **Germany,** a fixed amount is deductible per kilometer for the shortest route between the taxpayer's home and workplace.[3]

The same rule applies in **France,** as long as the distance is not "abnormal." The assumption, we think, is that when an individual lives abnormally far from work, true private choice is reflected. Otherwise, that individual could find similar work closer to home, or at least not "abnormally" far, or change to another line of profession within his capability. In other words, when the geographical distance involved is "abnormally vast," one could assume it is large enough to contain comparable choices for that particular taxpayer. Thus, choosing the furthest option means a true private choice.

Similarly, in **Sweden,** taxpayers are allowed to deduct either the cost of public transportation over a certain fixed amount or the cost of traveling by car if it can be established that the car saves at least two hours of commuting time per day.

In **The Netherlands,** only the cost of public transportation is deductible. Allowances provided by employers for travel by car are excludable from income if it does not exceed a fixed maximum distance.[4]

A similar approach is taken in **Israel.** While commuting expenses are not deductible, each Israeli resident is credited a fixed amount each year for such expense, and the value of employer-arranged transportation is excluded from income.

In **Japan,** commuting costs paid by employers are excludable up to a certain level, and self-employed taxpayers can deduct commuting expenses, but employees, until recently, were only given a large standard deduction against income from employment in order to save administrative expenses. This system was challenged on constitutional grounds as discriminating against employees, and even though the constitutional challenge ultimately failed, the statute was amended to allow employees commuting deductions if they exceeded the standard one.[5]

As for **Italy,** commuting costs are not deductible under the general principles governing deductions. Since Italy follows a schedular approach, these principles are different for every category of income, but they reach the same result of nondeductibility of commuting costs. As for the business income category, expenses are deductible if three

---

[3] AULT AND ARNOLD, *supra* note 2, at 208; KPMG, German Tax Card 2008.

[4] AULT AND ARNOLD, *supra* note 2, at 208–09.

[5] *Id.* 209.

requirements are met: (1) the expenses are necessary for the business, (2) the expenses are deducted in the taxable period in which they are accrued, and (3) the expenses have been previously deducted for accounting purposes. As for the self-employee income schedule, expenses also need to be necessary in order to be deductible. Since commuting costs are generally not considered necessary, they are not deductible. As for the immovable property income, the employee income,[6] and the capital income schedules, expenses are not deductibles; for the other income schedule, certain expenses may be.

## 2. Clothing

In the **United States,** the cost of clothing is only allowed for uniforms required by the employer, because clothing in general is considered an individual choice, even if in practice it is the kind of clothing that would not be worn outside the business context. The same rule applies in **Canada, France,** and **Germany.**

In **Israel,** the cost of clothing is deductible provided that the clothes specifically identify the employee as such and are inadequate for any non-employment purpose.

Similarly, in the **United Kingdom,** employees are allowed to deduct the cost of uniforms based on a fixed allowance that varies by occupation. Self-employed taxpayers are allowed the cost of uniforms (e.g., a barrister's wig and gown) but not ordinary work clothing (e.g., a suit worn under the gown, even if purchased exclusively for work).

**Australia** goes one step further and requires employees who wish to deduct the cost of uniforms or receive them from employers on a tax-free basis to register the uniform in a Register of Approved Occupational Clothing. The Register specifies requirements designed to distinguish uniforms from normal clothing that can be worn outside work (e.g., logos have to be a certain size).[7]

**Sweden** goes even further and prohibits deducting the costs of uniforms. The rationale is that the cost of business clothing saves the taxpayer the need to buy alternative non-business clothing, which they would otherwise incur and is a private consumption expense. On the other hand, **Sweden** and **The Netherlands** both permit employees to exclude the value of clothing provided by their employer from income.

In **Italy,** which follows the general rule described above, costs for uniforms are deductible for the employers from business income if the uniforms are provided by the employers. Costs for uniforms are never

---

[6] To a certain extent, prefixed deductions are generally available for employees.

[7] AULT AND ARNOLD, *supra* note 2, at 211–12.

deductible for employees. This is a consequence of the general rule that does not allow deductions from the employee income schedule.

## B. Child care costs

The decision to have children is generally viewed as personal, and therefore, child care expenses are not viewed as a necessary cost of earning business or employment income. Nevertheless, as more women have entered the workforce, most countries have moved to grant some form of credit or deduction for child care expenses in order to lighten the burden of combining work and child care. In addition, child care provided by employers is typically excludable. The choice also depends on the availability of free or subsidized public child care. It still remains an interesting and frequently debated issue since there is hardly a doubt that even if we consider such expense as a business one, there is a strong personal benefit involved. In other words, it remains a form of a hybrid expense, which has the potential of creating an astounding administrative burden deriving from the attempt to separate what is "private" from what is "business related."

Recently, the Israeli Supreme Court has discussed in the *Perry* case[8] this very question (i.e., whether child care expenses incurred by working parents should be deductible) and can serve us as a convenient reference point for the possible policy choices involved. The Israeli court allowed the deductions, basing its opinion primarily on the literal interpretation of the Israeli Tax Ordinance and its legislative history but in a dictum noted two relevant policy issues (It should be noted, however, that the Israeli Parliament has overturned the *Perry* decision. Israeli legislators were quick to respond and changed the law within a few months after the Supreme Court ruling. Following the amendment, the Israeli Income Tax Ordinance now explicitly prohibits deductions on account of child care expenses and instead provides some additional tax credits for working *mothers* only. Legal scholars in Israel generally agree that the Supreme Court got it mostly right, and that the later amendment is an example of poor tax policy and particularly bad drafting by the Knesset (the Israeli Parliament). Some nonprofit organizations have suggested they might bring the issue back to the Supreme Court, challenging the constitutionality of the new legislation. It seems that we have not heard the last on that issue).

First, the court noted that in not allowing child care deductions, the tax system is bound to create a horizontal distortion between similar income earners, only one of which has children. In doing so, the system creates a disincentive for parents who wish to join the workforce. Not surprisingly, as the court specifically noted, the "disincentived"

---

[8] CA 4243/08, The Dan District Assessment Officer v. Perry (4/30/2009).

taxpayers are almost always women. Thus, there is a general equality policy consideration here. Justice Rivlin particularly noted that "the practical outcome in eliminating these distortions might induce women… to join the workforce." He specifically saw it as a necessary outcome of "equality among spouses with respect to the right and duty to be a part of the workforce." Second, he specifically opined that such an outcome would, in turn, "increase the national product." Thus, according to the Israeli court, there is certainly a public sphere consideration here. These considerations represent a specific choice that might not be accepted by everyone (and indeed is not).

In the **United States,** the **United Kingdom,** and **Canada,** child care expenses are generally considered personal and not deductible. For example, the U.S. board of Tax Appeals specifically referred to child care as a form of "private duty" associated with being a parent by noting in *Smith*[9]:

> The wife's services as custodian of the home and protector of its children are ordinarily rendered without monetary compensation. There results no taxable income from the performance of this service and the correlative expenditure is personal… Here the wife has chosen to employ others to discharge her domestic function and the services she perform are rendered outside the home.

Interestingly, the Israeli Supreme Court in *Perry* specifically considered the *Smith* decision, calling it "archaic" and one that "ignores the feminization of labor."

**Canada** deviates a little from the **U.S.** scheme by allowing a limited deduction for some child care expenses, including day care and boarding schools or camps. In 1993, in *Symes v. Canada*,[10] the Canadian Supreme Court decided in a controversial decision, over the dissent of two women justices, that the denial of a full deduction for child care expenses did not discriminate against women because it was not shown that child care expenses were paid disproportionately by women (this is in sharp contrast to the Israeli Supreme Court opinion in *Perry*. Interestingly, the fact patterns in both *Symes* and *Perry* are almost identical).

Similarly, in **Australia** and **Japan,** child care expenses are not deductible. In Australia, employer-provided child care is in part excluded from the fringe benefit tax.

Child care is also not deductible in **Sweden** (although it previously was) because of the availability of a heavily subsidized public child care system. This shows that deductibility in not always necessary in

---

[9] Smith v. Commissioner of Internal Revenue, 40 BTA. 1038, (1939 WL 38), *aff'd*, Smith v. Commissioner of Internal Revenue, 113 F2d 114 (1940).
[10] Symes v. Canada, [1993] 4 S.C.R. 695.

order to achieve the policy goal of allowing both spouses to join the workforce. Deductibility is not necessary if the country simply pays for child care. We will encounter a similar example associated with health-care-related expenses below.

Also, in **China,** child care expenses are not deductible because they do not fall in the categories of income that may be free from individual income tax.[11]

In **Brazil,** only education expenses of the children are deductible.

In **Germany,** on the other hand, the Constitutional Court decided in 1988 that both child care provided by stay-at-home mothers and day care should be deductible. This decision was heavily criticized as allowing for the deduction of opportunity costs, and the legislature instead provided for a general deduction for child care without regard to actual expenses and a further deduction for actual costs.

**France** likewise provides a credit of 25 percent of the cost for caring for young children outside the home and a 50 percent credit for the salary paid for au pair and housecleaning services, even if only one parent works.

In addition, most of the countries surveyed provide for child credits that are designed to encourage childbearing without regard to the relationship to employment. Child credits are available in **Belgium, Canada, Germany, Israel, Italy, The Netherlands, Sweden, the United Kingdom,** and **the United States**.

Similarly, in Russia, taxpayers whose cumulative income during a taxable year does not exceed RUR 280,000 (RUR 40,000 before 2009) are eligible for a child allowance of RUR 1000 (RUR 600 before 2009). These allowances are granted only in respect of income taxable at the rate of 13 percent.

## C. Travel and entertainment

### 1. Business entertainment

Business entertainment expenses are in part personal consumption, and are also particularly susceptible to abuse. Because of these features most countries deny a full deduction and also impose special substantiation requirements. However, all the countries surveyed deny the full deduction rather than attempting to tax the consumption element to the recipient. This treatment can have different tax results if the employer and the employee are in different tax brackets (for example,

---

[11] *See* Article 4, *Individual Income Tax Law of the Republic of China* (English Version), revised in October 2007, *available at* http://202.108.90.130/n6669073/ n6669088/6888498.html (last visited on November 19, 2009).

where the corporate tax rate is significantly lower than the top individual rate, or where the employer is tax-exempt).

In the **United States,** business entertainment is subject to special substantiation requirements as well as percentage limitations.

The same strategy is followed in **Germany,** in which 80 percent of "reasonable" amounts are deductible. In **Canada,** the employer deduction is limited to 50 percent, while in **The Netherlands,** the limit is 90 percent. In **Italy,** business entertainment is subject to a gross profit percentage limitation.

In **Sweden,** there is no percentage limit, but the deduction must be "reasonable" and for restaurant meals it is based on standard amounts that have been gradually decreased. The large difference of the employer and employee rates in Sweden means that this approach still results in undertaxation compared to a full inclusion of the consumption element in taxable income. Similarly, in **Japan,** there is no percentage limitation, but the deduction is only allowed if the business purpose is clearly identified.

In **France,** the rule is more liberal and allows a full deduction with no requirement of reasonableness or percentage limitation. The French do, however, follow the other countries in denying a deduction for hunting, fishing, yachting, and the entertainment use of country houses and golf courses.

In **Australia,** on the other hand, no deduction is allowed for most entertainment expenses, although in-house dining facilities for employees are exempt. In addition, the entertainment of employees is subject to the fringe benefit tax, which in this case also applies to tax-exempt entities (thereby resolving to some extent the tax rate disparity problem mentioned above).


## 2. Business travel

The **United States** allows a deduction for business travel and meals "away from home" (interpreted as away from the taxpayer's usual place of business). The same rule applies in **Canada,** subject to the 50 percent limit on the cost of deducting business meals. In **Sweden,** travel expenses and lodging are fully deductible, while meals are allowed only if the travel involves an overnight stay. Germany reaches the same result with an extensive use of *per diem* amounts. In **Australia,** the fringe benefit tax applies to reimbursed travel expenses. Of course, these countries may still differ with respect to how far "away from home" is enough to justify the expense. Geographical size plays a key role here. In **Israel,** for example, a country approximately the size of New Jersey, 10 kilometers (about 6 miles) is considered distance sufficient to allow the deduction (or non-inclusion) for meals expenses.

In the **United Kingdom**, however, travel expenses are only allowed if they are incurred "wholly and exclusively" for business purposes. Thus, a lawyer was denied the deduction for attending a conference because he admitted that there were social and vacation aspects to the trip. In another case, however, an accountant successfully argued that the social aspect was incidental to the business purpose of the trip.

In **Italy,** travel and meal expenses are deductible, subject to certain limitations but only for entrepreneurs and self-employers. As for employees, these expenses are never deductible.

## D. Capital expenditures

In general, the distinction between an income tax and a consumption tax depends heavily on the treatment of capital expenditures. In an income tax, capital expenditures are not currently deductible but are instead added to basis and may be recovered over time or in some cases only upon realization. A consumption or cash flow tax, on the other hand, permits current expensing of all capital expenditures. Nevertheless, in most income tax systems, current expensing is allowed for some capital expenditures either as a way of stimulating investment or because of the difficulty of drawing the line between ordinary and capital expenditures.

In the **United States,** in principle, any expense that generates income beyond the tax year in which it is incurred must be capitalized, and this includes a pro rata share of expenses that generate both current and future income. But the general rule is subject to many exceptions. For example, research and development and advertising expenses are currently deductible even though they usually give rise to future income. Small businesses are allowed to expense a certain amount of capital expenditures.

The same pattern applies in **Israel, the United Kingdom, Canada, and Australia.** Capital outlays are not deductible, except where specifically authorized by statutes, and the test is whether the expenditure creates an enduring benefit for the business and whether it relates to a specific and identifiable asset of a capital nature. However, in some countries, courts are relatively generous in allowing deduction of expenses that give rise to intangible benefits, especially since goodwill is not amortizable in such countries.

In **Russia,** as a general rule, capital expenditures are added to the cost basis of an asset, and then depreciated.[12] However, a taxpayer has a right to expense capital expenditures in the current tax year, provided that such capital expenditure will not exceed the lesser of 10 percent of the original cost basis of an asset (or 30 percent if such asset belongs to

---

12 § 258 RTC.

certain classes of depreciatable assets) or 10 percent of such capital expenditures (or 30 percent if such capital expenditures are expended on an asset belongs to certain classes of depreciatable assets).[13]

In the continental European systems, the emphasis has been on the creation or acquisition of a distinct and legally identifiable asset or a substantial modification in the condition, character, or useful life of an existing asset. This is the rule in **France, Italy,** and **Germany.** In France, the courts have taken the position that all costs that create a steady and durable source of income must be capitalized.

In **Japan,** on the other hand, the emphasis is not on whether an asset or a source of income was created but on whether the benefits of the expenditure continue for more than one year. A detailed list of items whose cost must be capitalized is set out in guidelines issued by the tax authority.

The **Swedish** rule is more generous, allowing for expensing of the cost of any asset whose useful life does not exceed three years.

## E. Depreciation

In calculating depreciation deductions, the key issue is whether the system tries to approximate a deduction for capital costs over the actual useful life of the asset or whether it uses arbitrary formulas that are sometime designed to encourage specific types of business investment. Notably, whether accelerated or straight-line depreciation is used does not necessarily correspond to whether the depreciation is economically correct, because that depends on the pattern of income generated by the asset.

Even though some differences remain, many commentators have regarded the issue of cost recovery as one in which a remarkable degree of convergence had been achieved among jurisdictions.[14] All of these studies show quite clearly that since the mid 1980s, allowances for plant and machinery, in almost all countries tested, have become less generous, that is to say, almost all countries have broadened their tax base by relaxing the pace of capital expenditures recapture.

In the **United States,** the system began by attempting to approximate accurate deductions but gradually became formulaic and designed to encourage investment by coming close in some cases to expensing.

In **Brazil,** in the case of individuals deriving income from self-employed activity, certain expenses may be deducted, provided

---

[13] *Id.*

[14] *See, e.g.,* Alan J. Auerbach, Michael P. Devereux and Helen Simpson, *Taxing Corporate Income,* NBER WORKING PAPER No. 14494, 8 (2008). *Available at* http://www.nber.org/papers/w14494; *See also* Rachel Griffith & Alexander Klemm, *What Has Been The Tax Competition Experience Of The Last 20 Years?,* 34 TAX NOTES INT'L 1299 (2004).

some special accounting for that matter is maintained, but is generally very limited. Nevertheless, in no event is deduction allowed for the depreciation of installations, machinery, and equipment, or for leasing or transportation expenses.[15]

In **China,** enterprise income taxpayers can depreciate fixed assets following the straight-line depreciation method. In particular, the minimum depreciation time periods for fixed assets vary, for example: 20 years for housing, 10 years for train, steamship, machinery, and other production equipment; and 5 years for electronic equipment, transportation tools (other than train and steamship) and the devices, tools, and furniture relating to production and operation.

Another important issue is the treatment of intangibles and goodwill. In the **United States**, until 1993, intangibles were amortizable over their useful life but goodwill was not, resulting in extensive litigation over attempts by taxpayers to carve out intangibles from goodwill. From 1993, I.R.C. §. 197 permits amortization of both acquired intangibles and goodwill over a fixed period. In **Israel,** goodwill is depreciated at a 10 percent rate. In **Italy,** goodwill is depreciated at a 1/18 rate. Other rates apply to other intangibles.[16] In **China,** the value of intangible assets purchased by the taxpayer includes purchase price and related expenses arising in the course of purchase. In particular, for the intangible assets independently developed by the taxpayer, research and development expenses shall be accurately summarized. Expenses that have been directly deducted for research and development shall not be amortized in use of such intangible assets. Moreover, no depreciation or amortization generally shall be made for goodwill independently developed or purchased.

In some countries surveyed, depreciation deductions are based on formulas that attempt to approximate the useful life of assets. In **Canada,** for example, a comprehensive system of capital cost recovery applies to all tangible and intangible capital assets based on 46 different classes. Cost recovery deductions are determined on a declining balance basis for all assets in a given class. Goodwill and other intangibles are partially (75 percent) amortizable, and upon sale, only 75 percent of the gain is includable.

**Japan, Sweden,** and **Germany** likewise allow for depreciation and amortization, based on tables (including, except for **Italy,** amortization of goodwill).

In **Sweden,** however, the useful lives in the tables are appreciably shorter than actual useful lives, while **Japan** and **Germany** attempt to approximate actual lives.

---

[15] IBDF. Latin-American Taxation: Brazil. http://ip-online.ibfd.org/la/ and art. 75 of Brazilian Income Tax Law Regulations.

[16] *See* Presidential Law Decree n. 917/1986, art. 103.

In **Australia** and the **United Kingdom**, on the other hand, the rules are much stricter. In **Australia,** there is no amortization of goodwill and other intangibles, although 50 percent of the gain on the sales of small businesses is exempt to compensate for the effect of this rule. There is no comprehensive depreciation framework, and assets are examined on a case by-case-basis, resulting in the creation of non-depreciable "tax nothings." In the **United Kingdom**, the class of assets subject to depreciation is likewise quite limited. For example, no depreciation is allowed for office buildings and retail stores. These rules may be in reaction to a period in the 1970s when the U.K. corporate tax was essentially converted to a cash flow tax by allowing an immediate write-off for machinery, equipment, and 50 percent of the cost of industrial buildings.

## F. Business interest

In general, business interest should be deductible as a cost of earning business income. However, if the income generated by borrowed funds is either exempt or subject to a reduced tax rate, the full deductibility of borrowing costs can generate negative tax rates. A further complication is that since money is fungible, it is necessary either to trace the interest expense to the exempt or reduced rate income or to rely on formulas that deny a certain percentage of the interest costs to prevent tax arbitrage.

In the **United States**, interest on loans used to acquire or carry tax-exempt bonds (the interest on which is not includable in gross income), and investment interest used to acquire assets that generate capital gains (and therefore are taxed at a lower rate) is subject to deductibility limitations. In addition, thin capitalization rules limit the deductibility of interest paid to tax-exempt-related parties (usually foreign parent corporations).

In **Canada,** the deduction of expenses associated with tax-exempt income is specifically prohibited. Whether an expense is associated with exempt or taxable income is determined by using a tracing method. Expenses incurred to generate capital gains are not deductible even though capital gains are partially taxable, but expenses used to generate income apart from the potential capital gain are fully deductible. A similar rule applies in **Australia.**

In countries with schedular systems, such as **France, Italy, Germany,** and **Japan,** the denial of the deduction stems from the general rule that to be deductible, expenses must relate to a taxable category of income. In Italy, interest is deductible to the extent of the ratio between gross revenue plus other receipts included in business income and the total amount of all revenues and receipts .[17] In **Japan,** where an item relates to both taxable and exempt income, the deduction is prorated on a gross income basis. **Germany** also enacted a specific statutory rule denying deductions that have a direct economic connection with exempt income, like exempt dividends from foreign subsidiaries. In the **United States,** there has recently been a proposal for a similar rule.

In **Canada,** on the other hand, expenses incurred in connection with dividends are deductible even though the dividends are tax-free because dividends are expressly excluded from the definition of income.

In the **United Kingdom,** the schedular system likewise protects the tax base, but there is a specific rule denying the deduction for interest incurred for a trade that is carried on outside the scope of the U.K. corporate tax.

## G. Losses

### 1. Capital losses

In global systems, a capital loss limitation is frequently imposed to avoid "cherry-picking," i.e., the selective realization of losses while deferring the realization of gains. This introduces a schedular element into the global system.

In schedular systems, on the other hand, no special limitation is needed because losses are usually limited to gains in the same schedule. Loss deductibility limitation rules still dot most of the tax systems. Such rules are necessary since creative taxpayers used to devise many "loss-creating" schemes. Such schemes created tax deductible losses, even though they had little or no actual financial implication to the taxpayers. These losses were then used to shield real income. In the **United States**, one of the most infamous scheme was to create a real estate partnership in which borrowed funds were used to purchase property. The loan was usually a nonrecourse loan secured by the property itself, thus creating no real financial risk to the partners. Since the property was not intended to create any revenue, the depreciation and interest deductions taken by the partnership on account of the purchased property and the mortgage quickly created phantom losses and deductions that flowed directly to the partners. They, in turn, used their part of these losses and deductions to shield their real income from non-partnership sources.

In the **United States,** capital losses of individuals are limited to $3000, with the rest deductible only against capital gains. The same rule applies in **Canada,** where there is an additional limitation on losses from rented depreciable property (recoverable only from the income

---

[17] Art. 61, TUIR. Different rules apply for corporations. *See* art. 96, TUIR.

from that property) and for losses on certain personal use assets (the effect is similar to the passive activity loss limitation in the United States).

In **Brazil,** losses incurred in the sale of capital goods, as a general rule, are not deductible and cannot be used to offset gains on sale of other goods. There is an exception for losses incurred in the stock market. In the case of stocks traded in an exchange, the gain subject to tax is the positive output on a given month of all the trades carried out by the taxpayer. If the taxpayer has a net loss on a given month, that loss may be carried forward indefinitely and used to offset future gains in the stock exchange. There are no provisions regarding the carry-forward or carry-back of annual losses incurred by individuals. However, exclusively in the case of self-employed individuals that maintain special accounting for that matter, there are provisions authorizing the carry-forward of monthly expenses exceeding monthly revenues, during the same calendar year (i.e., until December).[18]

In countries with schedular systems, such as **Germany, France,** and **Italy,** losses can only generally be allowed against income from the same category. Obviously, in such a system, it is much harder to devise a "loss-creating scheme." However, this rule as been relaxed in Germany from 2004, and, instead, specific limits are applied to certain types of losses that are prone to abuse, for example, losses from livestock breeding. This makes the German system resemble a global system, but losses incurred by individuals with respect to capital property are still deductible only against profits from the same category of income.

In **France**, likewise, losses from one category can, in principle, offset income from another category of income, but anti-avoidance rules restrict this in cases of rental real estate, losses from activities in which the taxpayer does not participate on a personal and permanent basis, portfolio investment losses, and losses from hobby farming. In addition, long-term capital losses can only be deducted against long-term capital gains.

In **Russia,** losses arising from income that is taxable at the general rate of 13 percent may not be set off against income that is taxable at the other rates. Losses cannot be carried forward or backward. Losses from the alienation of securities traded on the open market may not be set off against gains from the sale of nonmarketable securities and vice versa.

In this regard, there seems to have been significant convergence between the global and schedular systems in this area of tax law.

---

[18] IBDF. Latin-American Taxation: Brazil. http://ip-online.ibfd.org/la and art. 76 of Brazilian Tax Law Regulations.

## 2. Other loss limitations

In the **United States,** both illegal payments (i.e., bribes) and fines are not deductible. In general, the same rules apply in the other countries surveyed, with a few notable exceptions.

**Canada** allowed a deduction for bribes until 1990 and still allows the deduction of fines for "minor" breaches such as exceeding regulatory quotas.

Similarly, in **Israel,** bribes and fines are not deductible. Previously, expenses in which the "illegality is only marginal" were deductible. However, an amendment introduced in 2009 changed that and now any payment that with respect thereof there is a "reasonable" suspicion of illegality, is not deductible. This stretches the indeductibility to payments that are not proven to be illegal but only potentially are.

**Australia** and **Italy,**[19] like the **United States,** now prohibit a deduction for both bribes and fines and for other costs connected with illegal activities.

**France** and **Japan** both prohibit deductions for fines but generally allow a deduction for bribes and other illegal payments related to business activity.

**Germany** prohibits a deduction for fines and also for bribes to domestic officials, but until 1999 allowed a deduction for foreign bribes if the recipient was named. This was changed under pressure from the OECD, which concluded a binding treaty forbidding deductions for bribes.

# II. PERSONAL EXPENSES

## A. Apportionment of personal/business expenses

In addition to the specific rules set out above for business expenses that have a consumption element like entertainment, most income tax systems outside the **United States** (which does not have a general rule) include a broad rule either disallowing or allowing in part "mixed" business and personal expenses.

Among the countries surveyed, **Germany, the United Kingdom,** and **Japan** all have a general rule that disallows deductions for mixed expenses.

In **Germany,** a statutory rule disallows any expenses of a mixed character unless it they are specifically permitted by statute (for example, business meals expenses are statutorily deductible). The prohibition is based on the idea that for horizontal equity reasons, all consumption must be included in the tax base even if it is incurred in a business setting.

---

[19] See art. 14, paragraph 4-*bis*, Law n. 537/1993.

The deduction is allowed only if the business and personal elements can be clearly separated, or if the personal element is de minimis.

Similarly, in the **United Kingdom,** deductions are allowed only if they are incurred "wholly and exclusively" in connection with trade or professional activities. The result is an absolute prohibition of the deduction of "dual purpose" activities. For example, courts have been reluctant to accept taxpayer assertions that the purpose of travel to conferences was entirely business oriented. In the context of employment income, the test is whether the expenses were incurred "wholly, exclusively, and necessarily" in the performance of employment duties. This strict language has been used to deny deductions for getting into a position to earn income (e.g., job searches), commuting, moving, and child care expenses.

In **Japan,** expenses that are not directly connected with the acquisition of income, such as contributions to schools, personal interest, and casualty losses are not deductible. The rule has also been used to deny expenses related to housekeeping.

On the other hand, **Italy, Canada, Australia, Sweden,** and **France** all allow for apportionment of mixed expenses so that the business or employment element is deductible. This again represents a view under which the private and public spheres are not completely separable.

In **Italy,** mixed expenses are generally deductible for half of their amount.

In **Canada,** where an expense can be apportioned on an objective, verifiable basis (e.g., mileage drive for a mixed use car), the tax authorities allow a deduction for the business portion.

Similarly, in **Australia,** the right to apportion is explicitly recognized, although the extent of it is still unclear in many cases. For example, hotel costs for a mixed business/personal trip must be apportioned, but it is not clear whether the cost of airfare can be.

In **Sweden,** the general approach is to identify the extra cost related to the business aspect of the deduction. For example, an instrumentalist in an orchestra was allowed to deduct dental costs that he established that he would not have otherwise incurred.

In **Israel,** a long set of regulations determines the deductible allowance for common mixed expenses (such as a cellular phone provided by the employer). The deduction of the business part of other mixed expenses (not set by the regulations) is allowed. However, the presumption is that a mixed expense is, in fact a personal one, and the taxpayer carries the burden of proof to show which part of the expense was in fact business related.

## B. Medical expenses

Medical costs are viewed as a personal expense, but they are nevertheless generally deductible on a cost recovery theory (they are necessary to restore the taxpayer's human capital) or as a matter or horizontal equity. However, under the theory that governments are at least somewhat responsible for the well-being of their citizens, different measures have been taken to ease the burden. The tax treatment of medical expenses may provide a good indicator as to the level that a government in any jurisdiction holds itself responsible to the health of its citizens.

In the **United States,** the deduction is allowed but subject to high limits so that only catastrophic out-of-pocket expenses are generally deductible. In most other countries, the availability of the deduction is limited and explained by the existence of publicly funded health care.

In **Canada** and **Australia,** a credit is available for costs in excess of a low threshold that are not covered by the public health system (e.g., because of new technological developments that take time to be covered).

As for **Italy,** 19 percent of medical expenses above a low threshold can be credited against personal income taxes.

In **The Netherlands,** likewise, medical costs are deductible if they exceed absolute and percentage-of-income limitations, even though only 12 percent of medical costs are not covered by public health insurance.

In **Russia,** the taxpayer may deduct medical expenses, including voluntary health insurance premiums, for himself and his spouse, children, and parents to a certain limit. Expenses for certain expensive types of medical care, as determined by the government, may be deducted irrespective of the limit.

Likewise, **Japan, Germany,** and **Brazil** provide for generous deductions for medical costs even though they have extensive public health systems. In Japan, costs that exceed $1000 or 5 percent of income are deductible up to $200,000. In **Germany,** all direct medical costs above a low minimum are deductible, as are medical insurance premiums and expenditures for home nursing care or permanent care in a nursing home (up to a limit). In **Brazil,** substantiated non-reimbursed medical, dental, and hospital-related expenses incurred by the taxpayer and his dependents are deductible. Expenses covered by insurance policies or reimbursed to the taxpayer are not deductible.[20]

In **France** and **Sweden,** however, medical deductions are not allowed because of the availability of public health care, although in France, mandatory contributions to the public health insurance scheme are deductible.

On the other hand, in the **United Kingdom,** medical costs that are not covered by the National Health Service are not generally deductible

---

[20] IBDF. Latin-American Taxation: Brazil. http://ip-online.ibfd.org/la/ and art. 80 of Brazilian Tax Law. Regulations.

unless they are work related, although coverage by employers of costs incurred outside the scope of national healthcare system (e.g., overseas) may be excluded.

Similarly, in **China,** medical expenses do not fall in the categories of income that may be free from individual income tax and thus are not deductible.[21]

Two completely different policy views are represented here. On the one hand, the **U.S.** view represents an approach that only places a mild responsibility at the footstep of the government for the health of its citizens. The government is willing to subsidize some health-related costs by allowing deductions but otherwise leaves the cost of health care to be determined by the free market. Evidently, such an approach is under heavy scrutiny and debate, as demonstrated by the recent health care legislation which included the imposition of so-called "health tax", and some broadening of low-cost healthcare programs. Some believe that given the unique nature of the health system in the United States, the "health tax" will be repealed before even taking effect in 2013. Other countries see the health-care issue as a public rather than private issue, thus providing for an extensive state-supported health system. In such a system, health expenses are not deductible (or tax-payers enjoy only limited deductibility) under the assumption that they are not really needed (since health care is free).

## C. Charitable contributions

All the countries surveyed except **Sweden** allow for a deduction or credit for contributions to charities, subject to certain limits, in order to encourage such activities.

In the **United States,** charitable contributions are allowed for a broad range of charities (including foreign charities through "friends of" organizations) up to 50 percent of a taxpayer's adjusted gross income. For gifts of appreciated property, the full fair market value can be deducted (although only the basis can be deducted for alternative minimum tax purposes).

Likewise, in **Canada,** individuals can deduct up to 75 percent of their income and the value of appreciated property.

Similar generous rules apply in **Australia,** although there are some limits on the type of gifts allowed and on the organizations that may receive deductible gifts.

Other countries, however, apply much stricter limits.

In **China,** for donations of individuals' income made to social organizations or government agencies in China, to the public welfare

---

[21] *See* Article 4, *Individual Income Tax Law of the Republic of China* (English Version). Revised in October 2007, *available at* http://202.108.90.130/ n6669073/n6669088/6888498.html (last visited on November 19, 2009).

undertakings, and to disaster-hit or poverty areas, the amount of donations under 30 percent of the taxpayer's taxable income may be deducted. Furthermore, some forms of donations made to educational or other specific causes may be totally deducted from the taxable income.[22]

In **Japan,** the total deductions may not exceed 25 percent of income, and deductions of donations of appreciated property are limited to the property basis. The same limit applies in **Russia**, where the law provides for a deduction of charitable contributions for income tax purposes, provided that they are paid to educational, cultural, scientific, or medical institutions, as well as certain payments made to institutions providing sports education. The deduction may not, however, exceed 25 percent of the taxpayer's total income in a calendar year. The limit in **France** is 20 percent. In **The Netherlands,** deductible donations may not exceed 10 percent of income, and in **Germany,** the general limit is 5 percent (10 percent for "especially meritorious cultural or scientific purposes").

Other countries adopt a credit system rather than a deduction one. For example, in **Israel,** there is a credit system in place. A donor is credited for 35 percent of the contribution amount, but there are caps, both in terms of the maximum absolute credit allowed and in terms of part of the gross income (no more than 30 percent of gross will be credited in a taxable year). Also, in **Italy,** there is a credit system. In fact, a donor is credited for 19 percent of the contribution amount, but as in Israel, there are also caps in terms of part of gross income. Similarly, in **Brazil,** there is a tax credit for the contributions made to funds controlled by the Municipal Councils, State and National Rights of the Child and Adolescent.[23] Brazil also grants tax credits for contributions to cultural, artistic, and audiovisual activities.[24]

Finally, **Sweden,** does not allow any contributions to charity to be deductible, viewing them as a purely personal expense. However, donations of appreciated property are not viewed as a realization event, and the appreciation therefore escapes taxation.

## D. Home mortgage and other personal interest

Most of the countries surveyed deny a deduction for personal interest, including home mortgage interest.

---

[22] Individual Income Tax of the People's Republic of China (English Version). Last amendment 2007. Article 6, http://www.lawinfochina.com/law/display.asp?ID=6575&DB=1.

[23] Article 87 of Brazilian Tax Law Regulations. https://www.planalto.gov.br/ccivil_03/decreto/D3000.htm.

[24] Articles 90 to 97 of Brazilian Tax Law Regulations. https://www.planalto.gov.br/ccivil_03/decreto/D3000.htm.

In the **United States,** however, while personal interest has not been deductible since 1986, home mortgage interest is, subject to very generous limitations ($1 million of indebtedness on up to two homes). This rule applies even to so-called "home equity loans" used to finance personal consumption. This approach represents a view that prefers home ownership over renting. Also, certain deductions are allowed for tuition-related interest.

In **Italy,** in sharp contrast, no form of personal interest is deductible. Also, in **Israel,** no form of personal interest is deductible. Several bills were brought forward over the years with the intent to allow mortgage interest deductibility, but none were legislated. With respect to tuition, the position of the Israeli Tax Authority is that such an expense improves the human capital, and hence, in essence, is a nondeductible capital expense.

In **Canada,** personal interest is not deductible, and proposals to allow a deduction for home mortgage interest have been rejected as too costly. Taxpayers routinely use savings for personal expenditure—and, at the same time, borrowing for income-producing purposes—and the courts have generally upheld the deduction as long as the amount used for the business purpose was equal to the amount of the loan, even if no actual tracing could be performed. The same rule applies in **Australia**. In **France**, however, to prevent such commingling, no deduction is allowed for either personal or investment interest.

In **Germany** and the **United Kingdom,** the rules have been tightened to disallow interest deductions that have previously been allowed. In Germany, personal interest has not been deductible since 1974, and home mortgage interest has not been deductible since 1994. Even business-related interest is not deductible if withdrawals from the business exceed equity plus profits, lest business indebtedness be used to finance personal consumption. In the United Kingdom, personal interest has not been allowed since 1969, and the home mortgage interest deduction was gradually restricted and finally abolished in 2000.

In **Sweden,** there are no restrictions on the general deductibility of interest, but business interest must be deducted from business income (generally taxed at a high rate) while all other interest, including personal and home mortgage interest, must be deducted from income from capital (taxed at a low rate). To prevent shifting of interest expense from capital to business income, tracing is generally required. In addition, if the amount of debt allocated to the business results in negative equity, interest is calculated on the negative equity, and that amount is treated as additional business income and capital expense, thus reallocating any excess interest expense from business to capital.

# 4

# The Taxpaying Unit

## I. INTRODUCTION

This chapter addresses the issues related to the identification of the taxable subject for individual income tax purposes.

A taxable subject can be defined as a taxpaying unit (individuals, married couples, families, business entities, and so on) that realizes taxable income, is liable to pay taxes, and is obliged to account for the income tax to tax authorities.

Usually, the realization of income and payment of tax and accounting to tax authorities is done by the same person (or unit), but in some cases, there may not be coincidence.[1] Take, for example, the case of withholding taxes. The payee of the income is the taxpayer, yet because the payer of the income controls the payment, it is obligated to act as a withholding agent for the tax authority and is liable for collecting and transferring the tax. In other words, the substantive taxpayer is the person entitled to the income, while the formal taxpayer is the person liable to withhold, pay, and account for the tax.

This chapter first discusses the basic issues at stake and the main models that countries may adopt as a solution, offering a comparative analysis. Then, it identifies the actual solutions adopted by the United States and by other countries.

## II. THE BASIC ISSUE AND THE TWO MAIN MODELS: HOW SHOULD WE DEFINE TAXABLE UNITS? INDIVIDUAL vs. FAMILY TAXATION

Once a country determines the concept of income and the concept of deductions, the main unavoidable policy question that every country with an (individual) income tax system faces is the definition of a

---

[1] The same tax may be due by two or more people and the payment of one person liberate the others. *See* MARIA CECILIA FREGNI, OBBLIGAZIONE TRIBUTARIA E CODICE CIVILE 243 (Giappichelli 1998) who deals with the Italian concept of "solidarietà tributaria".

taxable unit for purposes of linking the taxable income to a specific subject. There are two main models to define taxable units:

1. Under the *individual model* (or *separate taxation model*), each physical person is a taxable unit; therefore, everyone has to file tax returns, declare taxable income, claim expenses (and deductions), and pay income taxes.

2. Under the *family model* (or *joint assessment model*), the family is the taxable unit, and each individual is treated as part of its family; the family is thus required to file a tax return, declare income, and claim expenses (and deductions). Here the definition of a "family" for purposes of this model may pose additional controversies and complications.[2]

The definition of taxable unit brings in several equity and efficiency considerations.[3]

First of all, the horizontal equity principle requires equal treatment of equals. Who should we consider equals? If equals refers to families, then we should probably consider families as taxable units instead of individuals. On the other hand, if it refers to individuals, then we should probably consider individuals as taxable units.

This policy issue involves a social choice[4] and hence provides a fascinating comparative perspective. It is clear that the models can favor certain social values at the expense of others. For example, the adoption of the family model would result in unequal treatment of married couples as compared to unmarried partners. This, in turn, will require us to delve into questions regarding the definition of "marriage" for tax purposes[5] and will inevitably and promptly lead to the more general discussion of genders.[6] The individual model, on the other hand, does not provide that families with the same level of well-being are treated equally for tax purposes.

Second, a vertical equity issue may also be raised. From an income redistribution perspective, the choice between the two models would yield different results. Let's assume that Family A earns $60,000 a year (the husband earns $60,000, while his wife doesn't earn anything). Family B also earns $60,000 a year, but both husband and wife each

---

[2] Claudio Sacchetto, *La tassazione della famiglia: il modello italiano, in* La tassazione della famiglia: aspetti nazionali e comparati 72, (Rubattino 2010).

[3] *See* Mario Leccisotti & Vincenzo Patrizii, Il trattamento fiscale della famiglia nei paesi industrializzati, (Giappichelli 2002).

[4] Merlin Leroy, *Sociologie de la fiscalité de la famille, in* La tassazione della famiglia: aspetti nazionali e comparati 143, (Claudio Sacchetto ed., 2010).

[5] Maria Teresa Soler Roch, Family taxation in Europe 2, (Kluwer 1999).

[6] *See* Henry Ordower, *Comparative Law Observations on Taxation of Same-Sex Couples,* 111 Tax Notes 229 (2006); Dominique Grillet-Ponton, *La Famille et le fisc,* (PUF 1998).

earn $30,000. If a family model were adopted, Family A and Family B would be subject to the same amount of taxes. In contrast, if an individual model were adopted, the tax burden would be apportioned differently between the two families and most likely (assuming a progressive income tax system), Family A would be subject to significantly higher taxes than Family B.

Last, the choice between different models should also take into account efficiency considerations.[7] In fact, the incentive for an individual to engage in working activities (and to what extent) would also depend on the adopted model. Let's assume that Mr. Joe earns $250,000 a year and his wife, Mrs. Paula, is thinking about taking a $20,000 a year part-time teaching job. Mrs. Paula is more likely to accept the job in a progressive tax system that adopts an individual model than in a progressive tax system that adopts the family model, because under the latter approach, a significantly higher portion of her salary would be taxed.

Moreover, the family model can create a sort of tax penalty (so-called marriage penalty or marriage tax)[8] or tax privileges (so-called marriage bonus). "As long as we desire a progressive tax system based on family income, there is no way to make it also marriage-neutral. Any tax schedule will feature either a marriage bonus (single penalty), a marriage penalty (single bonus), or some combination of both bonus and penalty, depending on the tax schedules and circumstances of the people involved."[9]

In conclusion, the choice between the two models is associated with many policy considerations that each government has to address based on its policy priorities. Accordingly, if a government wants to be involved in determining the size of families, it should probably opt for the family model and structure its tax system in a way that makes marriage more or less convenient for tax purposes, depending on the desired family size. Alternatively, if a government wants to pursue the principle of marriage neutrality, according to which marriage does not have tax consequences, it should probably opt for the individual model.

It is noteworthy that there are also hybrid solutions that can be (and actually are) adopted. As we will see, many systems adopt elements of both models or give the taxpayers the option to choose whether to be taxed individually or as families.

---

[7] For a deep analysis, *see* Henrik Jacobsen Kleven & Claus Thustrup Kreiner, *The Taxation of Married Couples in OECD Countries: A Need for Reform?*, 2002, EPRU, *available at* http://ideas.repec.org/p/kud/epruwp/02-13.html.

[8] *See* Leslie A. Whittington & James Alm, *Marriage Penalty*, in THE ENCYCLOPEDIA OF TAXATION AND TAX POLICY 251 (Joseph J. Cordes, Robert D. Ebel, Jane Gravelle eds., 2005).

[9] JOEL SLEMROD & JON BAKIJA, TAXING OURSELVES. A CITIZEN'S GUIDE TO THE DEBATE OVER TAXES (The MIT Press 2008).

In the following discussion, we will examine how the tax systems of Australia, Brazil, Canada, China, France, India, Israel, Italy, Japan, Russia, Sweden, the United Kingdom, and the United States cope with the above-mentioned considerations. This analysis is not intended to give a complete overview of the technical mechanisms of each country but rather a flavor of how policy makers view the considerations developed above and solve the issues raised.[10]

## A. Concrete examples of countries adopting the individual model

Some of the countries adopting the so-called "individual model" are Australia, Canada, Italy, Japan, Russia, Sweden, and the United Kingdom. Most of them do not adopt a pure version of the model, in that they somehow take into account aspects of the family as a taxable unit model.

In **Australia,** the individual model is mitigated by a spousal tax credit, which is a credit that married taxpayers may claim when their spouse has no or limited income. This mechanism aims at treating families equally to a certain extent. However, this goal is not fully achieved considering that the credit is low, and it phases out when the spouse realizes a relatively small amount of income. Moreover, such a credit can create disparities between spouses and other couples. This is why the definition of spouses (*rectius* family) is crucial: for these purposes, spouses are two persons of the opposite sex, maintaining a living as husband and wife.[11]

Similarly, in **Canada**, there is a limited spousal tax credit.[12] The income of married couples or common law spouses of the opposite sex is aggregated for determining the entitlement to certain personal tax allowances.

In **Italy**, a tax credit for every dependent member of the family, defined as a family member with no or limited taxable income, is granted to the household.[13] However, a tax reform to adopt a sort of quotient familial is an issue of political discussion.

---

[10] *See* OECD, Taxing Working Families: A Distributional Analysis, (OECD 2005).

[11] On recent Australian tax family reforms, see Patricia F. Apps & Ray Rees, *Australian Family Tax Reform and the Targeting Fallacy* (May 5, 2010). Australian Economic Review, Forthcoming; Sydney Law School Research Paper No. 10/44. Available at SSRN: http://ssrn.com/abstract=1601088

[12] For example, in Canada, the spousal tax credit is equal to 15 percent of Canadian dollars: 20,640 if the taxpayer's only dependent is a spouse who has no income. The credit is reduced by 15 percent of the spouse's income and is eliminated once the spouse's income exceeds 10,320 Canadian dollars.

[13] Italy adopted a sort of "family" model until the Italian Constitutional Court (Corte costituzionale) considered this model unconstitutional (see Cort. cost.,

In **Japan**, there used to be a spousal allowance, but it was partially abolished in 2003 in order to encourage married women to work.

**Sweden** is an example of a country that moved from the family model to the individual model as part of a policy decision aimed at encouraging women to enter the job market. Therefore, today the marginal tax rate of an individual is not influenced by the income level of the other partner, and Sweden has now adopted a pure individual model.

In 1990, the **United Kingdom** also shifted from the family model (that attributed the wife's income to the husband, who was considered the only taxpayer) to the individual model. This shift was mitigated, however, by a series of tax credits aimed at assisting families.

As for developing countries such as **Brazil, China,** and **India**, it is worth noting that the individual model is more common. The reason behind this choice is that these countries prefer to be marriage neutral for efficiency reasons.

## B. Concrete examples of countries adopting hybrid solutions

Some of the countries adopting the "hybrid model" are the **United States, Germany,** and **Israel**. The "hybrid model" earned its name due to the fact that the tax systems allow taxpayers to elect to be taxed under the individual or family model.

In the **United States**, there are separate tax rates for single individuals and for married couples.[14] Married couples can opt to file a joint return. For these purposes, a taxpayer's marital status on the last day of the year determines his status for the whole year.

The effect of filing a joint return usually results in a lower tax liability (so-called marriage bonus) compared with a couple's tax liability had they not been married. However, under certain circumstances, a married couple filing a joint return can be subject to a higher tax liability (so-called marriage penalty) than an unmarried couple. The final effect (bonus or penalty) is determined by the amount of income that each

---

July 15 1976, n. 179, in *Riv. dir. trib.*, 1977, II, 112). *See* Franco Gallo, *Regime fiscale della famiglia e principio di capacità contributiva, in* RIVISTA DI DIRITTO FINANZIARIO E SCIENZA DELLE FINANZE 99, (1977). According to the Italian family model, the wife was never a taxpaying unit and her income was imputed to her husband, who was the only taxpayer, liable for paying the taxes and filing the tax return.*See, also,* MARIO NUSSI, L'IMPUTAZIONE DEL REDDITO NEL DIRITTO TRIBUTARIO, (Cedam 1996) and Enrico De Mita, *Il principio della tassazione soggettiva al netto e la tassazione della famiglia,* BOLLETTINO TRIBUTARIO 1413 (1997).

[14] *See* DOUGLAS A. KAHN & JEFFREY H. KAHN, FEDERAL INCOME TAX: A STUDENT'S GUIDE TO THE INTERNAL REVENUE CODE 573, (Foundation Press 2005); Marjorie Kornhauser, *Wedded to the Joint Return: Culture and the Persistence of the Marital Unit in the American Income Tax, in* 11-2 THEORETICAL INQUIRIES IN LAW - COMPARATIVE TAX LAW AND CULTURE 631 (2010).

partner realizes, by the rate schedule, by the possibility to reduce gross income with the other spouse's excess of deductions, and by the possibility to enjoy certain tax advantages reserved only to married couples filing tax returns (e.g., Code § 21(e)(2), 32(d)).

Filing a joint return may also have tax disadvantages. In fact, unless certain conditions apply, each spouse is liable for the entire tax on the joint income. Moreover, the aggregate amount of deductions available for a couple filing a joint return may be lower than the deductions available to each spouse filing separately (see Code § 179(b)(4)), even though the standard deduction for joint filers has recently been increased.[15]

In **Germany**, married couples can elect to sum up the total income, divide it by two, and apply the statutory rates. Children are treated as separate taxpayers for most tax purposes.

**Israel** is also a hybrid jurisdiction in this regard. The starting point of the Israeli Tax Ordinance is that a married couple's income is aggregated and taxed as a single economic unit. However, the ordinance provides exceptions to the general rule, which, if applicable, allow each spouse to elect his or her income to be taxed separately. Generally speaking, a married couple has the burden of proof to show that each spouse's income is unrelated and not dependent on the other spouse's income. This is intended to prevent a notorious, previously common abuse where one high-income earner spouse who owns a business would "hire" the other spouse for the job. Thus, the income would be "shared" among the two, effectively moving some of the same income from the same source to a lower tax bracket. In practice, years of judicial precedents have resulted in the exceptions surpassing the general rule. Today, most of Israeli married couples are taxed separately. It has been argued that this judicial stance represents a social development, which, over time, moved away from an archaic perception that treated the family as a cohesive unit, toward a perception that gives more weight to the self-transcendence of each individual within the family.[16]

In **Brazil**, spouses are required to file a joint tax return for the household. However, if they are married under a separate property regime, they have the option of filing individual returns in order to be taxed separately. Even if they are married under a community property regime, the spouse who is not the head of the household may file an individual return for certain types of income (e.g., employment income) and be taxed separately. A spouse who is taxed separately may not be considered a dependent for tax purposes. If the income of the spouses

---

[15] On the historical developments of this matter in the United States, see Stanley S. Surrey, *Taxation of the Family – The Revenue Act of 1948*, 61 HARV. L. REV. 1097 (1948) and Boris Bittker, *Taxation of the Family*, 27 STAN. L. REV. 1389 (1975).

[16] For a detailed account, *see* Rifat Azam, *Couples Taxation in Israeli Law: It is Time to Adopt the Separation Model*, 5 ALEI MISHPAT 179 (2006).

is taxed separately, deductible allowances that are common to the spouses may be taken by them proportionally to the income of each one, provided that the combined deduction does not exceed the normal limits.

## C. Concrete example of a country adopting the family model

**France** serves as an important example of a country that adopts the family model. The taxable unit is the family, defined as the husband, wife, dependent children, and any other qualified disabled persons who live with the family. Unmarried partners of the same or different sex may also qualify as a family for income tax purposes.

According to the French version of the family model, the income of all members of the family is aggregated and then split, based on a ratio (so-called *quotient familial*)[17]. The *quotient familial* is merely a family share. The taxable income of the household is divided into shares equal to the number of family members. Children are allocated half shares while wives, husbands, and other members of the family are each allocated one whole share. For example, a family consisting of a wife, a husband, a child, and a disabled person has a quotient familial of 3.5. Therefore, the aggregated income has to be divided by 3.5. Once the income shares are determined, the individual income tax rate schedule is then applied. The total tax (before any tax credits apply) payable by the taxable unit (the family) is the product of the tax on one share and the number of shares.

# III. ANTI-ASSIGNMENT OF INCOME RULES

## A. The reason for anti-assignment of income rules

Once the taxable unit is defined, specific anti-tax avoidance rules are necessary to prevent the reduction of the overall tax burden by shifting income between taxable units (usually related). The choice of the taxable unit and the so-called anti-assignment of income rules are particularly crucial in progressive income tax systems.

Let's assume, for example, that Country A has a proportional income tax system, and Country B has a progressive income tax system. Further, let's also assume that Mr. Joe earns $50,000 a year while his son earns nothing. If Mr. Joe and his son were residents in Country A, it would make no difference if they shifted income from Mr. Joe to his son.

---

[17] Pierre Beltrame, *Famille et impôt. La prise en compte des charges de famille en droit fiscal français, in* La tassazione della famiglia: aspetti nazionali e comparati 19 (Claudio Sacchetto ed., 2010).

On the other hand, if they were residents of Country B, it would be very convenient for Mr. Joe to shift part of his income to his son, reducing, therefore, their overall tax burden.

In order to prevent this shifting problem, a tax jurisdiction can either provide that related persons are treated as a single taxable unit (as is the case in **France**) and/or provide special rules that disregard transfers of income between related persons.

To sum it up, the basic issue at stake is the following: what kind of attribution rules can efficiently prevent the assignment of income phenomenon?

## *B. The solutions adopted by some industrialized countries: examples*

As we have already seen, there is no need for strict attribution rules in those countries that adopt the "family model" or in those countries with proportional tax systems. The shifting-of-income problem is present, however, in those countries with progressive tax systems adopting the individual model. In fact, the main purpose of the anti-assignment of income rules is to preserve the vertical equity level chosen by a given country.

The anti-assignment of income rules can be strict (as in **Canada**) or loose (as in the **United Kingdom**). Both approaches (strict and loose) provide that neither taxable income nor the tax burden can be shifted among different persons, yet they differ in how they treat the income derived from property.

In **Canada**, property-derived income that is transferred from one person to certain related persons is treated as income to the transferor. The same treatment applies to non arm's-length transfers of taxable income to nonrelated parties. Moreover, interest free loans may give rise to income to the lender if he and the borrower are related.

In the **United Kingdom**, on the other hand, transfers and gifts of property are respected for income tax purposes.

The **United States** adopts a solution that is sort of a compromise between the British system and the Canadian system. Transfers of property are treated differently depending on whether the property is irrevocably transferred. If so, the transaction is respected for income tax purposes. If the transferor/assignor retains certain rights in the property, the transaction is not respected for income tax purposes. This is also true even if the contract provides that the transferee/assignee has a right to the income from that property, unless the stream of income assigned to the assignee is of sufficient duration.

In **Australia**, there is a special provision that states that unearned income of children (e.g., parents' income shifted to children) is taxed at the highest tax rate, regardless of the parents' marginal income tax rate.

From a functional point of view, it can be demonstrated that preventing the shifting of income phenomenon can also be achieved using rules that are not technically anti-assignment of income rules but that have the same effect. In **Germany, Italy,** and **Sweden**, there are only specific rules governing the source of income. Therefore, the income from employment is assigned to the employee, the income from a trade or business is assigned to the entrepreneur, the capital income is assigned to the beneficial owner of the underlying capital, and so on. It is worth noting that in Sweden, source rules are governed by common law principles, while in Germany and Italy, they are governed by civil law principles.

Finally, the (non)solution adopted by **The Netherlands** is quite interesting: income and deductions can be freely assigned—and with no limitations—between partners.

5

# Tax Accounting

## I. THE TAXABLE PERIOD AND THE ACCOUNTING PERIOD: GENERAL DEFINITIONS

### A. Definitions, main issues, and possible solutions

The *taxable period* is the periodic basis on which income tax is imposed. The *accounting period* is the periodic basis on which the profits and expenses of a business are allocated for accounting and book purposes.

The taxable period is a fundamental concept for every income tax system. In fact, for obvious reasons, income and deductions are determined on a periodic basis and apportioned in taxable periods (or fiscal periods, tax years, basis periods, years of assessment). As each tax period triggers an independent tax obligation, the income tax is due periodically.

As a consequence, every income tax system has to deal with three issues: the definition of the taxable period, the specification of its starting and closing days, and the provisions applicable to certain taxpayers. The purpose of this chapter is to analyze possible policy solutions in light of the concrete responses given by several countries.

In most jurisdictions, income and deductions are generally determined on an annual basis. For taxpayers who do not maintain accounting books and records, this generally coincides with the calendar year.

The tax period is often determined on an annual basis for simplicity reasons and, in fact, the annual tax period will most likely relate to the government's budgetary year or coincide with the calendar year, thus reducing administrative costs.

However, in particular circumstances, certain taxpayers may be allowed to use different tax periods. This is true for taxpayers who have to keep accounting books and records and thus have to allocate profits and deductions based on accounting periods. In such cases, policy makers should investigate the possibility of imposing a taxable period that coincides with the accounting period; otherwise, an arguably undesired phenomenon of tax deferral schemes may emerge.[1]

---

[1] This is why in the **United States**, the Code strictly limits such schemes, by forcing partnerships to adopt taxable periods closer to their partners' periods.

As an example, let's consider an individual who pays taxes on a calendar year basis and is also a partner in a general partnership, whose accounting period starts on February 1 and ends on January 31 of the following year. Assume further that the partnership earns taxable profits (which flow to the partner) during the 11 months period between February 1 and the end of the calendar year. Taxes at the partnership level are accounted for, however, only when the partnership accounting period closes (i.e., January 31 of the following year). The partner will only have to account for his taxable portion of the partnership profits 11 months later (December 31) when his tax period closes. This mechanism will provide the partner with 11 months of deferral on his taxes due.

The need of coincidence between the taxable and accounting periods is even more evident when the taxable income depends on the amount of the book income. On the other hand, if book income and tax income are completely separate and independent, there is no specific need, other than reducing compliance costs, for the taxable and accounting periods to coincide.[2]

## B. The solutions adopted by some countries: examples

As a general rule, countries adopt the calendar year as a taxable period although there are many differences in each country's exceptions to the general rule.

Under **U.S.** tax law, income and deductions are determined on an annual basis under Code § 441, and the taxable period coincides with the calendar year. In fact, U.S. taxpayers, who are not required to maintain accounting books (or who do not use a permitted annual accounting period), are required to use the calendar year as their taxable period. However, under certain circumstances, a taxable period may be longer (Code § 441(f)) or shorter (Code § 441(b) and § 443(a)) than a calendar year. Under certain circumstances, U.S. taxpayers can also elect to report their income monthly. For corporations (and for entrepreneurs, in general), there is a coincidence between the taxable and accounting periods, even though book income and tax income are not related. Therefore, individual taxpayers compute their income tax liability using the calendar year unless they are entrepreneurs. In this case, they may also use the accounting year as taxable years.[3]

---

[2] On this issue, *see* Michelle Hanlon, Stacie Kelley Laplante & Terry J. Shevlin, *Evidence for the Possible Information Loss of Conformity Book Income and Taxable Income*, 48 J. LAW & ECON. 407, 2005.

[3] A 52- to 53-week year may be used if the taxpayer regularly keeps her books on that basis. A 52- to 53-week year is an annual accounting period that always ends on the same day of the week that is closest to the end of a calendar month.

Similarly, under **Italian** law, individual taxpayers have to report their income annually, based on a calendar year. Since tax income is strictly dependent on book income, the taxable period is defined by article 76, TUIR, as the "company's or entity's year or the operating period, as determined by law or by the articles of incorporation. Should the term of the year or operating period not be determined by the law or by the articles of incorporation, or should it be defined as two or more years, the tax period shall be the calendar year." In other words, taxable periods for corporations coincide with accounting periods (or operating periods) because of the fact that tax income depends on book income. In this case, a coincidence between accounting and fiscal periods reduces compliance costs.

In **Canada**, while for individuals the taxable period is the calendar year, for corporations the taxable period can coincide with its financial period, but it cannot be longer than 53 weeks. Once a taxable period has been set, any change has to be agreed upon with the Canadian tax administration.

In **France**, the taxable period for individual taxpayers is generally the calendar year. However, individuals who earn business income may opt to be taxed on the basis of the accounting period, freely chosen by the taxpayer. This general rule of the calendar year as the taxable period applies to corporations as well. However, if the taxpayer's accounting year is different than the calendar year, the taxable period coincides with the accounting period.

As for **Germany**, the taxable year is also the calendar year. For taxpayers who earn trade or business income, however, the taxable year may be different from the calendar year: in this case, the income of the financial year is formally taxed as income of the calendar year in which the financial year ends.

In **The Netherlands**, also, the taxable year is the calendar year. However, an entrepreneur may apply the accounting period for tax purposes or opt for a different taxable year in accordance with their statute.

In **Sweden**, the taxable year is the calendar year. As for corporations, the taxable year coincides with the accounting year, which is also annual, but can end on December 31, April 30, June 30, or August 31, unless another date is permitted by the Swedish tax administration.

Finally, in **Brazil**[4], **Russia, Israel,**[5] and **China,**[6] the taxable period is the calendar year.

---

[4] IBDF. Latin-American Taxation: Brazil. http://ip-online.ibfd.org/la.

[5] It is worth noting, that in Israel (generally speaking), as in some other countries, employees do not have to report their own income each year. Instead, income from employment is deducted at the source by the employer on a monthly basis, based on the expected yearly income. Differences between the expected and actual income are set off at the end of the year.

[6] IBDF. Asia-Pacific Taxation: China. http://www.ibfd.org/portal/Product_tiap.html.

In conclusion, most of countries under analysis have adopted the calendar year for physical persons, with an option to be taxed according to the accounting years for entrepreneurs. The reason behind this policy choice seems to be simplicity.

## II. CASH MODEL VERSUS ACCRUAL MODEL

### *A. The accounting methods: cash versus accrual*

As seen, taxable years have to be defined thoroughly. The next issue that policy makers have to deal with is how income and deductions should be apportioned (or allocated) to each taxable period.

Two main allocation models can be adopted on this regard: the *cash model* and the *accrual model.*[7]

Under the *cash model*, taxable income and deductions are allocated based upon cash receipts and disbursement. Therefore, under this model, income is imputed to the taxable period in which taxpayers actually receive cash or its equivalent. Expenses are deducted in the taxable periods in which taxpayers actually pay the expenses.

Under the *accrual model*, income and deductions are allocated based upon when the taxpayer earned the income or incurred the expenses, irrespective of when actually received or paid out. In particular, the income and expenses of a current period are taken into account as such whether or not payments have been received or made. Likewise, the income and expenses that have not been incurred in a current period are not taken into account in that period, regardless of whether or not payments have been received or made (unless otherwise stipulated by law).

Policy makers can also use a combination of the above-mentioned models either for different items of income (like in **Italy**) or for different kinds of taxpayers (like in the **United States**).

For example, the **Italian** legislator has chosen, albeit some exceptions, to adopt the cash method for employment income, self-employment income, capital income, income from land, and other income schedules, while it has adopted the accrual model for the business income schedule.

Under **U.S.** tax law, generally speaking, the cash model applies for individuals while the accrual model applies for corporations.

The difference between the **Italian** and **U.S.** approach is a consequence of the fact that Italy adopts a schedular definition of taxable income, while the U.S. adopts a global definition of taxable income.

---

[7] Michael Lang, ELLIOTT MANNING & STEVEN WILLIS, FEDERAL TAX ACCOUNTING, (LexisNexis Matthew Bender 2006).

Following is a brief survey of these models and some observations regarding the advantages and disadvantages they entail based primarily on the three mentioned economic principles of taxation (i.e., efficiency, equity, and simplicity).

First of all, the cash method is simpler than the accrual method for those taxpayers who do not have to keep accounting books. This means that policy makers can provide taxpayers with an opportunity to lower their compliance costs by adopting the cash rather than the accrual model. This is because, unlike the accrual method, the cash method does not require taxpayers to keep accounts of their expenses and profits, a task that frequently proves to be very complicated. However, this simplicity argument is not applicable for taxpayers (usually entrepreneurs) who, under the accrual method, are required to maintain accounting books and records.

As for administrative costs, it may be argued that the cash method is easier to administer, since it is easier for tax authorities to audit a taxpayer who follows the cash method[8] rather than a taxpayer who follows the accrual method. However, this is also true only for taxpayers who are not required to maintain accounting books and records according to the accrual method.

For the above-mentioned reasons, many countries allow taxpayers who are not required to maintain financial books and records, to utilize the (simplified) cash method. Indeed, in this case, it would be very costly both for taxpayers (compliance costs) and for tax administrations (administrative costs) to allocate income and deductions based on the accrual method.

On the other hand, most countries require the use of the accrual model (for income tax purposes) for taxpayers who are required to maintain accounting books and records. However, this is only true if the accrual method used for accounting purposes is equivalent to that used for income tax purposes.

In this context, an interesting issue is to what extent accounting rules used to apportion book income can be used for income tax purposes.[9] The answer depends on various factors: the definition of income, the definition of taxable period, the purpose of accounting rules versus tax rules, and so on. In fact, it is worth noting that accounting rules and tax

---

[8] For example, bank account investigations are more effective and immediate if taxpayers follow the cash method.

[9] The issue is part of a broader issue which deals with the relationship between corporate governance and taxation. See Nicola Sartori, *Corporate Governance Dynamics and Tax Compliance*, in XIII INTERNATIONAL TRADE AND BUSINESS LAW REVIEW 264, (2010) and Nicola Sartori, *Effects of Strategic Tax Behaviors on Corporate Governance*, 2009, available at SSRN: http://ssrn.com/abstract=1358930.

rules have to follow different principles, and this difference may have an impact on the allocation model.

For example, in the **United States,** the accrual method of accounting differs from the accrual method used for income tax purposes.[10] The obvious result is inconsistency between profits reported for tax purposes (which a corporation has a clear interest in keeping as low as possible) and the profits reported for accounting purposes (which a corporation, for market reasons, has a clear interest in keeping as high as possible).

Second, efficiency considerations may cause policy makers to impose the cash method for entrepreneurs as well, because the cash method—unlike the accrual one—can provide a substantial tax deferral by allowing taxpayers to expense all of their costs based on the disbursement and to tax their profits based on the cash (or equivalent) receipts.[11] This is why some jurisdictions allow small corporations, partnerships, and self-employees to apportion taxable income according to the cash method.

## B. The solutions adopted by some countries: examples

In the **United States,** the model for apportioning taxable income for individuals is the cash method with some exceptions (e.g., corporate bonds and other debt instruments issued for a discount price). Certain corporations, partnerships, and self-employees cannot adopt the cash method, but they have to apportion taxable income according to the accrual[12] method.[13]

A similar approach is taken by **Israel** and **Australia,**[14] where small businesses and individuals pay taxes in accordance with the cash method, while big businesses and corporations are required to report their income following the accrual method.

In **Brazil**, the cash method applies for the recognition of income and gains derived by resident individuals.[15]

---

[10] This approach is different from the one adopted by most European countries, which maintains consistency of tax and accounting purposes (this issue is discussed further below).

[11] It is worth noting that the efficiency reasons behind this choice are traded off with the equity issues that this choice may cause.

[12] As stated before, the accrual model used for tax purposes is different than the accrual model used for accounting ones.

[13] Douglas A. Kahn & Jeffrey H. Kahn, Federal Income Tax: A Student's Guide to the Internal Revenue Code 19, (Foundation Press 2005).

[14] Tax rules and accounting rules are completely independent in Australia.

[15] IBDF. Latin-American Taxation: Brazil. http://ip-online.ibfd.org/la.

In **The Netherlands**, business income is computed on the same accrual method for both tax and accounting purposes. Individuals are taxed on a cash basis.

On the other hand, in **Germany, France, Italy,** and **Sweden,** there is a strict relationship between tax accounting and book accounting: for this reason, earners of business income are allowed to use the same accrual method for both accounting and for tax purposes (with a few specific exceptions). As it has been underlined, this approach "tends to be pro-taxpayers, by allowing accounting reserves to be deducted for tax purposes and often allowing the unrealized losses to be recognized for tax purposes by valuation at the lower of cost or market value."[16]

Such a relationship is common in civil law countries because accounting rules are regulated under accounting laws rather than by independent professional bodies like in common law countries. This explains why the adoption of international accounting standards may have the effect of making corporate income tax rules more similar.

Moreover, in **Germany,**[17] **France, Sweden**, and **Italy,**[18] the method of tax accounting is determined by the category of income. Therefore, income other than business income is apportioned according to the cash method, while business income is allocated in time according to the accrual method. The adopted model is a consequence of two policy choices: the schedular system (rather than the global one) used to define taxable income and the strict relationship (rather than full independence) between tax accounting and financial accounting.

Similarly, in **Canada** and in the **United Kingdom**, income from business and property has to be apportioned according to the accrual method, while other items of income have to be apportioned according to the cash method. This is probably again a consequence of the fact that taxable income has book income as its starting point.

**Japan** and **China** have taken a different approach. As a general matter, the accrual model is mandated, and, therefore, taxpayers who are required to maintain accounting books and records—as well as those who are not—will utilize this method. Under certain conditions, however, small entrepreneurs and individuals have the option to elect the cash method.

---

[16] *See* Victor Thuronyi, Comparative Tax Law 268 (Kluwer 2003).

[17] Peculiar in **Germany** is that corporations' profits are determined following the so-called net worth comparison method (*Betriebsvermögensvergleich*): profits are the difference between net assets at the end of the previous year and net assets at the end of the current year (Sec. 4(1) EStG), reduced by capital contributions and increased by withdrawals.

[18] In **Italy**, as a general rule, the cash method applies to all categories of income except for business. Taxable business income is determined under the accrual method, with certain exceptions for dividends and social security contributions (Article 109(1) TUIR).

## III. NET OPERATING LOSSES

### A. Main issue and possible solutions

The independence of each taxable period may be subject to limitations if a taxpayer has profits in one taxable year that could be offset by losses from different taxable years. The issue, then, is to what extent a taxpayer can offset net operating profits utilizing the net operating losses.

Three approaches come to mind in this context. First, it is possible to consider different taxable periods as completely independent, thus not allowing taxpayers to carry back or carry forward net operating losses. Alternatively, it is possible to allow taxpayers only to carry back or only to carry forward net operating losses. Finally, it is possible to allow taxpayers both to carry back and carry forward net operating losses.

### B. The solutions adopted by some countries: examples

Most countries choose to allow taxpayers to carry back or carry forward net operating losses. The reason behind this is that taxpayers with losses (usually entrepreneurs) would be excessively penalized if they could not offset profits from one taxable period with losses from another.

In addition, such a limitation poses vertical equity issues. For example, let's assume a taxpayer realizes a loss in Year 1 of $1,000,000 and a net profit in Year 2 of $100,000. If the taxpayer were prevented from carrying forward his Year 1 loss to offset his Year 2 profit, he would be subject to taxes on the $100,000 despite his inability to pay, based on wealth accumulation at the end of Year 2.

A horizontal equity issue would also emerge, as this taxpayer would be treated differently from a taxpayer that realizes a loss of $900,000 at the end of Year 1 and zero income at the end of Year 2.

In the **United States,** net operation losses can be carried back for 2 years and forward for 20 years. For small businesses, the carry-back period for losses generated in 2008 may be increased to three, four, or five years. It is needless to mention that such extension of the carry-forward periods provides significant assistance to distressed businesses because it eases their cash flow burden (especially in the current economic turmoil where cash at hand is crucial for the survival of struggling businesses).

In **France**, losses may be carried forward for six years. However, for corporations only, losses may be carried forward indefinitely. Corporate taxpayers also have the option, subject to certain limitations, to carry losses back for the three preceding years.

In **Germany**, as a general rule, subject to certain limitations, net operating losses up to €511,500 may be carried back to the preceding year. Any excess losses may only be carried forward (albeit indefinitely) and utilized to offset up to €1,000,000 of net income; thereafter, any remaining losses may be used to offset up to 60 percent of the net income exceeding €1,000,000.

In **The Netherlands**, losses may be carried back for three taxable years or carried forward for nine taxable years. Such losses can only be used to offset taxable income of the same category.

In the **United Kingdom**, trade losses may be carried forward indefinitely and can offset profits of the same and continuing trade. As for corporations, trading losses can also be carried back for one year. Any other income losses can be carried forward and can offset only income of the same category.

In **Canada**, the rules for losses are the same for individuals and corporations. Ordinary losses may be carried back three years and forward twenty years for deduction against any form of income.

In **Italy**, losses cannot be carried back. Subject to certain limitations,[19] net operating losses may be carried forward for five years unless the loss is realized in the first three years of existence of the business (start up businesses). In this latter case, losses can be carried forward indefinitely. An anti-avoidance rule may apply in defining a start up business for this purpose.

Finally, in **Sweden**, the net loss deriving from one source of business can be carried forward to offset profits from the same source of business indefinitely. In this case, losses from one source of business income cannot be utilized to offset profits from another source, even in the same taxable period.

---

[19] 1. the majority of the voting rights of the company is transferred; 2. in the tax year in which the transfer occurs or in any of the two preceding or following periods, the activity of the company has changed.

# 6

# Taxation of Capital Gains and Losses

## I. GENERAL DEFINITIONS: CAPITAL GAIN AND LOSSES, REALIZATION, BASIS

### A. Definition of capital gain or loss

The definition of capital gains and losses and their treatment for tax purposes are, by far, two of the most controversial policy issues that every income tax system faces.

Here is one of the most common definitions of capital gain:

> It is "a gain on disposal of certain assets, e.g. assets held by way of investments. The qualification of a gain as a capital gain varies from country to country and is often strongly fact dependent. Capital gains may typically be contrasted with income from the sale of inventory in the course of a trade or business. In some countries capital gains are subject to a separate tax or no tax, while in other countries they may be subject to different tax treatment under the general income tax legislation (e.g. ring-fencing of losses). Gains may also be qualified as long-term capital gains or short-term capital gains according to the length of time held. Capital gains are generally taxed by reference to the difference between disposal proceeds and acquisition cost. Adjustments may be made, e.g. for inflation or for expenses of acquisition or disposal."[1]

This definition assumes that the capital gain arises upon *disposal* of an asset. Yet it is not at all clear from the contemporary tax literature that this is the preferred definition. In fact, many economists prefer to define capital gains as the income accrued on an asset at the time that an increase in value occurs.[2]

---

[1] BARRY LARKING, INTERNATIONAL TAX GLOSSARY 57 (IBFD 2005).
[2] *See* ROBERT M. HAIG , THE CONCEPT OF INCOME—ECONOMIC AND LEGAL ASPECTS, THE FEDERAL INCOME TAX 59 (Columbia University Press 1921); HENRY C. SIMONS, PERSONAL INCOME TAXATION: THE DEFINITION OF INCOME AS A PROBLEM OF FISCAL POLICY 5 (Chicago University Press 1938).

Two models can be adopted by policy makers to define capital gains and losses: the accrual model or the realization model. Here, too, hybrid solutions can also be adopted.[3]

According to the *accrual model*, a capital gain (or loss) can be defined as the increased (or decreased) value of an asset, regardless of whether the asset is converted into cash (or its equivalent).

According to the *realization model*, a capital gain or loss can be defined as the income (or loss) emerging by the disposition of an asset (or from any other "realization" event).

However, probably due to the fact that it is much simpler to administer, the second model (realization) is much more common. This is not to suggest that there is uniformity among countries regarding the concept of realization and the actual tax treatment of capital gains.[4] On the contrary, differences in the concept of realization exist due to the fact that various tax systems adopt different models for defining taxable income.

From an *equity* perspective, the realization model does not meet the test. Assume that there are two taxpayers: the first owns a house worth $100,000 at the beginning of Year 1, the value of which increases to $105,000 at the end of the year; the second has a $100,000 balance in a savings bank account at the beginning of Year 1, which earns $5,000 of interest during the year, resulting in a $105,000 balance at the end of the year. Horizontal equity requires equal treatment of these equally situated taxpayers. In our example, the two taxpayers, having the same level of well-being at the beginning and at the end of Year 1, are certainly equals. However, only the first model (accrual model) would treat them equally for tax purposes. At the end of Year 1, both taxpayers are $5000 wealthier (or a little less if we take into consideration inflation consequences). Nevertheless, according to the realization model, only the second taxpayer would be subject to tax on the interest income, while the first taxpayer would not be subject to tax on the appreciation in the value of the house. Consequently—assuming a 50 percent income tax rate—after applying the realization model, the first taxpayer would still have $105,000, while the second taxpayer would only have $102,500.

Unlike the accrual model, the realization model fails the *efficiency* test because of the so-called "lock-in effect": the holder of an asset is incentivized not to sell the asset to prevent triggering gain recognition.

---

[3] New Zealand taxes gains accrued on certain financial instruments, regardless of any realization events. Also, in the United States, France, and Sweden, certain gains are now taxed based on the accrual method, also known as "mark to market."

[4] *See* Joel Slemrod & Jon Bakija, Taxing Ourselves. A Citizen's Guide to the Debate over Taxes 279–82 (The MIT Press 2008).

Moreover, the realization model would cause an investment in appreciating assets to be much more attractive than other investments that pay out interests, dividends, or other taxable income of the like, just because of the tax deferral effect that the realization model allows. This is one of the main reasons for the development of complex financial instruments intended to imitate the cash flow of dividends in interest payments, without those payments being classified as dividends or interest for tax purposes.

If all this is true, one should wonder why most countries adopt the realization model (which is unequal and inefficient) rather than the accrual model. The main reason is simplicity: administrative and compliance costs would be significantly higher under the accrual model. Market value of assets is not easy to determine and, in some cases, even impossible to determine. Under the accrual model, taxpayers would get struck by (unnecessary) increased compliance costs (determining market values of assets), and tax administrations would suffer from a significant increase in their administrative costs (managing and monitoring their tax systems).

It has been argued that it would be relatively easy to adopt such a regime for the stock of publicly traded corporations because in that case, there are no liquidity or valuation concerns (the stock can easily be sold, and its value is established by markets on a daily basis).[5] Such a reform could enable countries to abandon the corporate income tax with its attendant complexities and inefficiencies. But no country we are familiar with has adopted this proposal despite its congruence with the Haig/Simons ideal. It may be that political resistance to paying tax on "phantom income" (which may disappear with the next market downturn) is too entrenched.

## B. The concept of realization and recognition

We have clarified in the previous subchapter why most of the jurisdictions use the realization model and why realization is here to stay. But what does realization mean? Generally speaking, *realization* is a term of art referring to an event that gives rise to a capital gain or loss.[6] However, the fact that an event gives rise to a capital gain or loss does not necessarily mean that the capital gain or loss is taxable (or deductible). In other words, while realization is often a taxable event, this is not necessarily true in all countries: a realized capital gain is taxable only if

---

[5] As we have seen, some countries (like New Zealand) are starting to adopt hybrid solutions, which means applying the accrual model whenever it is simple enough.

[6] It has already been underlined as realization has been described as the "Achilles' heel" of the income tax.

it is also recognized, and there is no available exemption under the controlling tax rules.

For example, in the **United States,** every realized gain or loss is also recognized (Code § 1001(c)) unless a statutory provision (like Code § 1031) provides that the gain or loss is not recognized. Moreover, recognized gains are also taxable unless a statutory provision states an exemption, while a recognized loss is not deductible unless a statutory provision authorizes the deduction.

The difference between nonrealization and nonrecognition deserves further clarification. While *nonrealization* simply means that there is no taxable event, *nonrecognition* is basically tax deferral (and not necessarily exemption). In fact, tax exemption is usually specifically prescribed.

Depending on the country, a realization event may indicate sales, exchanges, gifts, or bequests; leasing, surrender, or forfeiture; the receipt of insurance moneys or other compensation; the receipt of a sum for exploitation of an asset; the receipt of a sum for refraining from exercising rights; the destruction or abandonment of an asset; emigration of the taxpayer; and the transfer of the taxpayer's business property to his private property. These concepts, based on the realization model, are illustrated by the following scheme:

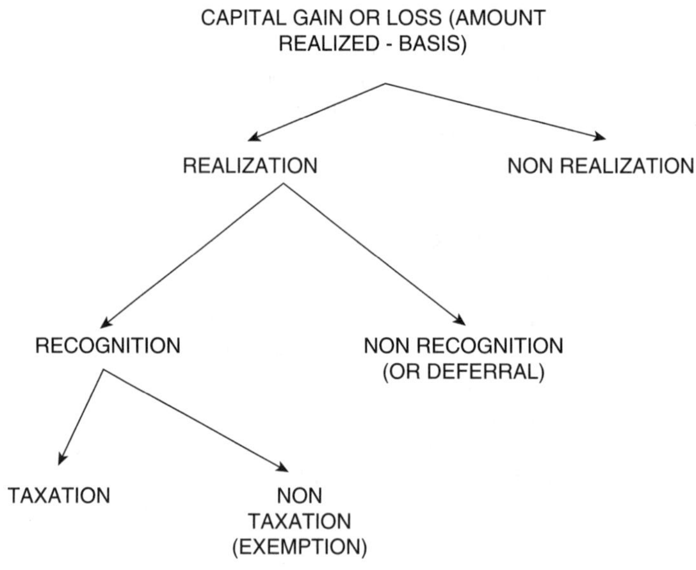


Capital gains or losses can be realized or not realized. Realized capital gains can be recognized or deferred to a subsequent realization event. For example, for policy reasons, corporate reorganizations (that are clearly realization events) are generally not recognized if certain conditions are met. Once a gain (or loss) is recognized, it is also taxable (or deductible), unless a tax rule provides for an exemption.

It is worth mentioning again (see Chapter 2) that realization is no longer considered a constitutional requirement in the **United States**, and there are several accrual or mark-to-market–based aspects in the U.S. tax system (e.g., the treatment of dealers in securities under Code § 475 and the elective mark-to-market regime for publicly traded PFICs under Code § 1296). Nevertheless, despite many indications to the contrary, the United States has largely remained a realization-based system. Moreover, as opposed to other countries, the aim of realization events in the United States has been limited to the actual sale or disposition of property, although the "realization trigger" bar has been lowered under the Supreme Court's decision in *Cottage Savings* to include various deemed realizations as well (such as debt modification).[7]

In both common and civil law countries, while the income tax remains a transactional tax and incorporates a realization requirement, the scope of realization events tends to be broader than in the United States. For example, gifts of property are considered realization events in **Australia**, **Canada** and **The Netherlands**. Gifts are also realization events in **Israel**, but gifts between relatives and gifts to the states are exempted. Death is a realization event in **Canada** and **The Netherlands** but not in **Italy** or in **Israel**. In the United States, death is not a realization event, but it gives rise to a step-up in basis under Code § 1014.

Other realization events involve attempts to police the jurisdictional scope of the income tax. Emigration, which involves for most countries the cessation of personal jurisdiction to tax, is a realization event in **Israel, Australia, Canada,** and **Germany** (for substantial stock holdings). Withdrawal from a business, which involves the end of business level of taxation, is a realization event in **Canada, France, Italy, Germany, The Netherlands,** and **Sweden**. Notably, the United States has recently (after many years or rejecting such proposals) adopted expatriation as a realization event for high net worth individuals (Code § 877A).

## C. The concepts of "basis" (or fiscal value) and "amount realized"

In order to determine the amount of a realized (and recognized) gain or loss under the realization model, it is necessary to clarify what a realization event is (see previous subchapter) and, more importantly, to define the concepts of basis and amount realized.

The basis is the fiscal value of an asset; in other words, the basis is the cost of an asset for purposes of computing a capital gain or loss (or the depreciation).[8] The concept of basis has two goals in income tax

---

[7] Cottage Savings Association vs. Commissioner, 499 U.S. 554 (1991).

[8] Douglas A. Kahn & Jeffrey H. Kahn, Federal Income Tax: A Student's

law: the determination of the taxable gains or deductible losses and the determination of the amount of depreciation (for assets used in trade or businesses—basically, allowing for cost recovery and preventing double taxation of the same income).

In most circumstances, the basis is the cost of the investments. For example, if a taxpayer buys a house for $100,000, the basis is $100,000.

The basis so determined can be adjusted (upward or downward) according to subsequent relevant events. For example, if a taxpayer makes a capital improvement of $30,000 into her house, this expense should be reflected in the basis of the house, which would therefore be increased to $130,000. If the same taxpayer has a deductible loss because of a casualty, such deduction should also be reflected in her basis, and the basis would therefore be reduced by an amount equal to the deduction. As we shall see, some countries have also adopted legislation that adjusts the basis to take into account inflation rates. Even though it can be quite burdensome to calculate such adjustments, it is definitely more accurate from a financial perspective.

In order to determine the gain or loss, the concept of amount realized is also fundamental. The amount realized is the amount of cash or its equivalent received in a transaction. The capital gain or loss is determined by calculating the difference between the amount realized and the basis in the asset transferred.

## II. NONRECOGNITION TRANSACTION AND EXEMPTION TRANSACTIONS

### A. Nonrecognition transactions

Certain transactions, which are clearly realization events, may be considered nonrecognition events for income tax purposes due to policy reasons (usually tax efficiency, *rectius* tax neutrality). By maintaining tax neutrality, policy makers try not to discourage certain economic choices. The most important example, which relates to corporate taxation, is the tax treatment of reorganizations.[9] Most jurisdictions consider reorganizations as nonrecognition events, deferring taxation to a subsequent recognition event (like a regular sale of assets). [10] Thus, tax

---

GUIDE TO THE INTERNAL REVENUE CODE 31 (Foundation Press 2005) define basis as "the maximum amount a taxpayer can receive in payment for an asset without realizing a gain."

[9] Each country has to decide whether (and to what extent) gains/losses resulting from transactions relating to assets or entities trigger the recognition of taxable capital gains or deductible capital losses.

[10] Four models can be adopted to solve the above mentioned issue (tax treatment of reorganizations):

law does not interfere with business restructuring decisions, and this is efficient and neutral[11].

---

- The first model is the full or partial taxation model: according to it, the taxable capital gains and the deductible capital losses resulting from cross-border corporate reorganizations are recognized, and immediately taxed in the hands of the assignor. The assets of the assignor will be valued in the hands of the assignee at the value that has been used to determine the assignor's tax liability, which generally corresponds with the market value. We have a full taxation if the capital gains are taxed at the same rate as ordinary profits, while we have partial taxation if capital gains are taxed at preferential rates.
- The second model is the roll over relief at fiscal value: according to it the taxable capital gains and the deductible capital losses resulting from cross-border corporate reorganizations are not recognized. The objective of this model is not to grant a tax exemption to the parties involved, but rather to "neutralize" the tax consequences of the reorganization, so that the reorganization involves neither a tax advantage nor a tax disadvantage. According to this model, taxation doesn't take place at the time of reorganization, but it is deferred and it will burden on the assignee when the gains are recognized. After the reorganization, the assets of the assignor will be valued in the hands of the assignee at the same value that they had before the reorganization, and the taxable profits of the assignee are calculated on the basis of tax elements that were present in the assignor company. In conclusion, there is not exemption on capital gains, but there is a deferred tax burden on the assignee on unrealized gains that exist at the time of the reorganization. This is the model adopted by the EU Merger Directive. According to the Merger Directive, we have relief if the assets, as a consequence of the transaction, become connected with a permanent establishment of the assignee in the home state of the assignor. The state of the assignor retains the right to tax gains on a subsequent disposal of the assets.
- The third model is the roll over relief at financial value: according to it, parties negotiate autonomously, if the unrealized gains have to be taxed immediately on the assignor or later on the assignee. The assignee will revaluate these assets for tax purpose only for the part that has been taxed on the assignor. In specific, to the extent that the assignor of assets has been tax free, the assignee will carry over the tax basis that those assets had before the reorganization in the assignor company; to the extent that the transfer of assets is taxed to the assignor, the assignee will revaluate these assets for tax purpose. This model, applied to cross-border corporate reorganizations, gives the hand to tax arbitrages.
- The fourth model is the participation exemption model. According to this model there is no taxation either on the assignor or on the assignee. In fact, the assignor is not taxed on unrealized gains and the assets (generally shares) of the assignor will be valued in the hands of the assignee at the contracted price of the assets (in terms of shares or cash), which should correspond to the market value.

[11] With reference to internal corporate reorganizations, the general policy view in most countries is that it is economically not efficient to tax corporate

Sometimes, nonrecognition regimes are also called rollover relief regimes, underlining the fact that nonrecognition does not grant a juridical exemption but rather a juridical deferral (which, in the long run, can be equivalent to an economic exemption). In order to grant the deferral, there is a carryover of basis so that after the nonrecognition sale or transfer of the asset, the assignee's basis is the same basis that the assignor had in the property prior to the sale or transfer.

A tax exemption, on the other hand, provides the assignee with a step-up-in basis, without triggering any taxes. This way, the inside capital gain on the asset is exempt from tax, and there is a so-called "jump of tax." Generally speaking, an exemption is set by a policy maker in order to promote and encourage certain behaviors, usually because they result in a positive externality or when it is necessary to grant systemic coherence to the income tax rules.

## B. Examples of concrete policy choices

Here are some examples of nonrecognition rules and of exemption rules actually adopted by some countries.

Under **U.S.** tax law, a *nonrecognition* regime in individual income tax is provided, inter alia, in the following circumstances:

1. where business or investment property is exchanged for property of a like kind (Code § 1031)[12];
2. where property is compulsorily or involuntarily converted into a property, which is similar or related in service or use (Code § 1033). The gain is deferred until the replacement property acquired in the above transactions is subject to a subsequent taxable event (as a disposition of the property in a non-like-kind transaction). In other words, the Code § 1031 and § 1033 transactions do not give rise to a tax exemption but rather a mere tax deferral; and
3. in the transfer of capital assets to a corporation in return for shares of the corporation (Code § 351).

An exclusion (or *exemption*) of $250,000 ($500,000 in the case of married persons filing a joint return) applies to gains from the sale of a home if it has been owned and occupied as the taxpayer's principal residence for at least two years during the five-year period preceding the date of sale.

---

reorganizations, because taxation would discourage reorganizations. For this reason, in the presence of certain conditions (for example, the continuity of business enterprise and the continuity of shareholder interest), most of the industrialized countries do not recognize taxable capital gains and deductible capital losses resulting from internal corporate reorganizations.

[12] This deferral regime does not apply to stocks, securities, or property held for sale.

In **Canada**, *nonrecognition* treatment is granted, inter alia, to the following main transactions:

1. transfers of capital assets to a corporation in return for shares of the corporation; and
2. transfers of capital property from a person to his/her spouse.[13]

As for *exemptions*, subject to many anti-avoidance rules, an individual resident in Canada may realize tax free capital gains up to $750,000 on the disposal of qualifying shares of a Canadian private corporation (with its primary active business in Canada) or on the disposal of qualifying farm and fishing property. Gains realized by a Canadian resident on the disposition of his principal residence and gains realized on the disposition of low-value personal-use assets, and compensation or damages received for personal injury are also exempt from taxation.

As discussed earlier, the **French** tax system defines taxable income in a schedular way. Such a policy choice reflects the tax treatment of capital gains.

As for the business income category, donations or bequests of an individual enterprise (self-employee) or of shares in a partnership are *nonrecognition* events (if certain conditions are met), and the taxation is thus deferred until a subsequent sale of the business (or until any other taxable event occurs). Long-term capital gains realized by entrepreneurs are usually *exempt* if two conditions are met: (1) the business activity has been exercised for at least five years, and (2) the taxpayer's profits do not exceed a certain amount.

As for the immovable property income category, capital gains on the disposition of the taxpayer's principal residence are *exempt* from tax, as in the **United States** and **Canada.** Moreover, immovable property gains are exempt if the sale prices are lower than €15,000.

In **Germany** and **Italy**, there is no specific definition of capital gain. Therefore, they are generally not subject to tax if they derive from private transactions. This choice is a mere consequence of the fact that both Germany and Italy define income in a schedular way based on the source model. However, certain speculative capital gains are subject to tax. For example, capital gains emerging in the conduct of a trade or business are included in the business income category if they are realized and recognized.

In **Germany,** capital gains (of at least €600) arising from the transfer of either immovable property held for less than ten years or movable property (not shares[14]) held for less than one year are subject to tax.

---

[13] This is an optional regime, since the transferor of the property can elect to tax the capital gain.

[14] From 2009, capital gains from the sale of shares and financial instruments are subject to tax notwithstanding the holding period.

Under **Italian** law, capital gains realized by individuals are taxable only if they are included in one of six categories of income.[15] Oftentimes, speculative capital gains fall under the category "other income" (Article 67, TUIR). This happens in the case of sales of stock, sales of securities and other derivative instruments, sales of subdivided land, or other immovable property held for less than five years.[16]

In **Brazil**, the taxation of capital gains of resident individuals upon disposal of real estate is subject to special rules. The income tax due on capital gains derived from the disposal of real estate acquired by an individual before 1988 is reduced by a certain percentage (up to 100 percent, 5 percent per year) depending on the year in which the individual acquired such real estate. A similar reduction applies with regard to real property acquired until 1995. Moreover, capital gains derived from the sale of low-value assets and rights are exempt if the sale price does not exceed BRL$35,000 in the month in which the sale is affected, with regard to assets and goods in general, or BRL$20,000, with regard to shares traded on over-the-counter markets. There is currently another special exemption for capital gains tax upon the sale of real estate by individuals. Pursuant to Article 39 of Law No. 11.196 of November 21, 2005, any gain from the sale of a residential real estate made by an individual resident in Brazil is exempted from income tax if the proceeds of the sale are used to acquire another residential real estate within 180 days from the date of the sale. Such exemption is irrespective of the value of the sale of the real estate and the amount of real estate owned by the taxpayer.

In **China**, gains arising from the disposal of assets are generally included as part of taxable income, i.e., the capital gain is the difference between the book value and the selling price of the asset. For individuals, certain exemptions are available to resident individuals such as gains on the sale of shares of Chinese listed enterprises and certain capital gains on houses subject to conditions, e.g., gains on disposal of a house self-occupied for at least five years.

In **The Netherlands**, capital gains are generally not taxable, with the exclusion of capital gains upon disposal[17] (substantial) of shares.

In contrast, under **Swedish** law, capital gains realized by an individual are generally included in capital income if, for private properties, they exceed Sek 50,000. *Nonrecognition* treatment has been set for donations and, under certain conditions, for capital gains derived from the sale of a building used as the main residence in previous years. In these cases, it is noteworthy that there is not carryover of basis for the

---

[15] For example, an Italian taxpayer selling a piece of art, privately, is not subject to tax on the realized gain, because such a gain is not included in any schedule of income.

[16] Capital gains on residential buildings are exempt from tax.

[17] Disposal has to be intended in a broad sense.

buyer, and the seller has to deduct the amount of the gain deferred from the basis in the newly purchased property as a condition for nonrecognition treatment.

In **Russia**, income from the alienation of private property is not taxable, provided that a minimum holding period of three years is fulfilled. If the holding period is not fulfilled, the excess of the gross sales proceeds over RUR 1 million (for immovable property) or RUR 125,000 (for movable property) is subject to income tax at the general rate of 13 percent.

Finally, in the **United Kingdom**, capital gains are exempt from tax if their amount is lower than Pounds 9600. Capital gains realized by the disposal of the main residence, as well as racehorses, government stock, and qualified corporate bonds are exempt from tax.


## III. TAXATION OF CAPITAL GAINS AND CAPITAL LOSSES: ORDINARY INCOME vs. SEPARATE INCOME

Once the concepts of realization and recognition have been defined, every policy maker will necessarily need to specify the taxation rules of capital gains. Two policy choices can be compared: the taxation of capital gains as ordinary income and the taxation of capital gains as separate income.

One way to treat capital gains is to include them in ordinary income and tax them accordingly (full taxation). This is the solution generally adopted by countries, like **Italy** and **Germany,** which do not have a specific definition of capital gains: if a capital gain is considered taxable income, it is generally fully taxed as ordinary income of the category it belongs to.[18] However, special rules, based on equity or efficiency considerations, may apply to accord a preferential tax treatment to certain taxable capital gains.

The other solution that can be implemented to tax a capital gain is the separate income model. According to this model, capital gains are taxed differently than ordinary income. An example of the separate income taxation model is given by nonspeculative capital gains.

As for capital losses, various solutions have been adopted. Countries that tax capital gains separately will generally allow capital losses to be deducted from capital gains. Following the same logic, countries that do not treat capital gains differently from ordinary income will generally allow capital losses to be deducted from both capital gains and ordinary income. These solutions prevent the erosion of taxes by utilizing low tax capital losses to reduce high tax ordinary income. It can be

---

[18] For example, specific exceptions may apply to capital gains derived by the sale of shares.

argued that, in recent years, there has been a convergence of the above models.

Three examples of countries adopting separate taxation of capital gains are the **United States**, the **United Kingdom,** and **Israel**.

In the **United States**, long-term capital gains (capital assets held for more than one year) are subject to a reduced rate of tax, capped at 15 percent (5 percent or 0 percent for low-income taxpayers).[19] Short-term capital gains (capital assets held for less than one year) are subject to tax at the ordinary income tax rates. Capital losses may be deducted only against capital gains. This is a consequence of the separate tax treatment to which capital gains are subject. However, excess losses can be deducted against ordinary income up to the amount of $3000 per year. Unused capital losses may be carried forward indefinitely and used to offset future capital gains.

In the **United Kingdom**, capital gains are subject to capital gains taxes (CGT), which are completely separate from the tax applicable to ordinary income. CGT is levied at a flat rate of 18 percent (10 percent for qualified business disposal). As in the United States, the natural consequence of the separate tax treatment of capital gains is that capital losses can only be deducted against capital gains[20] (and not against ordinary income), and unused losses can be carried forward indefinitely.

The case of **Israel** should also be mentioned. During the 1980s, Israel experienced a period of super-inflation (peaking at around 400 percent). This meant that most capital gains were generated because of inflation rather than real appreciation of the asset's value.[21] This required adjusting the tax laws. Since the 1980s, Israeli inflation rates have returned to rates comparable to those in other developed countries. Yet, beyond them being necessary, the inflation adjustment laws proved to be surprisingly operable, and hence Israel has preserved them. Since 1994, capital gains are apportioned to the part attributable to inflation and to the part attributable to real appreciation in value. Generally, only the

---

[19] Starting in 2011, the tax rates are going to be 20 percent and 10 percent (for low-income taxpayers).

[20] As an exception, losses on shares in unquoted trading companies can be deducted against ordinary income of the current or preceding year.

[21] Let's assume, for example, that Mr. Joe invested 100 New Israeli Shekels (NIS) in a nondepreciable capital asset. He held it for a year, and then sold it for 200 NIS. Presumably, he had a taxable gain of 100 NIS. However, assuming that inflation rates that year soared at 150 percent, his initial investment, adjusted to inflation, would have been 250 NIS (100 plus inflation of 150). If Mr. Joe sold the asset for 200 NIS, he would incur a financial loss of 50 NIS (200-250). Had inflation been ignored, Mr. Joe would have been required to pay taxes for the nominal gain of 100 NIS realized, even if he actually incurred into a financial loss of 50 NIS.

latter is taxed. This approach, even though more difficult administratively, is much more accurate from a policy perspective.

**Germany** and **Italy**, by comparison, have adopted the ordinary income model. This means that taxable capital gains are generally fully taxed. Capital gains from the sale of business assets are treated as ordinary business income and are thus fully taxed. Capital gains realized from the sale of private property (not business assets and not held for investment) are generally not subject to tax. Accordingly, capital losses realized by selling private property are not deductible.

More specifically, under **German** law, speculative capital gains derived from the sale of immovable property (held for less than ten years) and movable property (held for less than one year) are subject to tax if the total gains are above euros 600 per tax year. All capital investment income (including speculative capital gains and all gains derived from the sale of shares) accrued after December 31, 2008, is subject to a final withholding flat tax of 25 percent. Capital losses can be deducted against capital gains (to the extent they are taxable) realized in the previous year or in following years.

Under **Italian** law, certain nonspeculative capital gains realized from the sale of personal property are subject to separate taxation. Capital gains derived from the sale of business assets are fully taxed in the year they are realized unless they have been held for more than three years. In this latter case, taxpayers can elect to apportion the realized capital gains in five equal installments (the year in which the gain is realized and the four following years)[22]. As for capital gains realized from the sale of shares, a 12.5 percent final flat tax applies to individuals holding a nonqualified stock, while a 49.72 percent of the capital gain is treated as ordinary income for taxpayers holding a qualified stock. Capital losses can only be deducted against taxable capital gains. Capital losses from the sale of business assets can also be deducted against ordinary business income.

Other countries have adopted hybrid solutions.

For example, **Canada** treats one-half of net capital gains in ordinary income and taxes them accordingly. A special mechanism is adopted in order to exempt capital gains derived from the sale of property held for personal use. In fact, the basis of goods purchased for $1000 or less is deemed to be $1000, thus granting a substantial exemption. Capital losses can be deducted against capital gains realized in the current year, in the previous three years and indefinitely in the future years.

In **France**, short-term (less than two years) capital gains derived from the disposal of business assets are taxed as ordinary business income. An option to spread the gains over three years is available. Long-term (two years or more) capital gains from the disposal of business assets

---

[22] Art. 86, TUIR.

are subject to tax at a flat rate of 16 percent.[23] Capital gains realized from the sale of immovable property are also subject to tax at a flat rate of 16 percent. However, if such gains are long-term capital gains (five years or more), the tax treatment is more favorable, because the capital gain amount is reduced by 10 percent for each year of ownership beginning with the sixth year. Short-term capital losses can be deducted against business profits. If the enterprise's profits are not high enough, the loss can be deducted against other categories of income or carried forward for up to five years. Capital losses from the disposal of immovable property cannot be deducted. This includes capital losses from the sale of securities unless certain conditions are met. Long-term (e.g., nonspeculative) capital losses can be deducted against items of income that are taxable at the same rate. A ten-year carry-forward period is allowed.

In **The Netherlands**, capital gains are generally not taxable, except for business capital gains that are taxed as part of ordinary business income and for capital gains deriving from the disposal of shares by a substantial shareholder. As a consequence, business capital losses can be deducted against ordinary business income.

In **Sweden**, all capital gains realized by an individual are included in capital income to the extent they exceed Sek 50,000. Consequently, capital losses that cannot be used to offset capital gains can nevertheless be deducted from other capital income, up to a maximum of 70 percent of these losses.

---

[23] This rate is increased by 12, 1 percent of social taxes.

# 7

# Tax Avoidance

This chapter will provide a brief overview of the different approaches that countries pursue with regard to the concept of tax avoidance.

More specifically, first, we will define tax evasion, tax avoidance, and licit tax savings, and we will analyze the differences between civil law and common law countries in their approach to tax avoidance. Then, we will briefly compare the "substance-over-form" doctrines (typical of common law countries) with the "general anti-abuse" doctrines (typical of civil law countries).

## I. GENERAL DEFINITIONS: TAX EVASION, TAX AVOIDANCE, AND LICIT TAX SAVINGS

In the attempt to define tax avoidance, the starting point should be the concept of strategic tax behaviors (or aggressive tax planning strategies), which are actions designed solely to minimize tax obligations, the legality of which is questionable.

There are three categories of strategic tax behaviors: tax evasion, tax avoidance, and licit tax savings.[1] The definition of these behaviors is debated by academics, and it is not clear where the distinguishing lines should be drawn (i.e., when tax avoidance crosses the line and becomes tax evasion, for example). Despite this obscurity, we can nevertheless present the main ideas ingrained in each of the terms.

*Tax evasion* can be synthetically defined as intentional illegal behaviors, i.e., behaviors involving a direct violation of tax law, in order to escape payment of taxes.

*Tax avoidance* can be defined as all illegitimate (but not necessarily illegal) behaviors aimed at reducing tax liability. These behaviors do not violate the letter of the law but clearly violate its spirit. A typical example of tax avoidance is the fictitious conversion of ordinary income into nontaxable capital gains.

---

[1] *See* Francesco Tesauro, Istituzioni di diritto tributario. Parte Generale 239, (Utet 2009).

*Licit tax savings* can be defined as commonly accepted forms of tax behaviors that contradict neither the law nor its spirit and are intended to reduce the tax burden. This category can also be referred to as "legitimate tax planning."

This tri-partition is not generally accepted by economists. Professor Slemrod,[2] for example, splits strategic tax behaviors into two categories: tax avoidance when the behaviors are legal and tax evasion when they are not.[3]

The nature of each of these concepts varies from country to country depending on government's policies, court decisions, tax authorities' attitudes, and public opinion. As mentioned above, while it is clear that tax evasion is illegal—and that licit tax savings is legal—the legality of tax avoidance must be proven on a case-by-case basis. Each jurisdiction has its own anti-avoidance policies and rules, and, therefore, the same transaction could be classified as legal in one jurisdiction while simultaneously regarded as illegal in another.

Thus, the problem that every tax jurisdiction has to face is identifying the line that differentiates between legal tax behaviors and the illegal forms of tax avoidance. This is necessary not only for equity reasons but also for economic ones. A taxpayer who mischaracterizes a transaction creates inefficiencies that are manifested in higher administrative and compliance costs.[4] Tax evasion is easier to identify because it presumes a direct and intended violation of a law.

Theoretically, on the corporate side, the literature attempts to draw the line between licit and illicit activities based on the business purpose doctrine. Consequently, activities that have no business purpose and are aimed primarily, if not solely, at reducing taxes should be considered illicit and probably illegal. On the other hand, corporate transactions that are motivated by real business considerations and have important (yet secondary) tax advantages should not be considered illicit. This analysis becomes more complex when multiple transactions are involved, and the issue then is whether such transactions should be viewed as a whole, or separately, in order to consider the portion that gave rise to tax savings.

---

[2] *See* Joel Slemrod & Jon Bakija, Taxing Ourselves. A Citizen's Guide to the Debate over Taxes 144 (The MIT Press 2008).

[3] Therefore, following this approach, while the cost of tax avoidance is given only by expenditures on professional assistance, the cost of tax evasion is also the exposure to the uncertainty of an audit and any attendant penalties for detected evasion.

[4] As it has been underlined by SLEMROD & BAKIJA, *supra* note 2, at 173, this is one argument for replacing the income tax with a single consumption tax. In fact, consumption taxes seem to be much less susceptible to tax arbitrage.

The concept of tax avoidance is also related to the concept of tax shelter. There is no consensus among scholars as to how to define tax shelters. Broadly, they can be defined as transactions or arrangements "designed to reduce or defer taxation, typically in an artificial manner."[5] It is not clear, however, whether the term refers only to transactions that technically violate the letter of the law or whether it refers to all types of transactions engaged in for the sole purpose of reducing tax burdens and that lack any business purpose. Professor Bankman defines a tax shelter as a tax-motivated transaction unrelated to a taxpayer's normal business operations that, under a literal reading of some relevant legal authority, produces a loss for tax purposes in excess of any economic loss, in a manner inconsistent with legislative intent or purpose.[6]

It is therefore conceivable to consider tax shelters as transactions that conflict with the spirit of the law, usually lack any business purpose, and are pursued solely for tax reasons. They are often not foreseen by policy makers and are usually resolved ex post. In the meantime, they can produce high-tax savings for the single corporations, but presumably they create high costs for society. Professor Slemrod explains that tax shelters "use up real resources (including the time and effort of the lawyers, accountants, and investment bankers who devise the shelters) that could have otherwise been devoted to some socially productive purpose, they divert resources toward particular types of investments or other activities that help facilitate such avoidance behavior, and they require tax rates to be higher than they otherwise would have to be to raise a given amount."[7]

Common law and civil law countries initially adopted different models to address the above-illustrated issues: a substance-over-form doctrine developed by courts in common law countries and an abuse of law rule provided by statutes in civil law countries. However, it seems that many countries prefer hybrid solutions. On one side, common law countries are trying to codify a general anti-avoidance rule. On the other side, courts of civil law countries are trying to develop some sort of the substance-over-form doctrine.

---

[5] BARRY LARKING, INTERNATIONAL TAX GLOSSARY (IBFD 2005).

[6] Joseph Bankman, *The Tax Shelter Battle, in* THE CRISIS OF TAX ADMINISTRATION 7, (Henry Aaron & Joel Slemrod eds., 2004); and Joseph Bankman, *The Tax Shelter Problem*, LVII Nat'l Tax J. 925 (2004).

[7] *See* Joel Slemrod & Jon Bakija, Taxing Ourselves. A Citizen's Guide to the Debate over Taxes 280 (The MIT Press 2008).

## II. SUBSTANCE OVER FORM (THE EXPERIENCE OF COMMON LAW COUNTRIES)

The substance-over-form doctrine[8] has been developed by common law courts, with some variations among countries. Under this doctrine, tax authorities can look at the substance of a transaction disregarding the form. For example, if an item of income is clearly ordinary income, yet the taxpayer formally labels the item as capital gain (in order to benefit from privileged tax treatment), under the substance-over-form doctrine, tax authorities can re-characterize such an item as ordinary income, essentially disregarding the form of the transaction.

A development of the substance-over-form doctrine, albeit distinct, is the step transaction doctrine, which is a concept that was developed by courts in the United States. The step transaction doctrine provides that a taxpayer's form will generally be respected so long as it has legal and economic substance, even where a different route would have resulted in more tax. The doctrine will nevertheless treat a transaction that (in form) consists of multiple steps as a single transaction if the steps are all focused on the ultimate result. In other words, tax authorities can disregard economically meaningless steps and assess the tax treatment of the entire resulting transaction.

A further development is the economic substance[9] (or business purpose) doctrine. In order to be considered valid for tax purposes, a transaction must have a real business purpose (or bona fide purpose or economic substance) as opposed to the tax savings achieved.

Until very recently, **United States'** tax law did not have a general anti-avoidance rule. However, the substance-over-form doctrine has been developed by courts in order to disallow the tax benefits of transactions that are undertaken for mere tax avoidance purposes. The business purpose, economic substance, and step transaction tests have also been adopted by U.S. courts. In addition, specific anti-abuse rules dot the Internal Revenue Code and deal with specific fact patterns. The "economic substance" doctrine has recently been codified, and under the new law a transaction will be considered to have economic substance only if (i) the transaction changes in a meaningful way the taxpayer's economic position, and (ii) the taxpayer has a substantial purpose for entering the transaction (other than the tax purpose). If a transaction lacks economic substance, taxpayers are exposed not only to the possibility that the transaction will be ignored (or re-casted for what it really is). Rather, under the new law, a penalty of 40 percent is

---

[8] *See* CAHIERS DE DROIT FISCAL INTERNATIONAL, *FORM AND SUBSTANCE IN TAX LAW,* (Kluwer 1983).

[9] *See* Jinyan Li, *Economic Substance: Drawing the Line Between Legitimate Tax Minimization and Abusive Tax Avoidance,* 54 CAN. TAX J. 23 (2006).

imposed on any underpayment of tax which resulted from the transaction. Whether this codification has an impact that differs from the doctrine as developed by the courts, remains to be seen.

As noted, several specific anti-avoidance rules are present in the Code. Rules against wash sales, transfer pricing rules, Subpart F (or CFC legislations), and other anti-deferral provisions, thin capitalization rules, earnings stripping rules, anti-inversion rules, and partnership anti-avoidance rules (Treas. Reg. 1.701-2) are all example of specific anti-avoidance rules that nevertheless are not able to confront the tax avoidance phenomenon as a whole.

In the **United Kingdom**, a general substance-over-form principle has been developed by the courts. According to this principle, transactions that lack real economic substance will not be respected, for tax purposes, by courts. Nevertheless, and as clarified in *I.R.C. v. Duke of Westminster*,[10] the courts will respect legal rights of taxpayers when applying tax legislation to the facts. Specific anti-avoidance rules may also apply, and courts will interpret them broadly.

In **Israel,** there is a general (and very broad) anti-avoidance rule that enables the tax authority to disregard so-called "artificial transactions," step transactions, or even transactions that reduce tax obligations in an "inappropriate manner." Such a rule can actually facilitate the recast of "illegitimate tax avoidance" activities as illegal tax evasion. Given the broad definition, Israeli courts had to extensively deal with the interpretation of this rule, setting forth a number of considerations to be taken into account in deciding whether a tax avoidance scheme is legitimate or not[11], such as the deviation of the transaction from acceptable business patterns of similar transactions, the business justifications (other than tax avoidance) for the transaction, and the real substance of the transactions. All these arguments represent the general substance-over-form doctrine of the Israeli courts in this matter.


## III. ABUSE OF LAW (THE EXPERIENCE OF CIVIL LAW COUNTRIES)

The civil law doctrine, equivalent to the substance-over-form doctrine developed by common law countries, is the *abuse of law*.[12] Subject to

---

[10] Commissioners of Inland Revenue v. The Duke of Westminister, (1936) A.C. 1 (H.L.). *See* Assaf Likovsky, *The Duke and the Lady: Helvering v. Gregory and the History of Tax Avoidance Adjudication,* 25 CARDOZO L. REV. 953 (2003–04).

[11] *E.g.,* CA 3415/97 Rubinstein v. The Assessment Officer of Large Businesses, 57 P.D. 915 (2003).

[12] *See* Sebastian Moerman, *The Theory of Tax Abuse,* 27 INTERTAX 284 (1999); and Maurice Cozian, *What is Abuse of Law?,* 19 INTERTAX 103 (1991).

certain conditions that vary from country to country, the *abuse of law* doctrine empowers the tax authorities to disregard tax benefits of a transaction in which the form of the transaction adopted by a taxpayer is not specifically contemplated by law, and the same economic results could have been achieved differently.[13]

An important example of the adoption of the abuse of law doctrine can be found in the **German** system. If there is an abuse of law, the inappropriate legal structure is ignored for tax purposes and substituted by an appropriate legal form. As in most countries, Germany, as well, has specific anti-avoidance rules that are aimed at combating specific avoidance transactions.

In **France,** a specific section of the tax code adopts the abuse of law doctrine. Here, tax authorities can disregard, subject to certain strict conditions, artificial legal acts[14] or legal acts that the only purposes of which are granting tax benefits.

Under French tax law, there is also an additional anti-avoidance doctrine: the doctrine of abnormal acts of management. According to this latter doctrine, tax authorities may disregard management decisions that are contrary to the interest of the business. Specific anti-avoidance rules are also present in France.

Finally, **Brazil** offers another good example. In fact, it recently adopted a general anti-abuse provision.[15] Since January 2001 and under

---

[13] On the "abuse of law" doctrine within the EU, see Francesco Tesauro, *Divieto comunitario di abuso del diritto (fiscale) e vincolo da giudicato esterno incompatible con il diritto comunitario (nota a ord. Cass., 21 dicembre 2007, n. 26996)*, Giurisprudenza Italiana 1029 (2008); Peter A. Harris, *The Notion of "Abuse de Droit" and Its Potential Application in Fiscal Matter Within the EU Legal Order*, EC Tax Journal 187 (2001); Paolo Piantavigna, *Abuso del diritto e fiscalità nella giurisprudenza comunitaria: un'ipotesi di studio*, Rivista di diritto finanziario e scienza delle finanze 369, I (2009).

[14] Mainly, transactions that are disguised are other transactions that can grant substantial tax benefits.

[15] Generally, a comprehensive set of rules to fight tax evasion and fraud has recently been adopted. Other than the general anti-abuse provision, the following measures have been adopted:

> *Rules on bank secrecy.* Complementary Law No. 105, of Jan. 10, 2001 ("LC 105") sets forth the rules regarding the secrecy of financial transactions. Pursuant to Article 5 of LC 105, financial institutions are required to provide to the tax authorities general information on the financial transactions carried out by their customers. For this purpose, general information means the financial details concerning those transactions and the monthly amount(s) involved. Any information that may lead to the identification of the origin or the nature of the amount(s) inherent in the financial transaction(s) is strictly excluded and is not provided to the tax authorities.
>
> Tax authorities have the right to examine the customer's records maintained by the relevant financial institution. Such examination is indispensable in the following situations: (i) if there is subinvoicing of the amounts involved in a transaction

Art. 116 of the national tax code, the tax authorities may disregard legal transactions performed by a taxpayer that are intended to disguise or change the nature of a taxable event. Some commentators argue that such rule is not self-enforced, and that a new law is needed to specify what "disguise" means. Although no such law has yet been enacted, some courts have been applying the substance-over-form and business purposes doctrines in tax cases.

## IV. HYBRID SOLUTIONS

A typical hybrid solution has been adopted by **Italy**. In addition to specific anti-avoidance measures, there is a general anti-avoidance rule,[16] which is limited in its application to certain transactions (mainly reorganizations[17]). Italian tax authorities may disallow the tax

---

(cross-border commercial transactions included), or in the acquisition or in the resale price of goods and rights; (ii) if loans are obtained from nonfinancial entities or individuals without substantiation of the funds being received; (iii) if operations are conducted with a counterparty that is resident in a listed nil or low-tax jurisdiction; (iv) if there is concealment of the net income from fixed or nonfixed financial investments; (v) if there are expenses or investments that exceed a taxpayer's available income; (vi) if there are remittances abroad, through an account of a nonresident, of amounts incompatible with a taxpayer's declared income; (vii) if a taxpayer is subject to a special audit regime as a result of resistance to, or obstruction of, an auditing procedure; (viii) if there is a nonexistent or irregular company; (ix) if there is an individual who is not registered or who has a cancelled registration in the Tax Register of Individuals; (x) if there is a denial by the owner of the bank account of responsibility for the financial movement or ownership of the rights concerned; and (xi) if there is evidence that the legal owner is not the real owner. The tax authorities can only request the information referred in (i) to (vi) if the amounts involved exceed the declared value or the market value by at least 10 percent. The information requested from a financial institution may cover the preceding five years; and the tax authorities must maintain this information under secrecy.

In addition, Brazil has strengthened its CFC regulation. Since January 1, 2002, profits earned by CFCs or associated offshore companies will be included in the profits subject to Brazilian tax at the end of the fiscal year to which the profits refer, regardless of whether or not the profits are legally or economically available to the taxpayer.

[16] An overview of the application of general anti avoidance rules in different countries is offered by Tax Avoidance and the Rule of Law (G. S. Cooper ed., 1997).

[17] The followings are the transactions to which the anti-avoidance rule may apply:
– mergers, divisions, transformations, and liquidations and distributions to shareholders of reserves not consisting of profits;
– contributions to companies and transactions for the transfer or utilization of business assets;

advantages obtained through any act or transaction if three conditions apply: (1) there are no valid economic reasons for the transaction, (2) the transaction results in a tax benefit, and (3) there is a violation of obligations or prohibitions contained in Italian law. [18]

Recently, the Supreme Court[19] has been trying to apply a general anti-abuse of law doctrine based on constitutional grounds (the ability to pay principle) in order to allow tax authorities to disregard the tax benefits of transactions that do not have any economic substance besides obtaining the tax benefits.[20]

In **Sweden**, there is a general anti-avoidance provision, which is sort of a compromise between the abuse of law and the substance-over-form doctrines. Tax authorities may disregard a transaction if the following conditions are met: (1) the transaction grants a significant tax benefit to the taxpayer, (2) the taxpayer is directly or indirectly involved in the transaction, (3) the predominant reason of the transaction is the tax benefit, and (4) there is a violation of the purpose of law. However, as a matter of fact, this anti-avoidance rule has seldom been used because of these difficult to satisfy conditions.

**Japan** has also adopted a hybrid solution because even if it is a civil law country, its jurisdiction developed a limited substance-over-form doctrine. However, this doctrine applies only to specific (limited) circumstances such as transactions of family corporations. This is why most of the academics believe that Japanese courts cannot re-characterize legal acts for tax avoidance purposes without a specific provision.

**Canada** codified a general anti-avoidance rule (in 1987)[21] that provides that tax authorities can disregard the tax benefits of an avoidance

---

- transfers of debt claims and tax credits;
- EU mergers, divisions, transfers of assets, and exchanges of shares;
- transactions concerning securities and financial instruments;
- transfers of assets between companies within the same consolidated tax group;
- payments of interest and royalties eligible for the exemption under the EC Interest and Royalties Directive, if made to a person directly or indirectly controlled by one or more persons established outside of the European Union; or
- transactions between resident entities and their affiliates resident in tax havens and concerning the payment of an amount under a penalty clause.

[18] Article 37-*bis*, D.P.R. 600/1973.

[19] *See* Cass., Sez. Un., December 23, 2008, n. 30055 and n. 30057.

[20] *See* Angelo Contrino, *Il divieto di abuso del diritto fiscale: profili evolutivi, (asseriti) fondamenti giuridici e connotati strutturali*, DIRITTO E PRATICA TRIBUTARIA 463, I (2009).

[21] *See* Jinyan Li, *Tax Transplants and Local Culture: A Comparative Study of the Chinese and Canadian GAAR*, 11 THEORETICAL INQUIRIES IN LAW— COMPARATIVE TAX LAW AND CULTURE 655 (2010); Carlo Garbarino, *Comparative*

transaction, which is any transaction that (1) results in a reduction or deferral of tax (tax benefit), (2) does not have a bona fide purpose other than to obtain the tax benefit, and (3) results in a direct or indirect misuse of the statute or a direct or indirect abuse of the statute.[22]

As is the case of the United States and the United Kingdom, Canada has specific anti-avoidance rules that are prescribed by the statute, such as transfer pricing, thin capitalization, and controlled foreign companies legislation.

Courts have also developed a substance-over-form doctrine, which is more traditional for common law countries. For example, a taxpayer who actually achieves certain legal results different from the apparent results will be taxed in accordance with the actual legal results.[23]

In **Australia**, there is a general anti-avoidance rule, according to which tax authorities may disregard the tax benefit of certain transactions put in place with the primary purpose of obtaining a tax benefit. Three conditions are necessary in order to trigger the anti-avoidance rule: a transaction[24] has to be put in place, a tax benefit has to be obtained, and the primary purpose of the transaction is to reduce taxes.

---

*Taxation and Legal Theory: The Tax Design Case of the Transplant of General Anti-Avoidance Rules*, 11 THEORETICAL INQUIRIES IN LAW—COMPARATIVE TAX LAW AND CULTURE 765 (2010); Brian J. Arnold, *The Long, Slow, Steady Demise of the General Anti-Avoidance Rule*, 52 CAN. TAX J. 488 (2006).

[22] VERN KRISHNA, TAX AVOIDANCE: THE GENERAL ANTI-AVOIDANCE RULE, (Carswell 1990).

[23] *See Duke of Westminster* (1936), *Bronfman Trust* (1987), and *Shell Canada* (1999) cases.

In the first case, the House of Lords decision rejected that the legal form of a transaction could be disregarded in favor of its economic substance but recognized that the legal substance of a transaction prevails over the legal name used by the taxpayer.

In the second case (*Bronfman Trust*), the Supreme Court of Canada, without analyzing the connection with the *Duke of Westminster* case has stated: "The recent trend in tax cases has been towards attempting to ascertain the true commercial and practical nature of the taxpayer's transactions. . . . Assessment of taxpayers' transactions with an eye to commercial and economic realities, rather than juristic classification of form, may help to avoid the inequity of tax liability being dependent upon the taxpayers' sophistication at manipulating a sequence of events to achieve a patina of compliance with the apparent prerequisites for a tax deduction."

In the latter case, the Supreme Court held that re-characterization is only permissible if the label attached by the taxpayer to the particular transaction does not properly reflect its actual legal effect.

[24] Courts have held that the transaction has to stand and make sense on its own.

Australian courts have not developed a general substance-over-form doctrine. In fact, the High Court has rejected the applicability of a judicial substance-over-form doctrine on the grounds that it is unnecessary because a codified general anti-avoidance rule already exists.[25]

Here too, specific anti-avoidance rules have been adopted (for example, transfer pricing, controlled foreign companies, thin capitalization rules).

On the other hand, in **India**, there is no general anti-avoidance rule, and there are only a number of specific anti-avoidance provisions.

**Russia** has[26] anti-avoidance legislation, which allows tax authorities to reclassify deals and charge extra taxes. There are also special rules applicable in certain situations (namely, thin capitalization rules, transfer pricing rules, rules of calculating the term of excising the construction site, etc.).

A judicial anti-avoidance doctrine has been established in the Plenary Ruling No. 53 of the Supreme Arbitration Court of Russia. This ruling introduced the term "unjustified tax benefit," which replaced the "bona fide" concept. "Unjustified tax benefit" can apply to all taxes, and it is based on two doctrines: the substance over form and the business purpose.[27]

In **China**, there is a general anti-avoidance rule[28] for enterprises in the Enterprises Income Tax Law (EITL) but not in the Individual Income Tax Law. Article 47 of the EITL provides Chinese tax authorities with the power to make adjustments "through a reasonable method" where an enterprise enters into an arrangement "not for any reasonable business purpose." Article 120 of the EITL Regulations clarifies the meaning of "not for any reasonable business purpose," stating that it refers to an

---

[25] Tony Pagone, TAX AVOIDANCE IN AUSTRALIA (Federation Press 2010).

[26] Material for this question is based on review provided by Pepeliaev, Goltsblat & Partners (Russian law firm) for International Comparative Legal Guide. http://www.iclg.co.uk.

[27] The Court ruled that

1. officials should prove the circumstances on which their decision was based;
2. tax benefits can be recognized as unreasonable, in particular, when (a) for taxation purposes, operations are not considered according to their economic sense; and (b) operations have not resulted from justified economic or other factors (purposes of a business nature);
3. tax benefits cannot be considered as an independent business purpose, though a benefit may accompany transactions that have a real business purpose, because a taxpayer is free to achieve a desired economic result with a minimum tax burden; and
4. the fact in itself of infringement of the tax duties by the partner of the taxpayer is not proof that a tax benefit is unreasonable.

[28] *See* Li, *supra* note 21; Garbarino, *supra* note 21.

arrangement where the "main purpose is to reduce, exempt or defer the payment of taxes."

On January 8, 2009, the State Administration of Taxation (SAT) released circular,[29] regarding the *Implementation Measures of Special Tax Adjustments (Trial)* that details rules on administrating all the aspects of those anti-avoidance rules.

Chinese local tax authorities can, upon the approval of the SAT, launch general anti-avoidance investigation of an enterprise if it is found to be engaged in activities such as abusing tax incentives, abusing tax treaties, abusing corporation forms and structures, and avoiding taxes by using tax havens and other tax arrangements that don't have a reasonable business purpose. In determining if an enterprise is engaged in a tax-avoidance arrangement, the tax authorities shall adopt the principle of substance over form. Furthermore, the tax authorities may consider the following factors:

- form and substance of the arrangement;
- conclusion time and duration of the arrangement;
- how the arrangement is executed;
- connection between each step or part of the arrangement;
- changes of financial status of each party involved in the arrangement;
- tax consequences of the arrangement.

The tax authorities can also require the tax planner to submit the materials relevant to the tax avoidance arrangement under investigation. The tax authorities are empowered to recharacterize transactions based on the true economic substance and disregard the intended tax benefits under a tax avoidance arrangement. In particular, enterprises without any economic substance, including those established in tax havens for the purpose of tax avoidance, can be disregarded.

Corresponding adjustments shall be allowed in the case of a transfer pricing adjustment in order to avoid double taxation. If this involves an overseas related party resident in a treaty country, upon request from the enterprise, the SAT will enter into negotiations with the competent authorities of the treaty country pursuant to the Mutual Agreement Procedures Article in the treaty. The application of corresponding adjustments shall be made within three years after receiving the transfer pricing adjustment notice. In addition, corresponding adjustment rules shall not apply where the transfer pricing adjustment involves rental payments, interest, or royalties to overseas related parties. In this case, a nonrefundable excessive withholding tax is levied.

---

[29] *See Implementation Measures of Special Tax Adjustments (Trial) available at* http://www.chinatax.gov.cn/n8136506/n8136593/n8137537/ n8138502/8784619.html (Chinese version, last visited on November 19, 2009).

8

# Selected Business Tax Issues

## I. INTRODUCTION

**M**ost basic tax classes either completely ignore or only briefly cover the issue of business taxation. However, in this book, we do briefly address this issue for two reasons. First, most cross-border transactions—for which the comparative approach is probably most useful—are made via some form of business entity (usually *entities*). Thus, basic terms in comparative business taxation are useful for any future business lawyer. Second, it is of particular use to those students who find tax law interesting enough to pursue more advanced tax classes. For those, this chapter will cover some of the basic issues in business taxation from a comparative perspective.

We would like to start by noting that in 1953—quite some time before the word "globalization" had even been mentioned in relation to tax studies—Geoffrey Hornsey from Leeds University conducted a comparative study on the principles of corporate taxation in the United States, the United Kingdom, and France.[1] Even though not using the term "convergence," taking a true functional stance, he noted that "[T]he one striking fact which does emerge is the universality of the problems involved and the similarity of the solutions achieved."[2]

Notwithstanding Hornsey's five decades-old observations, there can be little doubt that many tax comparatists have argued that a meaningful trend toward convergence in the corporate tax arena emerged during the mid-to-late 1980s. Studying the response of several jurisdictions to the 1986 Tax Reform Act in the United States, Tanzi noted some common trends in tax reforms.[3] Specifically, in the area of corporate taxation, he argued that a trend could be identified "towards lowering the basic rate and broadening the base."[4] He also noted that the base-broadening measures taken by multiple jurisdictions had common characteristics of eliminating investment incentives and introducing less generous

---

[1] Geoffrey Hornsey, *Corporate Taxation—A Comparative Study*, 16 Mod. L. Rev. 26 (1953).

[2] *Id.* at 33.

[3] Vito Tanzi, *The Response of Other Industrial Countries to the U.S. Tax Reform Act* 40(3), Nat'l Tax J. 339 (1987).

[4] *Id.* at 355.

depreciation allowances.[5] Finally, he mentioned the fact that "classical systems" of corporate-shareholder integration was being challenged and gradually replaced by other systems of integration.[6] The trends identified by Tanzi in the midst of the reform movement have since become the subject of numerous studies.[7] That is to say, it is widely accepted that the process of reform in corporate taxation since the 1980s has some common features that are shared by most *industrialized* countries.

The remainder of this chapter examines the evolution of corporate taxation primarily (but not only) in the G7 countries with respect to the definition of a corporate taxpayer, corporate residency, corporate tax rates, corporate tax base, corporate/shareholder integration, and a few other categories. It questions whether this trend of convergence is still prevailing today.

## II. THE DEFINITION OF A BUSINESS ENTITY FOR TAX PURPOSES

### A. The importance of entity classification for tax purposes in the study of tax convergence

"The most basic decision in the design of corporate tax is the determination of what entities or organizations should be subject to tax."[8] In the absence of convergence in the definition of the kind of taxpayers that are subjected to the corporate tax regime, it is doubtful that convergence can be observed at all. Even if all other parameters explored later in this chapter are to be found fully converged, it does not make a whole lot of sense to argue that convergence exists when similar legal rules are applied to different legal entities in each jurisdiction. Interestingly enough, the issue of convergence in entity classification for tax purposes has only been seldom (and only briefly) explored, while other areas have received considerably more scholarly attention (for example, the convergence of corporate tax rates).

---

[5] *Id.*

[6] *Id.*

[7] For additional early observations of similar trends, *see* Robert P. Hagemann, Brian R. Jones & Roner Bruce Montador, *Tax reforms in OECD Countries: Economic Rational and Consequences*, OECD ECONOMIC DEPARTMENT WORKING PAPERS No. 40 (1987); DAVID W. WILLIAMS, TRENDS IN INTERNATIONAL TAXATION (IBFD Publications 1991).

[8] Hugh J. Ault & Brian J. Arnold, Comparative Income Taxation: A Structural Analysis 277 (University Press of Virginia 2004).

There are many distinct forms of conducting a business, each with its own advantages and drawbacks. It is important to note that most legal entities draw their legal vitality from areas of private law other than taxation. However, in some countries, taxable entities are also specifically defined, and these "tax definitions" do not necessarily correlate with general entity classifications. Arguably, there are some commonly held notions. In civil law systems, an entity is usually subject to corporate taxation if it is considered to be a "legal person." On the other hand, most common law countries adopt some sort of a "resemblance test" for tax purposes, namely, questioning the entity characteristics in order to determine which legal entity defined by law that it resembles the most.[9]

Many jurisdictions developed quite a formal approach when classifying for tax purposes domestic entities incorporated under their own laws. However, constant encounters with foreign entities forced all jurisdictions to revisit their substantive approach to the tax classification of legal entities. The survey does not pretend to be a comprehensive one but rather to question whether a trend toward convergence in corporate classifications for tax purposes may be pointed out.

## B. Corporate entity definitions for tax purposes: examples from the G7 countries

### 1. Canada

The Canadian Income Tax Act[10] (CITA) does not define "corporation" for tax purposes. Section 248(1) of the CITA does assert, however, that "a corporation *includes* an incorporated company." This very generic and unhelpful criterion has been in place for decades,[11] surviving all major reforms, including the adoption of the 1985 CITA. However, some interpretative doctrines of Canadian tax law do provide guidance. Under Canadian case law, when the CITA "uses, but does not define, private law terms or concepts, those terms and concepts generally take the legal meaning that applies under private law that governs the arrangement."[12] Thus, "corporation" for tax purposes should be interpreted to be a "corporation" under general corporate law. Surprisingly enough,

---

[9] Graeme S. Cooper & Richard K. Gordon, *Taxation of Legal Person and their Owners, in* VICTOR THURONYI (ED.), TAX LAW DESIGN AND DRAFTING, VOL 2 (Victor Thuronyi ed. 1998), Ch. 19, 78–82.

[10] Income Tax Act, R.S.C. 1985, c. 1 (5th Supp.).

[11] Income Tax Act, R.S.C. 1948, § 127(1)(h); Income Tax Act, R.S.C 1952, § 139(1)(h); Income Tax Act, RSC 1952, c 148 (am SC 1970-71–72, c 63), § 248.

[12] Also known as the "Complimentarity Doctrine." *See* Marc Darmo, *Characterization of Foreign Business Associations* 53(2), CANADIAN TAX J. 481, 484 (2005).

however, in spite of the existence of extensive case law and literature on the Canadian private law meaning of the term "corporation,"[13] it seems that at least until relatively recent times, Canadian tax courts revealed very little desire to address this substantive issue.

1980s Canadian cases, interpreting the term corporation for domestic tax purposes, addressed the issue primarily in relation to "deemed association rules."[14] Under the association rules, if two or more corporate entities are deemed to be "associated," some burdensome tax consequences may result. Even though the case law regarding the question of "association" was altered and developed over the years, the term "corporation" has not. Unfortunately, the term "corporation" received relatively little *substantive* attention in framework of 1980s case law, and the courts usually only questioned it in the connection with the other meanings, rather than as a standing-alone concept.

In *Allied Farm Equipment Ltd. v. MNR*,[15] in a somewhat tautological interpretation of the term, the court asserted that "the word 'corporations' as used therein must be given its plain, ordinary meaning . . . ." In its decision, the court mentioned another decision[16] that did give some weight to the fact that the corporations there were incorporated under the laws of Canada. This may imply a formal approach underlying the court's opinion, namely, that for tax purposes, a corporation is any entity incorporated under domestic corporate laws of Canada. Such a position was also implied in an earlier case,[17] where with regard to the interpretation of the term "corporation" for tax purposes, the court noted that "It can be assumed that, in enacting these sections [In CITA], Parliament had knowledge of the provisions of the Companies Act."

The Canadian Revenue Agency (CRA) released in 1977 an Interpretation bulletin (which has not been formally withdrawn since), adopting a single factor test for corporate classification, stating that:

> A corporation is an entity created by law having a legal personality and existence separate and distinct from the personality and existence of those

---

[13] For a historical survey on the development of the corporate entity in Canada, *see* John R. Owen, *Foreign Entity Classification and the Character of Foreign Distribution, in* REPORT OF PROCEEDINGS OF THE FIFTY-SEVENTH TAX CONFERENCE, 20:1 (2005).

[14] CITA § 256.

[15] [1972] C.T.C. 107. The decision was later reversed (cite), but on the ground that that the corporation were not associated with each other, *see* Allied Farm Equipment Ltd. v. Minister of National Revenue [1972] F.C. 1358.

[16] International Fruit Distributors Limited v Minister of National Revenue [1953] C.T.C. 342.

[17] Minister of National Revenue v. Consolidated Glass Ltd· [1954] C.T.C. 202, reversed on different issues; Minister of National Revenue v Consolidated Glass Ltd. [1957] C.T.C. 78.

who caused its creation or those who own it. A corporation possesses its own capacity to acquire rights and to assume liabilities, and any rights acquired or liabilities assumed by it are not the rights or liabilities of those who control or own it. As long as an entity has such separate identity and existence, the Department will consider such entity to be a corporation even though under some circumstances or for some purposes the law may ignore some facet of its separate existence or identity.[18]

CRA interpretive bulletins are not binding, yet, such a simplistic approach has been implied to a few times in Canadian case law as well.[19] Indeed, two commentators noted in 1987 the *sole* criteria for a legal entity to be regarded as a corporation for Canadian tax purposes is that the entity has a separate legal personality from its owners.[20] Today, the CRA still perceives a corporation to be "[a] form of business authorized by federal, provincial, or territorial law to act as a *separate legal entity*. Its purpose and regulations are set out in its articles of incorporation."[21] Unlike partnerships, joint ventures, and sole proprietorships in Canada, only the business corporation is recognized to have a legal entity separate from its owners.[22] Under such perspective, "all entities formed under corporation law are subject to the corporate income tax while those formed under partnership provisions are treated under pass-through rules."[23]

This simplistic approach would have been nice and easy to work with but then came globalization and ruined everything. Tax disputes involving foreign legal entities forced Canadian authorities to revisit their substantive approach toward the classification of entities incorporated under foreign laws, in order to determine whether they are to be regarded as corporations for Canadian tax purposes. This, in turn, forced the courts to reflect on the private law definition of the corporate entity.

In a series of cases,[24] Canadian courts developed a two-step approach to the classification of foreign entities. First, the entity's characteristics are determined in accordance with the entity's jurisdiction law of

---

[18] IT-343R, *Meaning of the Term Corporation* (1977). (Emphasis added.)

[19] *See generally* Vallée v. R., 2004 TCC 320; Holiday Luggage Manufacturing Co. v. Minister of National Revenue, [1987] 1 C.T.C. 23.

[20] James S. Hausman & George T. Tamaki, *Canada*, *in* 72 Cahiers de Droit Fisacl International 263, 263 (1987).

[21] Canada Revenue Agency Business Taxpayer Glossary, *available at* http://www.cra-arc.gc.ca/tx/bsnss/glssry/c-gn-eng.html#corporation.

[22] Doing Business in Canada § 14.01(Bruce Salvatore ed., 2008).

[23] Ault & Arnold, *supra* note 8, at 278.

[24] *See* Economic Labs (Can.) Ltd. V. MNR [1970] Tax ABC 303; Backman v. The Queen [2001] 2 CTC 11 (SCC); Spire Freezers v. The Queen [2001] 2 CTC 40 (SCC); Whealy et al. v. The Queen, 2004 DTC 2888 (TCC). All *cited in* Darmo, *supra* 12, at 484–86.

corporations. After these characteristics have been determined, they are compared with categories of Canadian business entities in order to assess which class for Canadian legal entities they resemble the most. Thus, Canadian courts have had to develop a substantive definition for the term "corporation." In a detailed historical survey, John Owen, defined characteristics of the modern Canadian corporation.[25] The main characteristics are (1) a separate legal existence of the corporation, distinct from its owners; (2) limited liability—shareholders/ members are liable only to the extent of their equity contribution to the entity; (3) centralization of management; (4) the entity's ability to pursue business in its own capacity; (5) shareholders of the corporation have no proprietary interest in the corporation's assets and vice versa but are entitled to a share of the entity profits; (6) perpetual life; and (7) shareholders may freely transfer their interest in the corporation. This is similar to the U.S. approach before the check-the-box approach came to life (which is explained below).

Amid this recent multifactored interpretation by courts and academics to the term corporation, the Canadian Revenue Agency traditional single-factored approach (the existence of a separate juridical personality) seemed be losing grasp. For example, the CRA used to utilize its single factor approach to assert that American LLCs—even if treated as conduits for U.S. tax purposes—are nevertheless "corporations" for Canadian tax purposes due to their distinct legal persona.[26] It is not certain that such a simplistic interpretation can still stand. Indeed, since the early 2000s, several advanced rulings and interpretative bulletins seemed to imply that the CRA is slowly adopting a more substantive approach when classifying foreign entities.[27] Finally, in the 2006 Canadian Tax Foundation Annual Conference, the CRA announced that it does not plan to update Interpretation Bulletin, which introduced the single factor approach, and instead will endorse the substantive two-step analysis advanced by the courts.[28]

---

[25] Owen, *supra* note 13, at 21–29.

[26] *See* Robert Kopstein & Leonard Glass, *Canadian Inbound Investment with Limited Liability Companies—A Trap for the Unwary*, 17 Tax Notes Int'l 1289, 1289 (1998).

[27] Darmo, *supra* note 12, at 488.

[28] Kristina Fanjoy, *CRA Views on Foreign Entity Classification*, KPMG's Canadian Tax Advisor 2007-3, *available at* http://www.kpmg.ca/en/ services/tax/GlobalTaxAdviser/issues/200709/article2.html (last visited Dec. 12, 2008).

## 2. France[29]

French corporate legislation differentiates between "commercial companies" (Société commeciales) and "civil companies" (Sociétés Civiles).[30]
As a very general rule, entities that extend only limited liability to their
owners are deemed to be commercial companies and may engage in
any activity. A civil company many not engage in commercial activities
(as defined under French Commercial Code), or otherwise their owners
may be held liable for the company obligations.[31] This distinction
is important for tax purposes, since under the French tax code, civil
companies are tax transparent.

Put generally "[A]ll legal entities that carry out operations in
France . . . are subject to corporate income tax."[32] French tax legislation
further stipulates specifically which commercial legal entities, which
have been incorporated under domestic French legislation, are subject
to corporate tax. According to the French tax code, corporate taxes are
levied on both corporations (Société Anonyme or S.A.) and limited
liability companies (Société à Responsabilité Limitée or SARL).[33] The
S.A. is a corporation that is created to engage in commercial activity
and composed of at least seven members. Its shares represent the
equity participation of their shareholders and are transferable. Shareholders in an SA are only subject to liability to the extent of their capital contribution.[34] The SARL is a company composed of at least two
but no more than the one hundred members. Each member is liable to
the SARL obligation only to the extent of his or her capital contribution.[35] In addition, the code contains a "basket" provision, prescribing
that all legal entities other than partnerships (for which specific rules
apply, as described immediately below) are subject to corporate taxation if carrying for-profit activities.[36]

Some limited partnerships are also taxed as corporations. French law
recognizes two kinds of limited partnerships. The first is the regular
limited partnership (*Société en Commandite Simple* or SCS). An SCS
(rather than its partners) is subject to corporate taxes on the part of its

---

[29] Unless specifically stated otherwise, all data regarding France is taken from
LOVELLS & PAUL, HASTINGS, JANOFSKY & WALKER (EUROPE) LLP, DOING
BUSINESS IN FRANCE (2008) [Hereinafter DBF]. All court cases and legislative
materials cited are mentioned therein. The French Unified Tax Code (*Code
général des impôts*) is abbreviated CGI.

[30] DBF §5.01.

[31] DBF §5.01[2].

[32] DBF § 13.01 (emphasis added).

[33] CGI §219(I)(2), *cited in* DBF § 13.01[3][b].

[34] DBF §5.02.

[35] DBF §5.03

[36] AULT & ARNOLD, *supra* note 8, at 279.

taxable income attributed to its limited partners.[37] A second form of limited partnership, the limited partnership with shares (*Société en Commandite par Actions)* is subject to corporate taxes on its entire net profits (rather than only the profits attributed to limited partners).[38]

It is quite clear, we think, that the general rule stemming for the above is that in France, the price of having a distinct legal personality accompanied by limited liability for the owners is entity-level tax.[39] It should be noted that in addition, the French tax code also extends to some pass-through entities—such as general partnerships and single-member limited liability companies—an opportunity to *elect* to be treated as corporations for tax purposes.[40]

France's domestic criteria for entity classification for tax purposes are also implemented to foreign entities operating in its territory.[41] Meaning, similar to the Canadian foreign entity classification, foreign entities' characteristics are viewed in the prism of French domestic tax law. Thus, for example:

> [E]ven when . . . partnership is established in a [foreign] State which applies a fiscally transparent approach, the fact that the partnership is a legal person precludes the view that income simply 'flows through' this entity to the partners. Since a partnership constitutes a separate legal entity [according to French law], it cannot be ignored [in France] for tax purposes.[42]

## 3. Germany[43]

Similar to French law and loyal to its continental tradition, German tax legislation specifically lists which legal entities (as defined by German corporate legislation) are subject to corporate income taxation. The Corporation Tax Act of 2002 (KStG) prescribes that the following legal entities are subject to corporate tax:[44] German Stock Corporations (*Aktiengesellschaft* or AG); Limited Liability Companies (*Gesellschaft mit*

---

[37] CGI §206(4), *cited in* DBF § 13.01[3][c][ii].

[38] CGI §206(1), *cited In* DBF § 13.01[3][c][ii].

[39] Ault & Arnold, *supra* note 8, at 279.

[40] DBF § 13.01[3][c][i].

[41] *See generally* OECD, The Application of the OECD Model Tax Convention to Partnerships: Issues in International Taxation No. 6, 63–65 (1999). [Hereinafter OECD Partnerships Report.]

[42] *Id.* at 64.

[43] Unless stated otherwise, all references are taken from Business Transactions in Germany (Bernd Ruster ed., FRG 2008), [hereinafter BTG]; The German Corporation Tax Act of 2002 (*Körperschaftsteuergesetz*) is abbreviated hereinafter as KStG.

[44] KStG § 1, BTG §32.05[1].

*beschränkter Haftung*, known as GmbH); partnerships limited by shares (*Kommanditgesellschaft auf Aktien* or KGaA); business cooperatives (*Erwerbs und Wirtschaftsgenossenschaften*); mutual insurance associations (*Versicherungsvereine auf Gegenseitigkeit*); other legal entities under private law; an association (*Verein*), institution (*Anstalt*), foundation (*Stiftung*), and other property without separate juridical personality (*Zweckvermogen*); and commercial businesses run by legal entities under public law.

The Stock Corporation Act (*Aktiengeset,* or AktG) sets the legal framework for the creation of both AGs (the stock corporation) and KGaAs (partnership limited with shares).[45] Section 1(1) of the AktG provides that a stock corporation possesses legal personality of its own.[46] As such, it may possess legal rights and obligations. Stockholders are only liable to corporate obligations to the extent of their equity contribution as represented by their stock holdings.[47] The KGaA is a hybrid entity, combining characteristics of both limited partnerships and corporations.[48] It is composed of at least one general partner, who is personally liable for all of the KGaA's liabilities. The general partner can be a stock corporation or a limited liability company, thus getting around the disadvantage of unlimited personal liability. The KGaA members who are not personally liable are called "shareholders" and treated the same way as shareholders in an AG. Just as an AG, the KGaA is treated as having a distinct legal personality, i.e., it is not transparent for tax purposes.

The GmbH, which is the most common form of corporate entity in Germany, was originally "designed to permit the simple formation and easy administration of companies with a small share capital."[49] While GmbH offers its owners much more flexibility in managing their affairs and at the same time maintaining their limited liability, it is nevertheless treated as having a separate legal entity.[50]

As in the French case, entities incorporated under laws other than German laws are treated as corporations for tax purposes if they resemble more a corporation (either AG or GmbH) than a partnership under the governing German law.[51] The test for characterizing foreign entities for German tax purposes has developed in case law, which magnificently evolved to be a "Canadian style" two step approach to the issue.[52]

---

[45] BTG § 24.01[2][a].

[46] *Id.*

[47] *Id.*

[48] AktG §§ 278 *et. seq.,* BTG § 24.01[2][d].

[49] BTG § 23.01[1][b].

[50] BTG § 23.02[1].

[51] BTG § 32.05[1][b].

[52] Stanley C. Ruchelman et al., *European Approaches to Hybrid Entities and Financing Structures: An Introduction,* 14 Tax Notes Int'l 1487, 1494–95 (1997).

First, the characteristics of the foreign entity are considered. Second, taking these characteristics into account, the foreign entity is put through a sort of a "resemblance test" questioning to which German legal entity it resembles the most. If such entity is subject to corporate tax under German law, so would be the foreign entity.

## 4. Italy[53]

Italian tax legislation prescribes in quite a straightforward manner which entities are subject to domestic corporate tax. It provides a definition of (both domestic and foreign) "persons" (*rectius* entities) subject to corporate tax.[54]

Italian entities subject to corporate taxation are joint-stock companies (*società per azioni*, S.p.A.), limited partnerships with share capital (*società in accomandita per azioni*, S.a.p.a.), limited liability companies (*società a responsabilità limitata*, S.r.l.), cooperative companies, mutual insurance companies, and public and private entities other than companies.[55] Foreign entities of any type are also subject to Italian corporate tax on their source-base income.[56]

The (S.p.A.), which is the functional equivalent of the U.S. C-corporation, is a juridical entity separate from its owners and only extends limited liability to its shareholders (to the extent of their capital contribution), and its shares are freely transferable.[57] The main distinction between the S.p.A. and the limited liability company (S.r.l.) is that the latter also provides its members with flexibility and autonomy with respect to the S.r.l. corporate governance requirements,[58] and thus in many corporate law aspects is equivalent to the U.S. LLC. The partnership limited by shares (S.a.p.a.) is a legal entity (unlike other kinds of partnership entities in Italy) that is composed of limited shareholders (liable only to the extent of their capital contribution) and unlimited shareholders, who are the only ones which may exert managerial powers.[59] If certain conditions are met, the Italian corporations can be treated as pass-through entities for income tax purposes.[60] Other resident entities subject to

---

[53] *See* IBFD's CARLO GALLI, EUROPE—CORPORATE TAXATION—ITALY (2008), *available at* http://online2.ibfd.org/gii/. [Hereinafter IBFD Italy]. *See also* Roberto Schiavolin, *I soggetti passivi, in* L'IMPOSTA SUL REDDITO DELLE PERSONE GIURIDICHE. IMPOSTA LOCALE SUI REDDITI 35 (Francesco Tesauro ed., Torino 1996).

[54] Income Tax Code (*Testo unico delle imposte sui redditi*), TUIR, art. 73.

[55] *Id.* Articles 73(1)(a)–73(1)(d).

[56] *Id.* art. 73(2).

[57] IBFD Italy § 1.2.1.

[58] IBFD Italy § 1.2.2

[59] IBFD Italy § 1.2.7.

[60] *See* art. 115 and 116, TUIR.

corporate taxation (cooperative, mutual insurance companies, public and private entities other than companies) are all sharing the common characteristic of being treated—under Italian law—as having a distinct juridical personality.

## 5. Japan[61]

Both domestic and foreign entities are classified under Japanese law into several categories for tax purposes.[62] Of these categories, only entities classified as "Ordinary Corporations" (*Futsu Hojin*) are fully liable to Japanese corporate income tax.[63] Domestic Ordinary corporations consist mainly of legal entities established pursuant to either the Japanese Commercial Code or the Japanese Limited Liability Company Act.[64] These include Stock Companies (*Kabushiki Kaisha*, SC); Partnership Companies (*Gomei Kaisha*, PC); Limited Partnership Companies (*Goshi Kaisha*, LPC); and Limited Liability Companies (*Yugen Kaisha*, LLC).

Stock companies represent the "traditional" view of a corporation, i.e., an entity with a separate juridical personality, whose shareholders are only liable to the extent of their equity investment in the firm.[65] The limited liability partnership is comprised of general partners and limited liability partners[66] and thus may be treated as the equivalent of an LLP in the U.S. Limited liability companies extend, as their name imply, only limited liability to their equity members and characterized as an entity where "the internal relationships within the company involve a very high degree of personal association, much like limited partnerships."[67] Partnership Companies are the functional equivalent of the common law general partnership, where all partners are fully liable, jointly and severely, to partnership obligation.[68]

The fact that partnerships are liable to corporate tax is unique from a comparative perspective. This explains why Japan has such substantial revenue from corporate tax. No other G7 country subjects such an entity—having no separate personality from its owners and extending full liability to its owners (in the case of PCs)—to unlimited corporate taxation. In other words, "for tax purposes, corporations include not

---

[61] All references in this subchapter are taken from DOING BUSINESS IN JAPAN (Zentaro Kitagawa ed., 2008) [hereinafter DBJ]. The Japanese Corporation Tax Act is abbreviated JCTA.

[62] DBJ Part X § 2.01[1].

[63] *Id.*

[64] *Id.*

[65] DBJ Part VII § 2.02[1].

[66] DBJ Part VII § 2.02[2].

[67] DBJ Part VII § 2.03[3].

[68] DBJ Part VII § 2.03[1][a].

only those in the ordinary sense (e.g., a joint stock company) but also co-operative associations and certain specific organizations."[69]

This "take it all" approach makes life very unpleasant for entities doing business in Japan but incorporated outside of Japan, as they will usually be treated as corporations for tax purposes for the reason of their mere existence. Yet, foreign entities may approach the Japanese Ministry of Finance for classification other than "Ordinary Corporation."[70]

## 6. United Kingdom

Section 832(1) of The Income and Corporation Tax Act[71] (ICTA) defines a "company" for tax purposes as "any *body–corporate* or *unincorporated association* but *does not include a partnership*, a local authority or a local authority association." This general definition is subject to some exceptions, in cases where entities are defined otherwise for the purpose of specific ICTA provisions.

We should thus approach two terms: "unincorporated association" and "body corporate." The term "unincorporated association" has been interpreted to mean:

> two or more persons bound together for one or more common purposes, not being business purposes, by mutual undertakings, each having mutual duties and obligations, in an organization that has rules which identify in whom control of it and its funds rests and on what terms and which can be joined or left at will. The bond of union between the members of an unincorporated association has to be contractual.[72]

In many aspects, this broad definition seems to capture a sensible view of what a "partnership" is, which as noted above, is specifically exempt by section 832(1) from corporate taxation. A later case[73] however, makes clear the tax distinction between unincorporated associations and partnerships by asserting that a partnership is a profit-seeking entity in which partners are entitled to share profits. Members of an unincorporated association only enjoy membership privileges as defined in the association's rules.

Some questions still remain. For example, as a matter of general law, the term "unincorporated" implies that an unincorporated association

---

[69] HIROMITSU ISHI, THE TAX SYSTEM IN JAPAN, 169 (3rd ed., 2001); AULT & ARNOLD, *supra* note 8, at 279.

[70] DBJ chapter X § 2.01[2].

[71] U.K. ST 1988.

[72] Conservative and Unionist Central Office v. Burrel [1982] STC 317.

[73] Blackpool Marton Rotary Club v. Marti, [1988] STC 823, *rev'd on other grounds*, in 62 TC 686 (1989). *Cited in* SWEET & MAXSWELL'S TAXATION OF COMPANIES AND COMPANY RECONSTRUCTIONS, § A2.1.2 (2008).

is not a legal entity for general law purposes. If an unincorporated association does not share profits with its members, how should such associations' profits (in case they do accrue), be taxed in the absence of a legal entity deemed to have earned them?

Related questions were discussed In *Worthing Rugby Football Club v. Commissioner*.[74] The club, acting as an unincorporated association by its own bylaws, acquired two parcels of land and conveyed them to the club's board of trustees to be held for the club's use. The land was later sold by the trustees to a third party. In assessing the transactions, the Commissioner of Inland Revenue determined that the club, and alternatively its trustees, is liable for corporate taxes, capital gains tax, and land development tax. The trustees challenged the assessments on the ground that an unincorporated association is not a legal entity capable of acquiring, owning, and disposing of the property. Specifically, in the issue of the corporate tax assessment, they argued that even though unincorporated associations are clearly subject to corporate taxes under section 832(1), the fact that the club could not in itself perform the transactions meant that it had no capacity to produce the taxable gains assessed. Hence, the assessments should have been made to the members of the club, each in its own individual capacity, as the true beneficiaries of the land. The commissioner did not challenge the argument that the club is not a legal entity for general law purposes but argued that it is a legal creation specifically for purposes of tax law.

At first, a special commissioner accepted most of the trustees' arguments, discharging both the capital gains tax and the corporate tax assessments, and holding the trustees (rather than the club) liable to the land development tax. On appeal, the Chancery Division—accepting the Revenue arguments—reversed, noting that (emphasis added):

> There can be no doubt that . . . an unincorporated association such as a club *is not a legal entity* however real its existence may seem to the club member and to the man in the street.
>
> . . .
>
> It is clear that under the general law, the association *is incapable of owning property.*

However, the Chancery Division also stated that:

> It is clear that unincorporated associations have long been treated *for income tax purposes as entities in themselves, as distinct from their constituent members,* to which income can accrue.

---

[74] [1985] STC 186.

The Chancery Division decision was affirmed by the Court of Appeals.[75] It is clear then, that in spite of having no legal personality, unincorporated association are "companies" capable of producing profits for U.K. income tax purposes.

We now turn to question the meaning of the term "body corporate." The term "body corporate" is the English Law term for "corporation." The core meaning of the term "corporation" in English Law has remained very much unchanged since the celebrated *Salomon* case.[76] In spite of this fact, the issue of classification of entities as "bodies corporate" has been widely litigated in the United Kingdom, particularly with regard to the classification for tax purposes of foreign entities operating in the U.K. The landmark case here is *Memec*.[77] The factual background in *Memec* is extremely complex, but for our purpose, it is enough to mention that the court addressed the legal nature of a German silent partnership (in which the silent partner was a U.K.-based company), in order to determine whether it should be characterized as transparent or opaque for U.K. tax purposes. The way the Court of Appeals approached the issue—which by now should come with no surprise to the reader—is by considering the characteristics of the German partnership and then comparing them to English legal concepts of what a partnership is. The court concluded that the silent partnership is not transparent, primarily on two grounds: First, unlike an English partnership—where the profits and losses are the profits and losses of the partners—in a silent partnership, the silent partner's interest in profits is indirect and contractual. Second, in an English partnership, the partners are jointly and severally liable for the partnership's debts, while in the case of silent partnership, the silent partner has no liability toward a third party doing business with the partnership.

The U.K. Revenue Service (Her Majesty's Revenue and Customs—HMRC) was quick to adopt the court's position in *Memec*.[78] Since then, the HRMC published several interpretive bulletins dealing specifically with entity classification for tax purposes.[79] These bulletins both specified the substantive questions to be asked when classifying an entity for tax purposes and listed certain foreign entities that are viewed by the revenue to be "tax transparent" or "tax opaque." According to HRMC, the questions to be asked when classifying a foreign entity for tax purposes are: (a) Does the foreign entity have a legal existence separate from that of the persons who have an interest in it? (b) Does the entity issue share capital or something else, which serves the same

---


[75] [1987] STC 273.

[76] Salomon v. Salomon Ltd. [1897] AC 22, (HL).

[77] Memec plc v. Commissioners [1998] STC 754 (CA).

[78] 39 TB 627 (1998).

[79] *See, e.g.,* 50 TB 809 (2000); 83 TB 1295 (2006).

function as share capital? (c) Is the business carried on by the entity itself or jointly by the persons who have an interest in it that is separate and distinct from the entity? (d) Are the persons who have an interest in the entity entitled to share in its profits as they arise; or does the amount of profits to which they are entitled depend on a decision of the entity or its members, after the period in which the profits have arisen, to make a distribution of its profits? (e) Who is responsible for debts incurred as a result of the carrying on of the business: the entity or the persons who have an interest in it? (f) Do the assets used for carrying on the business belong beneficially to the entity or to the persons who have an interest in it?

Finally, it should be noted that in spite of *Memec*, U.K. tax law still provides some ambiguity with respect to the definition of "company" for tax purposes, as evident from the later *Bishopp* case.[80] *Bishopp* involved two of the world's most renowned accounting partnerships—Price Waterhouse Coopers (PWC) and Ernst & Young (E&Y). Both PWC and E&Y wished to reregister their London-based partnerships as a Jersey limited liability partnership (LLP), primarily for nontax reasons. However, that may have caused some tax problems. It is certain that under the ICTA a U.K. partnership is not subject to corporate taxes, but the status of a Jersey LLP is not as clear. Some of its characteristics may bring it under the definition of "body corporate," and since there was no question that the new partnerships would be resident in the U.K. (in spite of their foreign registration), their worldwide income would be subjected to U.K. corporate taxes if indeed designated as "bodies corporate" by the U.K. tax authorities.

PWC and E&Y wished to avoid these unfortunate results by seeking a confirmation from the HMRC that a Jersey LLP would not be regarded as a company for tax purposes. The HMRC refused to give such assurances and implied that it would treat a Jersey LLP as a company, liable to corporate taxes. PWC and EY sought court relief by appealing for a declaration that even if they registered as Jersey LLP, the entities would continue to be classified as partnerships for U.K. tax purposes. The court refused to grant such a declarative relief, primarily on procedural grounds (such as that the issue is a theoretical one) and refused to discuss the substantive question at hand, thus maintaining some ambiguity.

## 7. United States

The U.S. Internal Revenue Code[81] does not define a corporation for tax purposes but does assert that it *"includes* association, joint stock

---

[80] R v Commissioners, *ex parte Bishopp* [1999] STC 531.
[81] 26 USCA [hereinafter I.R.C.].

companies and insurance companies."[82] In spite of this somewhat generic reference in the code itself, of the countries in the G7, the United States has probably seen some of the most dramatic legal evolution with respect to the definition of entities subject to corporate taxation. Over the past two decades, this issue has been heavily explored,[83] and it is almost unfair to summarize it in only a few paragraphs.

Generally speaking, the classification of entities for corporate tax purposes should be divided into two main periods: before and after the implementation of the so-called "check-the box" regulations[84] in 1996 (the Regulations). Prior to the adoption of the Regulations, the guidelines for determining whether an entity is deemed to be a corporation for tax purposes were laid in 1935 by the Supreme Court in *Morrisey v. Commissioner*.[85] In *Morrisey*, the court adopted a "resemblance test" that "determined an entity's classification for tax purposes by examining the features of the entity and determining whether its characteristics more nearly resembled those of a corporation"[86] than another entity. The court counted six characteristics of a corporate entity, two of which also characterize partnerships. Thus, four characteristics were left for purposes of the resemblance test: (1) continuity of entity's life; (2) centralization of management; (3) the entity's owners are only liable to the entity's debts to the extent of their capital contribution; and (4) free transferability of the owners' interests in the entity.

In many aspects, the "resemblance test" is the equivalent of the "two-step approach," still in effect in some other countries surveyed here. Albeit, it is not unreasonable to assume that the 1935 "resemblance test" provided at least some inspiration to other countries' tax systems, the jurisdiction that pioneered it (the United States) eventually neglected it for a more formal classification embedded in the check-the-box regulations. The problem with the resemblance test was that it left much room for the taxpayers' discretion. Even though the test was substantive, a

---

[82] I.R.C. § 7701(a)(3).

[83] Just to name a few: *Cp. 2: The Definition of "Corporation," in* Boris I. Bittker & James S. Eustice, Federal Income Taxation of Corporations and Shareholders, (Warren Gorham Lamont 2008); *What is a Corporation?, in* Douglas A. Kahn & Jeffrey S. Lehman, Corporate Income Taxation (5th ed. 2005), 50–53; Victor E. Fleischer, *If it Looks Like A duck: Corporate Resemblance and Check-The-Box Elective Tax Classification*, 96 Colum. L. Rev. 518 (1996); Patrick E. Hobbs, *Entity Classification: The One Hundred-year Debate*, 44 Cath. U. L. Rev. 437 (1995); Joseph A. Snoe, *Entity Classification under the Internal Revenue Code: A Proposal to Replace the Resemblance Model*, 15 J. Corp. L. 647 (1990); William J. Rands, *Organizations Classified as Corporations for Federal Tax Purposes*, 59 St. John's L. Rev. 657 (1985).

[84] 26 CFR §§ 301.7701-1–301.7701-3.

[85] 296 U.S. 344 (1935).

[86] Kahn & Lehamn, *supra* note 83, 84, at 50.

sophisticated taxpayer could easily construct its business to be characterized as that or the other for tax purposes, especially amid the growing legal recognition of new forms of legal entities—such as the limited liability companies—in many U.S. states. This created a huge administrative burden for the IRS, and in addition, there was hardly any point of forcing taxpayers to adopt certain classification, when they actually could—with some planning—adopt whatever classification they chose. These unnecessary complexities have eventually led to the adoption of the Check-the-Box regulations in 1996.

The Regulations provide a completely technical set of tests for classification for tax purposes. First, the Regulations expressly provide a list[87] of entities, both United States and foreign, which are treated as "associations" (and hence, corporations) for U.S. tax purposes. Among those which we mentioned when surveying other countries, the list notes the French *Société Anonyme*, the German *Aktiengesellschaft*, the Italian *società per azioni*, and the Japanese *Kabushiki Kaisha*. Even though this approach is very formal, it is important to note that all entities mentioned in the list would have probably been characterized as "corporations" under the resemblance test as well. This is so because they all carry most, if not all, four characteristics of a corporation as described in *Morrisey*.

If an entity is not listed and is categorized as "eligible entity," it may elect (by "checking-the-box") to be treated as a corporation for U.S. tax purposes, or otherwise it is treated a partnership (in some case, the default is association treatment, and an election is needed in order to be treated as a partnership).[88] The rule of thumb is thus very simple: if an entity is listed— it is a corporation; if it is not and it is eligible—it may elect how it should be treated for tax purposes.

## C. Summary

The description of the ways by which the G7 countries classify legal entities for tax purposes shows at least some degree of convergence in the types of entities subject to corporate taxation. Yet, there are some noteworthy exceptions, such as the fact that the United States is the only jurisdiction not to tax limited liability companies, Japan is the only jurisdiction subjecting partnerships to corporate level tax, and that the United Kingdom subjects unincorporated associations to corporate tax.

With respect to domestic entities, all countries surveyed adhere closely to their own general corporate legislation when classifying an entity for tax purposes. Even though each country adheres to its own corporate law, there are some similarities in the characterization of entities classified as corporations. Some countries would characterize more

---

[87] 26 CFR 301.7701-2(b).
[88] 26 CFR § 301.7701-3(a).

entities than others as corporations (most notably, Japan, which taxes more kinds of entities than other countries, while the U.S. taxes less), but all countries would tax entities that hold the four characteristics described in the *Morrisey* case. In other words, per se corporations are always subject to corporate taxation, in all countries surveyed.

With respect to foreign entities, all countries surveyed apart from the United States and Japan apply some sort of a two-stage "resemblance test." First, the entity characteristics are portrayed, relaying on the laws of the entities jurisdiction. Second, these characteristics are compared to those of the jurisdiction in question, to determine to what sort of domestic entity the foreign entity resembles the most. This practice is observed not only in the G7 but throughout the OECD countries.[89] It seems that most countries put great emphasis on the existence of separate legal being—and to a lesser extent—the existence of limited liability.


## III. CORPORATE RESIDENCY

### A. Conventional determinants of corporate residency

We should start by noting the reason that corporate residency is at all important from a comparative perspective. Under the now widely acceptable global approach to taxation (discussed in Chapter 2), most countries tax their residents' worldwide income and foreign residents' income sourced within the taxing jurisdiction. Thus, it is important to determine whether a corporation is a resident at a specific jurisdiction, in order to assess the scope of its taxable income in that territory (i.e., global or territorial).

There are two commonly shared methods used to determine corporate residency, as two leading commentators recently noted:

> Although different jurisdictions determine corporate location in different ways, the range of options is rather limited. Basically, in locating a corporation, a legal system can adopt either the "place of incorporation" ("POI") rule or some version of the "real seat" ("RS") rule. Under the POI rule, the corporation's location is determined by where it was incorporated, a purely formal criterion. Under the RS rule, a corporation's location depends on some combination of factual elements, such as the location of the administrative headquarters or the location of the firm's center of gravity as determined by the location of the employees and assets. The place of incorporation can also bear on this question, but it is not determinative.[90]

---

[89] *See also* OECD PARTNERSHIPS REPORT, *supra* 41, at 9.

[90] Mitchell A. Kane & Edward B. Rock, *Corporate Taxation and International Charter Competition*, 106 MICH. L. REV. 1229, 1235 (2008). *See also* Richard Vann,

It is obvious then that any given jurisdiction faces the options to adopt a formal approach (place of incorporation), a substantive approach (real seat, also known sometimes as "place of effective management"), or some combination of the two. On its face, this makes our comparative task rather easy. All we have to ask is which of the two methods is adopted in each jurisdiction. Unfortunately, as shall be explained below, in the real world, comparative work is never easy.

Table X summarizes which of the two methods (or any other method) was adopted by each of the G7 countries over the course of the past two decades. It does so by examining the question in two points of time: 1987 (just when the wave of tax reforms started to sweep the world) and today. The POI question is easy to compare since POI strictly looks at formalities. The comparative hardship arises, of course, by the fact that many countries adopted the substantive test as well, which compels us to question how these countries interpret substantively the "place of effective management" question. This question is discussed briefly in the next part, but before doing so, it may be useful to provide a little background by examining some acceptable criteria for determining the "place of effective management."

Such criteria can be found in the OECD model tax convention,[91] which is a widely adopted benchmark for tax treaties drafting. Even though the OECD model convention is primarily a source for drafting treaties for the prevention of double taxation (DTCs), its effects probably stretch far beyond this or the other specific treaty, as it provides a standardized benchmark of tax legislation.[92] Article 4(1) of the OECD convention provides that a person's[93] residency is determined, among others, by references to the "place of management or any other criterion of a similar nature." Article 4(3) asserts that "where by reason of article (1) . . . a person other than an individual is a resident of both Contracting States, then it shall be deemed to be a resident only of the State in which its *place of effective management* is situated.

The commentaries to section 4(3)[94] have undergone some meaningful changes throughout the years, the most recent of which was as recent as

---

*International Aspects of Income Tax, in* Tax Law Design and Drafting Vol. 2 (Victor Thuronyi ed., Cp. 18, 1998), 15–16.

[91] OECD, Model Tax Convention on Income and on Capital (2005). [Hereinafter OECD Model Convention.]

[92] *See generally* Reuven S. Avi-Yonah, International Tax as International Law: An Analysis of the International Tax Regime 2–5 (Cambridge University Press 2007).

[93] Which is defined to include "an individual, a company and any other body of persons," OECD Model Convention § 1(1).

[94] OECD Model Convention, Commentary to § 4(3).

July 2008.[95] Prior to the 2008 amendments, the commentary asserted that (italics added):

> The place of effective management is the place *where key management and commercial decisions* that are necessary for the *conduct of the entity's business are in substance made.* The place of effective management will ordinarily be the place *where the most senior person or group of persons (for example a board of directors) makes its decisions,* the place where the actions to be taken by the entity as a whole are determined; however, no definitive rule can be given and all relevant facts and circumstances must be examined to determine the place of effective management. An entity may have more than one place of management, but it can have only one place of effective management at any one time.[96]

The criterion is thus quite simple. Place of effective management is deemed to be where managerial discretion is exercised, which usually correlates with the place in which board members regularly meet or where the executive officers are located. However, the 2008 amendments introduced some far-reaching changes to the commentary. First, rather than looking at the place where decisions regarding the "conduct of the entity are in substance made," the commentary now looks at the place where decisions with respect to the "conduct of the entity—*as a whole*—are in substance made."[97] The following question then arises: what does the term "as a whole" means? The new commentaries are ignoring this issue, but our guess is that the idea is to make sure that in the age of multinational activity, one should only look at decisions significantly affecting the entire multinational entity, rather than decisions that only affect a specific branch in a specific jurisdiction.

A far more important change is the complete deletion of the place of the board meeting and senior management location as relevant criteria at all. The new commentaries simply leave the place of effective management to be determined according to the notoriously difficult to define "facts and circumstances" test. As we shall see, most countries have yet to follow this path. The reason for this modification, we think, is the relative ease by which the "place of board meetings" factor is manipulated. After all, it is not unreasonable to assume that airport hotels were invented primarily for two reasons: accommodating air crews and to aid corporate tax planning.

---

[95] 2008 Update to the OECD Model Tax Convention (July 18, 2008). [Hereinafter OECD 2008 Convention Amendments.]

[96] *Supra* note 95.

[97] OECD 2008 Convention Amendments, at 7.

**Table X** Definitions of Corporate Residency for Tax purposes in the G7

| Jurisdiction | 1987 Residency Definition[98] | 2008 Residency Definition[99] |
| --- | --- | --- |
| Canada | Any corporation incorporated in Canada; corporation not incorporated in Canada if its central management and control are exercised in Canada. | Corporation incorporated in Canada; Corporation not incorporated in Canada if its central management and control are exercised in Canada. |
| France | The country in which the company is registered (the legal seat test). | Companies that have their legal seat (*siège*) in France or which have their place of effective management (*siège social effectif*) in France. |
| Germany | A corporation is resident in Germany for tax purposes if either its legal seat (*Sitz*) or its management is located in Germany.[100] | A corporation is resident in Germany for tax purposes if either its legal seat (*Sitz*) or its place of management (*Ort der Geschäftsleitung*) is located in Germany. |
| Italy | A company is considered resident if its legal seat, place of effective management, or main business purpose is in Italy for the greater part of the financial year. The place of incorporation is not relevant. | A company is considered resident if its legal seat, place of effective management, or main business purpose is in Italy for the greater part of the financial year. The place of incorporation is not relevant. |
| Japan | A company incorporated under the laws of Japan or a company not incorporated under the laws of Japan if its principal office is in Japan or its chief purpose is to carry business in Japan. | Any corporation having its head office in Japan is a domestic corporation. A corporation organized under the laws of a country other than Japan and has its head office in Japan is regarded as a domestic corporation. [101] |

*Continued*

---

98 Source, unless stated otherwise: 72 Cahiers de Droit Fiscal (1987).

99 Source, unless stated otherwise: PWC, Corporate Taxes—Worldwide Summaries (2008), *available at* http://www.taxsummaries.pwc.com/uk/wwts/wwts.nsf?Open; IBFD, Europe—Corporate Taxes Database, *available at* http://online2.ibfd.org/gii/.

100 *Doing Business in West Germany*, 3 Foreign Tax L. Bi-Weekly Bull. 1, 6 (1985).

101 DBJ *supra* 61, at Ch. X § 2.01[1.]

**Table X** (*Contd.*)

| Jurisdiction | 1987 Residency Definition | 2008 Residency Definition |
| --- | --- | --- |
| United Kingdom | Place of effective management.[102] | Companies incorporated under U.K. law and companies incorporated abroad if their central management and control is situated in the U.K. |
| United States | Any corporation incorporated under U.S. federal or state law.[103] | Any corporation incorporated under U.S. federal or state law. [104] |

## *B. Characterizing "real seat" of a corporate entity in the G7*

Since the United States does not apply a real seat test, but only the place of incorporation test, the United States is not discussed here.

In questioning the "place of central management and control," *Canadian* courts have always closely followed English courts.[105] Hence, some English jurisprudence on the matter will be described here in conjunction with the Canadian one. In doing so, we will draw substantially from Robert Couzin's excellent study on corporate residency.[106]

There are only a handful of tax cases that can be titled as seminal as *De Beers*,[107] in which the question was whether a company registered and having its main office abroad can be assessed in England on the grounds of having a London office, and that its principal managers are U.K. residents.[108] The House of Lords rejected the place of incorporation test as the only determinant for corporate residency for tax purposes and asserted—in an eternally remembered phrase—that:

> [A] company resides for purposes of income tax where its real business is carried on . . . I regard that as the true rule, and the real business is carried on where the central management and control actually abides.[109]

This "central management and control" test has since seen an overwhelming volume of interpretation both in case law and in administrative

---

[102] DOING BUSINESS IN THE U.K. (Barbara Ford ed., § 25.01[2], 2008).

[103] I.R.C. § 7701(a)(4).

[104] I.R.C. § 7701(a)(4).

[105] ROBERT COUZIN, CORPORATE RESIDENCE AND INTERNATIONAL TAXATION 25 (IBFD Publications 2002).

[106] COUZIN, *id.*

[107] De Beers Consolidated Mines, Limited v. Howe [1906] AC 455 (HL).

[108] For a comprehensive review of the case, *see* COUZIN, *supra* 106, at 25–47.

[109] *De Beers, supra* note 108, at 458.

rulings.[110] To summarize it in a few paragraphs would be futile. We thus shall briefly describe the current legal situation in Canada with respect to the interpretation of the "central management and control" test. Under current Canadian jurisprudence, the place where the board regularly meets establishes a rebuttable presumption of residence.[111] Additional facts to be taken into account are the place in which the individual company managers exercise their discretion, the place where the corporations operates its real business, and the place to which laws the corporate entity adheres in maintaining its corporate governance practices.[112]

A striking fact is that the CRA, in its own interpretation of corporate residency (last updated in March of 2008), still cites the 1906 *De Beers*[113] Case. The CRA opinion is that the place in which the central management and control "abides" is where the directors regularly hold their board meetings.

In *France*, the place of effective management is located in the state in which the management discretion is exercised. The effective place of management is determined on a case-by-case basis but "generally corresponds to the place where the directors conduct the board meetings."[114] It should be noted that the question of corporate residency is of less importance in France than in other countries, since France still adheres to a territorial approach with respect to corporations. Namely, any corporation doing business in France, domestic or foreign, is only subject to tax on its French operations.[115]

Entities organized under *German*[116] commercial law are compelled by law to have their legal seat and their place of management (*Verwaltungssitz*) in Germany. However, the question of "place of management" remains relevant with respect to entities incorporated under foreign laws and is normally defined as "the place where the persons who have final authority make the decisions concerning the management of the business are located."

*Italy*[117] applies two alternative substantive tests: The place of effective management (*sede dell'amministrazione*) and the place of the main business purpose (*oggetto principale dell'attività*). The place of effective management is the place from where the company's directors manage the

---

[110] *See* Couzin, *supra* note 105, at 48–102.

[111] Couzin, *supra* note 105, at 93.

[112] *Id.*

[113] Canadian Revenue Agency, *Residency of a Corporation* (2008), *available at* http://www.cra-arc.gc.ca/tx/nnrsdnts/bsnss/bs-rs-eng.html.

[114] Mathieu Lescot, *France Issues CI.R.C.ular on Branch Tax Exemption*, 17 Tax Notes Int'l 77, 77 (1998).

[115] DBF, *supra* note 29, at § 13.01[3][b].

[116] IBFD, Europe—Corporate Taxes Database—Germany, § 8.2.1.1 (2008).

[117] IBFD, Europe—Corporate Taxes Database—Italy, § 8.2.1.1 (2008).

company and in which managerial decisions are made; hence, it usually corresponds to the place where board meetings are held. The place of the main business purpose is the place of the purpose indicated in the articles of incorporation. If not indicated in the articles of incorporation, the place of main business purpose is determined by the actual activity of the company.

*Japan's* "real seat" test concerns the place where the principal office is located. Concurrent with civil law principals, a corporation incorporated under the laws of Japan must have its principal office registered in Japan. With respect to entities incorporated in another jurisdiction, the place of principal office is deemed to be the place where the office is registered according to the company's documents of incorporation or where the main business purpose of the company is located.[118] If the corporation's documents fail to provide such a place, then the place of the principal office is "the place where representatives or managers are situated . . . its business is planned and accounting and budgeting is controlled."[119]

As already noted, in the *United Kingdom*, the principles of *De Beers* dictate the substantive issues of corporate residency. Until 1982, it was generally accepted that a company is resident in the place in which board meetings are held.[120] However, numerous cases where the situation of the board meetings had little connection with substantive management induced the Inland Revenue to issue in 1983 a Statement of Practice,[121] indicating that the Revenue intended to "investigate the question of corporate residence in borderline cases perhaps more thoroughly . . . The determination of the place where a company is managed and controlled was, in the final analysis, a question of fact."[122]

The 1983 statement was superseded by a 1990 statement,[123] still in effect, which inter alia interprets case law concerning the "central management and control" test. Specific reference is made to both *De Beers* and to *Unit Construction Co. LTD. V. Bullock.*[124] In *Unit Construction*, three subsidiaries of a U.K. company were registered in Kenya, and all had board members situated in Kenya. Over the course of several years, the subsidiaries suffered significant losses. With a desire to utilize the losses, it is not surprising that this time, it was the taxpayer's stance that the Kenyan companies should be deemed to be resident in the U.K. The taxpayer argued that the Kenyan directors did not exercise any real

---

[118] Hideo Matsumura, *Japan, in* 72 Cahiers de Droit Fiscal International 389, 391 (1987).

[119] *Id.* at 395.

[120] Ford, *supra* note 102.

[121] SP 6/83.

[122] Ford, *supra* note 102.

[123] SP 1/90.

[124] [1960] A.C. 351 (HL).

discretion and received all their instructions from the management of the U.K. parent. The House of Lords determined that the subsidiaries were in fact all domiciled in the U.K. for tax purposes, noting that "only authorized . . . management and control are relevant to an inquiry as to the residence of a company."[125]

The statement of practice then continues to portray HRMC's view regarding the place of "central management and control" test. According to the HRMC, the place where the board of directors meets is important but not decisive. For example, attention should be also paid to a situation in which most discretion is exercised by a single individual and to the location of such individual. It is also noted that a mere formality of holding board meetings outside the U.K. will not suffice to have the corporation regarded as foreign. There has to be some sort of substantive business and management decision making in these meetings.

## C. Summary

Some jurisdictions have for a long time maintained that corporate residency translates to the place of board meetings as an indicator to the place of central management. Even though the United States does not apply similar tests to corporate residency, it does question similar issues when determining whether corporate income is "effectively connected" to "United States trade or business", thus rendering it taxable in the United States.[126] The U.K. applies a somewhat more substantive approach to the issue than other countries, but the place of board meetings still retains its importance even there.

These similarities all adhere closely to the OECD commentaries in the model tax convention, as were in effect before the 2008 amendments. This benchmark is now gone, replaced by the obscured "facts and circumstances" test. It should be interesting to revisit the question of corporate residency in a couple of years, to see how this important change affected corporate residency definitions around the globe.


# IV. CORPORATE TAX RATES


One the most notable features of the tax reform wave of the 1980s was the reduction of both personal and corporate income tax rates. In the case of corporate income tax rates, which shall be investigated in this part of the chapter, the reductions have been referred to as nothing less

---

[125] *Id.* at 369.
[126] I.R.C. §881.

than "dramatic."[127] Indeed, there is ample quantitative evidence showing that since the 1980s, corporate tax rates have been gradually eroding throughout the world.[128]

A recent OECD report provides us with a detailed account of recent trends in OECD countries.[129] The report shows that since the late 1980s, there has been a continuous drop in statutory corporate tax rates: data available for 17 OECD countries demonstrates a significant drop of the average statutory rate in these countries from 50.9 percent in 1982 to 38.3 percent in 1997.[130] Data for all OECD countries showed a further drop from an average statutory corporate tax rate of 33.6 percent in 2000 to an average of 28.4 percent in 2006.

Similar trends can be observed with respect to corporate effective marginal and effective average tax rates. Out of the 19 countries tested in the OECD report in this regard, the marginal effective tax rates (METR) have been reduced in 14, in a period lasting from 1982 to 2005. The mean METR has decreased from 27.9 percent in 1982 to 20.3 percent in 2005.[131] As for average effective corporate tax rates (AETR), the majority of OECD countries have reduced their AETR over a period lasting from 1982 to 2005. The mean AETR among OECD countries has decreased from 34.2 percent in 1982 to 24.4 percent in 2005.[132]

This movement toward lower corporate income tax rates can be observed not only in OECD countries. Studies of tax policies in developing countries report similar findings. For example, a World Bank study notes that tax reforms in developing countries also have been characterized by the reductions of corporate tax rates.[133] Another study gives a full account on 1990s tax reforms in Latin America and notes that "most of the [Latin American] countries joined the world-wide movement towards lower marginal tax rates on individuals and on enterprises."[134] It further demonstrates that the top marginal corporate

---

[127] Richard Vann, *General Report*, 88a CAHIERS DE DROIT FISCAL INTERNATIONAL 23, 25 (2003).

[128] Just to name a few: Duane Swank & Sven Steinmo, *The New Political Economy of Taxation in Advanced Capitalist Democracies*, 46 AM. J. POL. SCI. 642 (2002); Tanzi, *supra* note 5 at 104–05, 112–13; Michael P. Devereux, Rachel Griffith & Alexander Klemm, *Corporate Income Tax Reforms and International Tax Competition*, 17 ECON. POL'Y 449 (2002).

[129] OECD, FUNDAMENTAL REFORM OF CORPORATE INCOME TAX (OECD 2007).

[130] *Id.* at 20–21.

[131] *Id.* at 26–28.

[132] *Id* at 28–29.

[133] Wayne R. Thirsk, *Overview: The Substance and Process of Tax Reform in Eight Developing Countries*, *in* TAX REFORM IN DEVELOPING COUNTRIES, 1, 18–19 (Wayne R. Thirsk ed., 1997).

[134] Vito Tanzi, *Taxation in Latin America in the Last Decade*, CENTER FOR RESEARCH ON ECONOMIC DEVELOPMENT AND POLICY REFORM, WORKING PAPER

income tax rates in Latin American countries fell from an average of 43.3 percent in 1986 to 28.6 percent in 2000.[135] As you might recall, the average statutory tax rate in OECD countries was 33.6 percent in 2000, so the difference is not huge. Finally, one study concluded that parallel trends have been the lot of South African countries, noting that the mean statutory rate of corporate tax rates in South African Development Community (SADC) countries fell from approximately 44.3 percent to 33 percent in a period lasting from 1980 to 2004.[136] To sum up, the erosion of corporate tax rates can be easily referred to as a global phenomenon.

Yet, the mere fact that there is an undisputed worldwide erosion of corporate income tax rates tells us very little about rate *convergence*.[137] In order to argue that tax rates are "converging," we should show that the rate reduction is moving toward a common mean. To put it in a statistical language, we should question whether dispersion indicators (such as standard deviation) of corporate tax rates also are shrinking.

One argument in this regard could be that as countries compete to attract FDI (Foreign Direct Investment) from multinational enterprises (MNEs), corporate taxes are racing toward a bottom zero (or a nominal) tax rate, which of course means total convergence at that rate. This argument would originate in the "doomsday" scenario of tax competition, which is most likely to take place in the absence of international cooperation. Such "prisoner's dilemma"-type arguments were indeed made.[138] These arguments of convergence at zero rates can, at the least, be countered. Some commentators assert that it is highly unlikely that tax competition will lead to such a dramatic "race to the bottom" of tax rates. This is so because there are several domestic factors (the size of public sector debt being one example) that creates counterweights to international competition factors.[139] Another set of counterarguments relates to the fact that tax holidays are hardly the only consideration in MNEs investment decisions. Zero tax rates—the argument goes—will eventually harm tax revenues and minimize public spending. This will harm the countries' infrastructure and create a deterrent for FDI.

---

No. 76, at 5 (2000).

[135] *Id.*, at 24–26.

[136] Zorika Robinson, *Corporate Tax Rates in the SADC Region: Determinants and Policy Implications*, 73:4 S. AfricAn J. Econ. 722 (2005).

[137] *Cf.*, Jennifer Gann, *Comparing Top Rates Does Not Prove Convergence*, 19 TAX Notes Int'l 743 (1999).

[138] *See, e.g.*, Vito Tanzi, *Globalization, Tax Competition and the future of Tax Systems*, International Monetary Fund Paper No. WP/96/141, at 18 (1996); For a summary of the tax competition/prisoner dilemma conundrum (and contradictory arguments), *see* Julie Roin, *Competition and Evasion: Another Perspective on International Tax Competition*, 89 Geo. L.J. 543, 549–54 (2001).

[139] Swank & Steinmo, *supra* note 128.

In other words, "because MNEs benefit from tax expenditures and provisions of public goods and services, they are unlikely to drive the rates to zero."[140]

Some economists studied the dispersion indicators of corporate tax rates over time, the most obvious of whom is Slemrod, who studied which noncompetitive factors can be found to influence countries' corporate tax rates.[141] His single most important finding for our purpose is that throughout the world, in a period lasting from 1980 to 1995, the mean as well as the *standard deviation* fell for both statutory and average corporate tax rates. This trend of rate convergence during the last two decades of the twentieth century is also supported by other studies.[142] It is not clear whether this trend of convergence is still persistent, and recent data suggests that with respect to nominal corporate tax rates at the least, the past decade was characterized by a trend of *divergence* in corporate tax rates.[143]

## V. SOME GENERAL REMARKS ON CORPORATE TAX BASE

The question of convergence in the corporate tax base (or any tax base for that matter) among different jurisdictions can be understood in one of two ways (which are of course interrelated but still distinct from each other). The first is convergence in the measures, according to which corporate tax base is defined. We shall refer to this feature as *base*

---

[140] Johsua D. Moore, *The Economic Importance of Tax Competition for Foreign Direct Investment: An Analysis of International Corporate Tax Harmonization Proposals and Lessons from the Winning Corporate Tax Strategy in Ireland*, 20 Pac. McGeorge Global Bus. & Dev. L.J. 345, 357 (2007).

[141] Joel Slemrod, *Are Corporate Tax Rates, or Countries, Converging?* 88 J. Pub. Econ. 1169 (2004).

[142] *See, e.g.,* Reint Gropp & Kristina Kostial, *FDI and Corporate Tax Revenue: Tax Harmonization or Competition*, 38:2 Fin. & Develop. 10 (2001), showing that the standard deviation of corporate tax rates, both nominal and average, in OECD countries is decreasing over time; Rosanne Altshuler, Harry Grubert & T. Scott Newlon, *Has U.S. Investment Abroad Become More Sensitive to Tax Rates?*, in International Taxation and Multinational Activity 9 (James Hines Jr. ed., 2001), showing that the average effective tax rate paid by American CFCs in 58 countries have decreased over time, and that the dispersion of these rates had been reduced as well; Harry Grubert, *Tax Planning by Companies and Tax Competition by Governments: Is There Evidence for Change in Behaviour?*, in International Taxation and Multinational Activity 113 (James Hines Jr. ed., 2001).

[143] Omri Marian, *Do Tax Laws Truly Converge? A Case Study of Corporate Tax Rates in 11 Industrialized Countries, in* The Discursive Failure in Comparative Tax Law, S.J.D. Thesis presented at the University of Michigan Law School 121, 137–43 (2009).

*definition convergence.* The second is convergence with respect to the measures according to which the tax base is allocated among different jurisdictions. We shall refer to this feature as *base allocation convergence.*

The question is how different countries define the corporate base of taxation. To put it in more practical terms, we should ask what each country considers to be corporate income according to its domestic tax laws. What deductions are allowed to corporations? What methods of depreciation do domestic laws prescribe? Are there any specific exemptions? It is impossible to address these issues in a manageable length in a subchapter (or for that matter, in an entire book). As for the question of base allocation, it would discuss how countries define corporate residency, as well as passive and active income in similar ways. These questions were partially addressed in our exploration of corporate residency.

So, how can we compare domestic corporate tax bases? Nominal rates are usually a given factor. Even effective rates, both marginal and average, are (at least arguably) objectively measurable using economic data. The definition of tax base, on the other hand, is usually a quagmire of multiple code sections, regulations, authorities' rulings, and court decisions. In sum, there is no simple method to summarize the way by which a specific county defines the tax base for its corporate taxpayers. Thus, we shall confine ourselves to some general observations regarding corporate tax bases.

We would like to start our general comments by noting that the global trend of reduction in corporate tax rates has not been accompanied by an erosion of corporate tax revenues, as one might expect. Analyzing corporate tax receipts for the G7 countries over a period of 1970 to 2004, a recent NBER study reports that in all G7 countries—other than for Japan—there is no evidence of a substantial decline in the share of corporation tax revenues in total tax receipts, amid the reduction of tax rates.[144] Some studies even demonstrate that corporate tax revenues actually increased in most OECD countries during the same period.[145] In other words, economic literature makes it quite clear that there is no

---

[144] Alan J. Auerbach, Michael P. Devereux & Helen Simpson, *Taxing Corporate Income*, NBER Working Paper No. 14494, 8 (2008). *Available at* http://www. nber.org/papers/w14494; *See* also Rachel Griffith & Alexander Klemm, *What Has Been The Tax Competition Experience Of The Last 20 Years?*, 34 Tax Notes Int'l 1299, 1306–07 (2004), showing that corporate income tax revenues as a share of total taxation analysis suggest no marked downward trend in corporate tax revenues and concluding that governments have managed to keep corporate income tax revenues pretty constant as a share of GDP.

[145] Michael P. Devereux, *Development in the Taxation of Corporate Profits in the OECD Since 1965: Rates Bases and Revenues*, Oxford University Center for Business Taxation Working Paper No. 07/04, 12 (2006), *available at* http:// users.ox.ac.uk/~mast1732/RePEc/pdf/WP0704.pdf.

statistically significant correlation between corporate tax rates and corporate tax revenues.[146]

A few possible explanations to the stability of corporate tax revenues have been introduced. For example, it has been suggested that increased corporate profitability over the past few decades significantly contributed to higher corporate tax revenues.[147] Another possible explanation relates to both the ever-increasing size of the corporate sector and the tendency of taxpayers to favor the incorporated mode of doing business.[148] Larger corporate sectors may imply that there are more corporate taxes to be collected. The last explanation for revenue stability, which is the most pertinent for our purpose, is that the reduction of corporate tax rates has been accompanied by corporate tax base broadening. Significantly, the corporate tax base broadening movement, just as tax rates reductions, is viewed as a wide international phenomenon, particularly in OECD countries.

Numerous accounts imply that convergence in the measures taken for the sake of tax base broadening apparently prevailed. Generally speaking, since the mid-1980s, most industrialized economies implemented very similar reforms in their tax base. An IMF survey reports that "In OECD countries, the decline in statutory rates has generally been accompanied by a broadening of the tax base through a scaling back of generous deductions and exemptions . . . , e.g., by cutting back on investment tax credits, loss offset rules, and interest deductibility."[149] Another study gives a detailed account of the corporate tax base broadening in the U.K., summarizing that since the 1980s, one of the primary measures of base broadening has been the reduction in the value of deductions allowed for capital expenditures (i.e., reduction in the value of initial allowances allowed, as well as replacing accelerated systems with more moderate depreciation methods).[150] The same study also asserts that "the base-broadening . . . reforms to the structure of the U.K. corporation tax in the mid-1980s have also been carried out in other countries" and demonstrates that the value of depreciation allowances have been falling across the G7 economies.[151]

These studies imply that since the mid-1980s, most industrialized economies introduced similar reforms aimed at corporate tax base broadening. The most commonly shared reforms included

---

[146] *Id.* at 14–25.

[147] *See generally* Devereux, *id,* at 12–13.

[148] *See* Ruud A. De Mooij & Gaetan Nicodeme, *Corporate Tax Policy and Incorporation in the EU,* CEB Working Paper No. 07/016 (2007); Michael Devereux, Rachel Griffith & Alexander Klemm, *Why Has the U.K. Corporation Tax Raised So Much Money?* 25(4) Fiscal Studs. 366 (2004).

[149] John Norregaard & Tehmina S. Khan, *Tax Policy: Recent Trends and Coming Challenges,* IMF Working Paper No. WP/07/274, 8 (2007).

[150] Auerbach, Devereux & Simpson, *supra* note 144, at 5.

[151] Auerbach, Devereux & Simpson, *supra* note 144, at 7.

(1) elimination (or significant reduction) of credit-producing investment incentives; (2) replacing generous accelerated depreciation methods with methods that more closely relates to the useful life of the depreciable assets; and (3) introducing limitations on interest deduction of debt financing, i.e., thin capitalization rules.

Most of these changes took place during the late 1980s, in the wake of the worldwide tax reform movement[152]; however, recent surveys indicate that many countries have been introducing similar reforms as late as the late 1990s and even well into the 2000s.[153] In other words, modern tax legislators continue to copycat old base-broadening trends, rather than implementing new (and maybe more creative) broadening instruments.

# VI. CORPORATE/SHAREHOLDERS TAX INTEGRATION OF DISTRIBUTED PROFITS

## A. Definition of integration and general issues

An area of corporate taxation in which trends of convergence have been identified by many commentators is in the extent by which the taxation of corporations and their individual shareholders are integrated.

Integration of the individual and corporate tax systems means that corporate income should be taxed only once, integrating individual income tax and corporate income tax in order to eliminate double taxation of corporate income and the connected economic distortions (most commonly referred distortion are the incentive to invest in noncorporate rather than corporate structures, the incentive to invest in debt rather than equity, and the incentive to retain corporate profits within corporations).

There is an overwhelming variety of practical and theoretical methods to integrate corporate/shareholder taxation and an almost equally overwhelming abundance of literature describing them.[154] For our purpose, it is not necessary to provide a detailed description of all methods but rather to understand that all of them operate in an easily described spectrum.

---

[152] See, *e.g.*, Auerbach, Devereux &Simpson, *supra* note 144, at 5; Devereux, Griffith & Klemm, *supra* note 148, at 1302–03.

[153] *See, e.g.*, OECD TAX POLICY STUDIES NO. 9: RECENT TAX POLICY TRENDS AND REFORMS IN OECD COUNTRIES, 31–126; 157–58 (2003).

[154] Some examples include OECD REPORT, *supra* note 130, at 85–90; DOUGLAS A. KAHN & JEFFREY S. LEHMAN, CORPORATE INCOME TAXATION, 5th ed., 28–36 (Foundation Press, 5th ed. 2005); Graeme Cooper & Richard K. Gordon, *Taxation of Enterprises and their Owners, in* TAX LAW DESIGN AND DRAFTING, VOL. 1, ch. 19 (Victor Thuronyi ed., 1996). *Colloquium on Corporate Integration,* 47 TAX L. REV. 427–723 (1992).

One end of the spectrum is marked by the Classical Method, under which full tax authority is exerted both on companies and their shareholders; namely, there is no integration. Under such a system, all corporate profits are taxed twice at full rates. The first instance of taxation is at the corporate level, on corporate profits, at corporate tax rates. The second collection of taxes is being done at the shareholder level, at individual tax rates (assuming shareholders are individuals), when the corporate profits are being distributed.

At the other end of the spectrum, this double taxation is completely eliminated. The most extreme way to eliminate double taxation is to treat corporations as conduits for all tax purposes, while all of their profits, losses and other tax attributes are allocated to their shareholders, as it is usually done in the case of partnerships and their partners. Such a radical system of corporate/shareholder taxation has never been adopted, as a general rule, in any country,[155] and hence, we shall embrace some more relaxed versions of integration as the other end of our spectrum.

These relaxed methods of integration are also dedicated to the elimination of the double tier taxation. Such systems appear in many forms. The most obvious one is the Full Imputation System. In cases of full imputation, corporate taxes are being levied, but in essence, they are nothing more than a partial withholding regime on shareholders' taxation. When corporate profits are being distributed, shareholders are taxed at their individual capacity but also receive full credit for their proportional share of the taxes already paid by the corporation. Another way to achieve a relief in double taxation is by Dividend Exclusion/ Exemption. In such a system, the corporate taxes are levied, but shareholders' level taxation is eliminated by excluding distributed profits from the individual tax base.

An article by Yariv Brauner provides us with a full account on some recent trends of corporate/shareholder integration.[156] Exploring evidence from several jurisdictions,[157] Brauner concludes that "[d]uring the second half of the last century, many countries gradually replaced their so-called classical corporate tax regimes, under which corporate earnings were taxed twice . . . with an integrated regime (imputation), which taxed such earnings only once."[158] However, he also asserts that "[t]his clear and gradual trend has been abruptly reversed with the turn of the century."[159] This reversal of trends is also supported by a 2003 IFA

---

[155] KAHN & LEHMAN, *Id.* at 36.

[156] Yariv Brauner, *Integration in and Integration World*, 2 N.Y.U. J. L. & Bus. 51 (2005).

[157] *Id.* at 68–76.

[158] *Id.* at 51.

[159] *Id.*

study arguing that a "significant move away from the imputation system" can be observed throughout the world.[160] Brauner argues that the primary reasons for which imputation has been abandoned are the difficulties to extend its benefits across borders.[161] If a country, in which a company is resident, grants credits to foreign shareholders for taxes paid by the resident company, the result is zero revenue for the source country (with respect to the part of the stake held by foreign shareholders). Of course, it is technically possible to maintain imputation as a strictly domestic policy (i.e., extend the credits only to local shareholders), as was being done during the 1990s,[162] but such policies create preferential treatment to domestic shareholders. These policies both scared investors away (to other countries which did extend the credits across borders)[163] and also contradicted international nondiscrimination rules.[164]

The theoretical scheme to maintain imputation at the international level requires the source country to give up any taxation of the foreign shareholders,[165] in fact, to move from a full imputation system to a dividend exemption system. This can be maintained in one of two ways: unilateral or coordinated. Under a unilateral approach, the source system would simply exempt shareholders (both foreign and domestic) from any taxation on dividend and compensate for the revenue loss by rising corporate tax rates. This is not a feasible solution in the prisoner-dilemma-like environment of global taxation. Such a tactic would probably divert FDI away to lower-rates jurisdictions.

Under a cooperative method, the source country will not raise corporate taxes but will share information with the residence country in order to assure that the residence country will only tax the difference between the corporate tax rate in the source country and the individual tax rate in the residence country. Thus, the source country is able to collect some revenue. It requires any country that is a partner to such a scheme to completely forego withholding on dividends and trust the other country to share complete and accurate information (in order for the former to be able to tax its own residents holding stakes in foreign corporations). Such a level of cooperation is not easy to achieve. With inadequate level of international cooperation and information sharing, countries had to find middle solutions to the problem as they moved

---

[160]  Richard Vann, *General Report, in* 88a Cahiers De Droit Fiscal—Trends in Company/Shareholders Taxation: Single or Double Taxation?, 21, 30 (2003).

[161]  Bruner, *supra* note 156, at 7, 78–86.

[162]  *Id.* at 84.

[163]  *Id.* at 84–85.

[164]  *Id.* at 82–83.

[165]  *Id.* at 80–82.

away from the imputation method, while trying to maintain some of its merits.

If we adhere to a functional approach, it is arguable that even though a set of corporate tax reforms in the 2000s implemented different integration methods throughout the world, jurisdictions have all some remarkably similar ends. In almost all jurisdictions, imputation systems have "been replaced by the less accurate reduced dividend tax rate system, which, in a way, is a hybrid of dividend exclusion and the classical system."[166] By lowering tax rates on dividends (but still taxing them), countries were able to keep some virtues of imputation (since it is not eliminated completely); avoid being categorized as discriminatory toward foreign shareholders (by exerting the same "partial dividend taxation" to both foreign and domestic shareholders); maintain reasonable tax revenues; and at the same time, maintain their competitive standing in comparison to other jurisdictions.

Thus, even though the movement away from imputation has been executed in different directions, eventually, all roads have led to Rome. Placing this global movement on our previously noted spectrum, many countries have moved from the imputation end to a midlevel position between imputation systems and classical systems. One commentator specifically stated that "[T]here can be detected a general convergence of countries' company shareholder tax systems in an international setting. The convergence is towards dividend relief systems that are more neutral than imputation internationally yet retain some of the domestic benefits of imputation."[167]

## B. Some specific integration methods adopted by countries

As we have seen, every country has to deal with the following basic tax issue: how (and to what extent) double dividend taxation caused by the overlapping of personal and corporate income taxes should be avoided. In other words, every country has to decide how to deal with integration.

Summarizing the discussion so far, four models can be identified as tax solutions to the above-mentioned tax problem:

1. the classical system (modified or unmodified);
2. the imputation system (full or partial);
3. the reduced taxation of distributed profits (split-rate method, dividend deduction method, zero rate method); and
4. the participation exemption.

---

[166] *Id.* at 77–78. *See also* Vann, *supra* note 160, at 68–69.

[167] Vann, *supra* note 160, at 69.

According to the unmodified classical system, all distributions are taxed as any other items of income. In other words, this system provides no or little relief for personal income tax on dividends. Traditionally both the United States and Switzerland have adopted this method. The assumption of this model is that there is no real double taxation behind taxing distributions.

The modified classical system provides shareholders with relief of various kinds for personal income tax on dividends unconnected with corporate income tax paid on distributions. This is the system adopted by Italy for individuals.

According to the partial imputation system, partial credit is given for shareholder personal income tax liability in respect to corporate income tax paid on distributed dividends. This system is adopted by the United Kingdom and France.

A full imputation system grants partial credit to shareholder personal income tax liability in respect to corporate income tax paid on distributed dividends. In other words, tax-credit shareholders are provided full-tax credit on tax liability for the corporate tax attributable to the dividends they receive. This system has been adopted by Australia. It was also adopted by Italy before 2004.

The reduced taxation of distributed profits model can be split into three submodels: (1) the split-rate method, according to which a lower rate is applied to distributed profits than to retained profits: it was adopted by Germany before it moved to the participation exemption model; (2) the dividend deduction method, which provides a deduction of distributed income from the corporate income tax base; and (3) the zero rate method (or full integration), according to which distributed profits are exempt from corporate income tax.

The fourth model of solving the integration problem is the participation exemption model, under which dividends are not subject to tax for the receiving shareholders. Today, this model is the most common one in **Europe**, due to the fact that European tax law prescribed this method for cross-border EU distributions, and, therefore, many countries also adopted it domestically. For example, in **Italy**, under the current system, corporate shareholders can exclude 95 percent of the dividend from taxable income (partnership shareholders and sole proprietorship shareholders can exclude 60 percent of the dividend from taxable income). However, individual shareholders are subject to a reduced rate on dividends (and capital gains) of 12.5 percent. In other words, Italy adopts the participation exemption model for corporate and partnership shareholders, while it adopts the modified classical system for individuals. It is worth noting that Italy, before 2004, used to adopt a full imputation system, which granted a full integration. The current model provides only a partial integration.

In the **United States,** a dividend tax rate cut, adopted for individuals in 2003, provided a partial integration because it reduced the extent of double taxation of corporate income. However, this system, which is currently under revision, can be criticized with many arguments:

- It does not reach a full integration.
- It creates distinctions among taxation of different forms of income.
- It could give rise, through corporate income tax avoidance (tax shelters and loopholes) and evasion to (quasi) double nontaxation, and only a small part of the benefits given by such tax avoidance activities are recaptured upon payment of dividends.
- It increases incentives for individuals to convert (through tax avoidance) ordinary income to capital gains.
- Price adjustments could grant unjustified (and undeserved) benefits to people who already owned stock before the reform.

As for corporate shareholders, the United States has adopted a dividend received deduction method, which can be considered an evolution of the participation exemption model. Generally, the United States has not adopted this method for dividends from foreign corporations.

# 9

# Selected International Tax Issues[1]

Most basic tax classes do not address international taxation issues. However, as it has been done for business taxation issues in comparative tax work, it is nevertheless necessary and important to briefly deal with some basic international tax issues for (at least) three reasons.

First, many current transactions are cross-border transactions. As such, a basic understanding of international tax issues is certainly useful, let alone required, for any future corporate, tax, or international lawyer.

Second, such knowledge is of particular use to students who find tax law interesting enough to pursue more advanced international tax classes.

Third, the international aspect of income taxation is an area where one would expect to find the most convergence between national systems because this is where tax systems interact directly with each other.

Indeed, as discussed in the conclusion of the book, there is a significant degree of convergence among tax systems, and this has led some observers to argue that a coherent international tax regime exists, embodied in the income tax treaty network, in customary international law and in domestic law.[2]

Others have disputed this characterization, because the persistence of international tax arbitrage (i.e., transactions designed to take advantage of the divergence between national tax laws) proves that convergence is far from complete, even in this area of tax law.[3]

---

[1] This chapter, as far as it relates to policy considerations and the U.S. perspective, is mainly taken from REUVEN S. AVI-YONAH, INTERNATIONAL TAX AS INTERNATIONAL LAW: AN ANALYSIS OF THE INTERNATIONAL TAX REGIME, (CAMBRIDGE UNIVERSITY PRESS 2007).

[2] *Id.* The practical implication of the existence of an international tax regime is that countries are not free to adopt any international tax rules they please but rather operate in the context of the regime, which changes in the same ways that international law changes over time.

[3] H. David Rosenbloom, *Tax Arbitrage and the International Tax "System,"* 53 TAX L. REV. 137 (1998); Reuven S. Avi-Yonah, *Comment on Rosenbloom,* ibid at 167.

Within the field of international tax law, convergence is evident mainly in the treaty network. There are currently over 2500 bilateral income tax treaties, mainly designed to prevent double taxation and fiscal evasion, and they cover most countries in the world (e.g., all OECD countries have treaties with each other). Moreover, all the treaties follow the same OECD and UN models, and that means that about 80 percent of the wordings of the tax treaties are identical. This is a remarkable phenomenon, and it poses significant constraints on a country's tax laws. For example, a country may generally not impose tax on business income earned by a corporation of another country with which it has a tax treaty, unless that corporation has a "permanent establishment" (i.e., a fixed place of business, directly or through a dependent agent) in the taxing country.

The convergence goes beyond the text of the treaties. Courts around the world tend to consult the OECD commentary when interpreting the meaning of tax treaties. Tax administrations in both OECD and non-OECD countries attempt to follow the OECD transfer pricing guidelines in auditing prices from transactions between related parties (with the exception of **Brazil**, which disregards the OECD guidelines in using formulas to allocate profits between related parties, as do the U.S. states).

## I. THE BASIC DISTINCTION: GLOBAL JURISDICTION MODEL vs. TERRITORIAL JURISDICTION MODEL

Despite the significant degree of convergence in international tax law, important differences remain when comparing domestic tax laws as well as other areas outside the income tax treaty network. The most important example is the contrast between global and territorial jurisdictions.

From the perspective of a single country, two basic international tax problems should be dealt with: (i) whether tax residents should be taxed on their worldwide income (or only on the income sourced within the residence country) and (ii) whether nonresidents should be taxed on the income sourced within the (nonresidence) country.

The solution to the above-mentioned issues gave rise to the emergence of two major models: the global jurisdiction and the source (or territorial) jurisdiction models.

Global jurisdiction provides that the residence country has the right to tax its residents on their worldwide income (i.e., residents are taxed on both their domestic source and foreign source income). Theoretically, non-residents should also be taxed on their worldwide income, but this creates a practical obstacle in collecting taxes and may raise theoretical questions relating to jurisdiction of tax (based on customary international law).

Therefore, countries following the global jurisdiction model generally tax nonresidents only on their domestic source income.[4]

Territorial jurisdiction provides that the residence country has the right to tax all persons (residents and nonresidents) only on domestic source income, meaning income derived within the country.[5]

As exceptions, countries that sought to attract foreign investments (usually tax havens) have adopted laws that exempt foreigners from income tax.

This division between global and territorial jurisdictions has historically controlled.

The **United States**, the **United Kingdom,** and **Italy** are examples of countries that chose to follow the global jurisdiction model and, therefore, tax their residents on worldwide income "from whatever source derived" (in the United States, Code § 61).

**France** and **the Netherlands,** as well as other continental European countries, are territorial jurisdictions and, therefore, tax residents and nonresidents only on income derived from sources within their respective taxing jurisdictions.

Other countries tended to fall into the global or territorial camps depending on which European country colonized them.

This division can be seen in the OECD model treaty as well, because it has two alternative articles to prevent double taxation: a foreign tax credit article for global jurisdictions and an exemption article for territorial jurisdictions.

Admittedly, this distinction was always somewhat superficial because global jurisdictions generally do not tax their residents on all foreign source income (e.g., income earned through subsidiaries that they control[6]), and, in practice, source jurisdictions do not limit their taxing powers only to domestic income. For these reasons, a sort of convergence between the two models is observable in practice.


## II. DEFINITION OF RESIDENCE AND SOURCE


Residence and source are fundamental concepts in international tax law that every country is tasked with defining.[7]

---

[4] This approach is preferred by Reuven Avi-Yonah, *see* R. AVI-YONAH, *The Structure of International Taxation: A Proposal for Simplification,* 74 TEX. L. REV. 1301 (1996).

[5] *See* Fadi Shaheen, *International Tax Neutrality: Reconsiderations,* 27 VIRGINIA TAX REV 203 (2007).

[6] There are, however, antideferral regimes.

[7] *"Nothing is more fundamental under the federal income tax system than determining whether an individual is a domestic or a foreign taxpayer." See*

*Residence*–Nearly every country has, as a practical matter, two types of jurisdictions to tax: one applicable to residents and the other to non-residents. This is a consequence of the international tax regime. As a result, the definition of residence for tax purposes plays a significant role in determining the tax consequences, namely, which country has the initial right to tax.

While it is clear why global jurisdiction countries need to define residence (only residents are taxed on their worldwide income), it is less obvious how the definition is relevant for territorial jurisdiction countries. The likely reason is because one of the principal goals of the international tax regime is to allocate income between residence and source countries, in order to meet both the single tax and the benefits principles (described below). In addition, as indicated above, territorial jurisdiction countries are moving away from the pure territorial model and toward hybrid systems; in this case, the distinction between residents and nonresidents is more relevant.

Separate rules are used to determine tax residency of individuals and corporations.

Individuals' residency is generally determined based on physical presence tests, such as the number of days during the year (or longer look-back periods) that they are present in one jurisdiction (*formal model*) and/or based on their substantive connection to the certain jurisdiction (*substantive model*).

Most countries we examine here combine the two models.

In **Italy**, in order for an individual to become a tax resident, she must have either her habitual abode or her domicile within Italy for more than half of a year. Therefore, if a German tourist sojourns on Lake Garda (Italy) for 200 days, she is still not considered an Italian resident, for tax purposes, unless she has a habitual abode or a domicile in Italy.[8]

In **France**, an individual is a resident if she has her permanent home in France, or if she is physically present in the country for 183 days or more.

In **Canada**, there are a series of factors that are taken into account: residence of family members, physical presence, and social and economic ties. In any case, Canada's approach is similar to the French one (and different than the Italian one) in that every person who sojourns in Canada for more than 183 days is considered a resident for tax purposes.

---

David Tillinghast, *A Matter of Definition: "Foreign" and "Domestic" Taxpayers*, 2 INT'L TAX & BUS. LAW. 239 (1984).

[8] Art. 2, T.U.I.R. *See* Maria Cecilia Fregni, *La residenza fiscale delle persone fisiche*, GIURISPRUDENZA ITALIANA 2564 (2009).

Under the **Australian** tax system, if a person sojourns for more than 183 days in Australia, she is presumed to be an Australian resident unless she can prove that her place of abode is outside of Australia. A substantive presence test also applies.

A unique solution is offered by the **United States**. Under Code § 7701, U.S. residency can be obtained by an individual in two ways: by *status* (U.S. citizen or permanent resident[9]) or by *physical presence* (more than 183 days, partially counting days of presence in the two previous years). While the *physical presence* test is common, almost no other country uses the *status* test. This broader "catch" of residents is justified by the fact that the United States provides services to its citizens and permanent residents even if they reside outside the country.[10]

In conclusion, most countries have a more flexible notion of physical domicile that is based on the location of the usual habitual abode (where the person usually lives), where her family is, where her social connections are, where she has a driver's license, and so on. Historically, the United States had a similar rule, and the American States still do. In 1984, the federal government changed the nature of the test primarily due to the administration difficulties associated with it. However, in treaties (signed both by the United States and by other countries), this test for fiscal domicile still exists.

As we have seen in previous chapter, corporations, there are many ways in which tax residency status is obtained: the place of incorporation (United States, United Kingdom, and Sweden), the place of registry, (Sweden, Italy), headquarters or principle or legal office location (Japan and Italy), the place of effective management (United Kingdom), the place of the principle business location (Italy), and the place of residence of the shareholders.

The first three models follow a formalistic legal connection approach, while the other models take into account the substantial connection between the country and the corporation.

Many jurisdictions combine the above-mentioned models. For example, the commonwealth countries (**United Kingdom, Canada, and Australia**), which traditionally focused on the place of effective

---

[9] Green card holders. Reuven S. Avi-Yonah, The Case Against Taxing Citizens (March 25, 2010). U of Michigan Law & Econ, Empirical Legal Studies Center Paper No. 10-009; U of Michigan Public Law Working Paper No. 190. Available at SSRN: http://ssrn.com/abstract=1578272, has pointed out as the United States *"is the only developed country to tax citizens living permanently overseas on their worldwide income. This rule was created at a time when the income tax applied only to the rich and when some of the rich moved overseas to avoid the draft. We do not have a draft any more, the income tax applies to the middle class, and many more US citizens live permanently overseas for non-tax reasons. In a globalized world, citizenship-based taxation is an anachronism which should be abandoned."*

[10] Cook v. Tait, 265 U.S. 47 (1924).

management test, now apply a combined test of substantial connection and place of incorporation. **Germany** and **The Netherlands** combine the two approaches as well.

In **Italy**, art. 73, TUIR, states that *"for income tax purposes, partnerships, companies and entities which for the greater part of the tax period have their legal or administrative office, or their principal business activity in the territory of the state shall be considered resident."*

A unique formalistic solution has been adopted by the **United States**. Under Code § 7701, the residency test for corporations is the *place of incorporation*. In other words, corporations incorporated in one of the American States are considered to be American, whereas corporations incorporated anywhere else in the world are considered to be foreign (nonresident)[11]. The policy rationale for this rule is that a corporation owes some sort of allegiance to the state of incorporation.

Formalistic solutions seems to be apparently better in terms of simplicity. In fact, these solutions are easier to administer than substantial solutions (i.e. administrative costs are lower adopting formalistic rather than substantial solutions); moreover, formalistic solutions also reduce tax litigations as well as other administrative disputes with Tax Authorities.

Compliance costs are also very low adopting formalistic solutions, because taxpayers can easily determine their *status*.

The downside to this, however, is that such formalistic rules are easy to manipulate. In fact, U.S. residents take advantage of this rule, by forming wholly owned foreign corporations to hold their foreign source income, causing a substantial tax deferral. For this reason, many anti-deferral rules have been adopted, which, as a result, have aggravated the Code's complexity.

This is not to say that the place of management and control test cannot be manipulated. On the contrary, this is possible based on the interpretation of the test. For example, if "managed and controlled" refers to the location in which the board of directors conducts its meetings, then it would be relatively easy to set up directors' meetings in an offshore island; this is, after all, one of the primary purposes of airport hotels.

*Source*–The source concept is also fundamental in international taxation. The issue of defining the source of income has to be dealt with by any country with an income tax system (both global jurisdictions and territorial jurisdictions). The concept of source is important both for nonresidents (because it determines whether an item of income of a

---

[11] This rule allowed U.S. corporations to invert. *See* Reuven S. Avi-Yonah, *For Haven's Sake: Reflection on Inversion Transactions*, 95 TAX NOTES 1793 (2002); R. Avi-Yonah, *Law Professor Testimony on Corporate Inversions*, (2002) TNT 201, Nicola Sartori, *Tax Dynamics of (U.S.) Corporate Expatriations*, 10 GLOBAL JURIST, Iss. 3 (Topics), Article 2 (2010).

nonresident is connected with a specific country) and for residents (because it controls the operation of the foreign tax credit—or exemption or deduction—method). Rules governing source are generally identical for residents and nonresidents.

There are two major approaches for defining source: (i) the formal approach (i.e., rules under the control of the taxpayers, as technical or mechanical tests) and (ii) the substantive approach (more geared at the economic substance—not under the full control of the taxpayer).

Usually, the formal approach is adopted for passive (investment) income.[12] This choice is coherent with the benefits principle (passive/investment income is taxed primarily by the residence country, and active/business income is taxed primarily by the source country). As mentioned, the formal approach is easier to administer and enforce, yet taxpayers have a substantial amount of control over the rules and can therefore manipulate them.

The substantive approach is mainly adopted for active income, because countries constantly seek to tax foreigners on their active (business) income sourced within their respective jurisdictions. Again, this follows the basic concept of the benefits principle that attempts to trace the economic source of the income.

Following the above distinction, the **U.S.** Code takes the formalistic approach for interest (sourced according to the residence of the payer), dividends (residence of the payer), resale inventory (location of ownership passage), and capital gains (residence of the seller). On the other hand, the Code adopts the substantive approach for income derived from services (place of performance); rents and royalties (place of use of property); sales of real estate (location of real estate); manufactured inventory (one-half in the location of manufacture and one-half in the location of sale); and, more important, business income (connection with a U.S. trade or business).

In **Italy**, active income of a foreign person is taxed only if the foreign person has a permanent establishment in Italy, as defined in art. 166, TUIR. The concept of permanent establishment involves the presence of a fixed business location (store, office) or the presence of agents with certain types of legal authorities.

The formalistic approach has been also adopted for income from capital (residence of the payer) while a substantive approach has been adopted for income from immovable property (location of the property), income from employment or self-employment (location of the job), and other income category (location of the productive source).[13]

There are exceptions to this general distinction. **Australia**, for example, taxes dividends based on the substantive approach: the source rule

---

[12] See below for a definition of passive and active income.
[13] Art. 23, TUIR.

is the location in which the corporation earns its income rather than the location in which the corporation is resident.

## III. THE TWO PRINCIPLES OF INTERNATIONAL TAXATION: THE SINGLE TAX PRINCIPLE AND THE BENEFITS PRINCIPLE

Before discussing the two main principles of the international tax regime, it is necessary first to address a basic distinction upon which the international tax regime lies: the distinction between active and passive income.

The roots of this distinction trace back to the League of Nations in the 1920s. The League of Nations became aware of the potential double taxation problem that could arise based on the application of domestic laws of different countries. For example, if a resident of Country A (a global jurisdiction country) derives income sourced in Country B, both countries could assert their right to tax the income: Country A based on the residency and Country B based on the source of the income. Therefore, the League of Nations came up with a compromise: the division between active and passive income and the attribution of the former to the source country and the latter to the residence country.

*Active income* is the income over which a taxpayer has control (basically business income and income from services performed).

*Passive income* is the income over which a taxpayer has no control (basically investment income, e.g., dividends, capital gains, royalties).

The two principles that inform the international tax regime are the *"single tax principle,"* which deals with the appropriate level of taxation that should be levied on income from cross-border transactions and the *"benefits principle,"* which deals with the way the taxable base should be divided among various jurisdictions.

According to the *single tax principle*, income from cross-border transactions should be subject to tax once (that is, neither more nor less than once). This principle incorporates the traditional goal of avoiding double taxation, in addition to the developing goal of avoiding double nontaxation (or undertaxation).

The single tax principle can be justified as a goal of the international tax regime, on both theoretical and practical grounds.

From a theoretical perspective, if income derived from cross-border transactions is taxed more heavily than domestic income, the added tax burden creates an inefficiency manifested in the incentive to invest domestically. The corollary also holds true in the reversed scenario where income from cross-border transactions is taxed less heavily than domestic income, in which case this creates an economic inefficiency manifested in the incentive to invest internationally.

In addition, there is a strong equity argument against undertaxation of cross-border income, which applies to income earned by individuals. From an equity perspective, undertaxation of cross-border income violates both horizontal and vertical equity when higher tax rates are imposed on domestic source income.

On a practical level, the single tax principle can be justified because double taxation leads to tax rates that can be extremely high and tend to stifle international investment. Double nontaxation, on the other hand, offers an opportunity to avoid domestic taxation by investing abroad and therefore threatens to erode the national tax base.

The appropriate rate of tax for purposes of the single tax principle is determined by the second principle of international taxation, the *benefits principle*. This principle assigns the primary right to tax active business income to source jurisdictions and the primary right to tax passive income to residence jurisdictions. Therefore, the rate of tax is generally the source rate for active (business) income and the residence rate for passive (investment) income. When the primary jurisdiction refrains from taxation, however, residual taxation by other (residence or source) jurisdictions is possible, and may even be necessary to prevent undertaxation.

This distinction, which stems from the work of the League of Nations in the 1920s, can also be justified on both theoretical and practical grounds.

On a theoretical level, the benefits principle has its logic because individuals are the primary investment income earners, while corporations are the primary business income earners.

It follows that residence-based taxation of individuals makes sense. First, residence is relatively easy to determine in the case of individuals. Second, because most individuals are usually part of only one society, distributive concerns can be addressed more effectively in the country of residence. Third, residence overlaps with political allegiance, and in democratic countries, residence taxation is a proxy for taxation with representation.

In the case of multinational corporations, source-based taxation seems generally preferable.

First, the grounds for taxing individuals on a residence basis do not apply to corporations. In fact, the residence of corporations is frequently difficult to establish and relatively meaningless. Multinationals are not part of a single society, and their income does not belong to any particular society for distributive purposes. Also, multinationals can exert significant political influence in jurisdictions other than the residence jurisdiction of their parent company, therefore causing the concern about taxing foreigners who lack the ability to vote to lose relevancy.

Second, source-based taxation is consistent with a benefits perspective on justifying tax jurisdiction. Source jurisdictions provide significant benefits to corporations that carry on business activities within them. Such benefits include the provision of infrastructure or education, as well as more specific government policies such as keeping the exchange rate stable or interest rates low. These benefits justify source-based corporate taxation in the sense that the host country's government bears some of the costs of providing the benefits that are necessary for earning the income.

On a more pragmatic level, since the source jurisdiction has—by definition—the "first bite at the apple," that is, since it has the first opportunity to collect the tax on payments derived from within its borders, it would be extremely difficult to prevent source jurisdictions from imposing the tax. This is particularly the case for business income derived from large markets, in which case there is little fear that the foreign investor will abandon the market because of source-based taxation. For portfolio investment, however, even large source countries like the United States have tended to abandon it so as not to drive away mobile capital. Thus, business income is a better candidate for source-based taxation than investment income.

## IV. OUTBOUND TRANSACTIONS

There is an outbound transaction when residents of one jurisdiction derive foreign source income. Domestic tax law rules deal with outbound transactions by preventing both double taxation and double nontaxation.

### A. International tax rules that prevent double taxation

Double taxation may arise when both the residence-based and source-based taxing claims are asserted on the same item of income. Historically, the source country, has the "first bite of the apple"; this is why the main burden of providing relief from double taxation falls on the residence country.

There are three major models that have been adopted in order to prevent double taxation.

*Foreign tax credit*–A credit equal to the amount of the foreign taxes paid in the source jurisdiction is granted by the residence jurisdiction to offset the domestic tax liability.

Under this mechanism (adopted by countries following the global jurisdiction approach, such as the **United States**[14] or **Italy**[15]), a taxpayer's

---

[14] *See* REUVEN S. AVI-YONAH, DIANE M. RING & YAVIR BRAUNER, U.S. INTERNATIONAL TAXATION—CASES AND MATERIALS, (Foundation Press: New York, 2005), at 310.

[15] *See* A. Contrino, *Il credito per le imposte assolte all'estero, in* IMPOSTA SUL REDDITO DELLE SOCIETÀ 1033 (F. Tesauro ed., 2007).

foreign income is included in her tax base, yet the initial right of the source country to tax the income is preserved because the residence country provides a credit for the foreign taxes paid. If the foreign tax rate is lower than the domestic rate, a residual domestic tax is collected, but there is no double taxation. If the foreign tax rate is higher than the domestic one, domestic taxes are not due, and, therefore, double taxation has been once again prevented.

By implementing the foreign tax credit, we are also able to maintain foreign export neutrality, an economic concept stemming from the efficiency argument, providing that the choice between domestic and foreign investment should not be affected by tax considerations (and this is efficient).

The foreign tax credit raises many other issues that we will not address here such as what taxes are creditable, how should we treat losses, and what limitations should apply.

*Exemption*–According to this model, adopted mainly by territorial jurisdiction countries (such as **France**), the residence country exempts the foreign item of income, and it is therefore excluded from the tax base.

Countries adopting this model generally provide the exemption for active foreign income only. For example, in **Australia**, an exemption is provided for active foreign income while a credit is provided for passive income. The exemption model is considered the simplest model because the administrative and compliance costs are lower.

The exemption model raises many subissues as well, such as what classes of foreign income should be taxable, how should deductions be allocated, and how should foreign losses be treated.

*Deductions*–According to this third model, foreign taxes would be treated as deductible costs. Many economists argue in favor of implementing the deduction method over the credit method. These methods result in different tax liabilities. A tax deduction is basically an expense that taxpayers may deduct from their gross income, therefore lowering their taxable income, which, in turn, lowers their overall tax burden. The amount of tax savings from the deduction depends on the taxpayer's tax rate. For a corporation subject to a 35 percent tax rate, each dollar of deduction produces 35 cents of tax savings.

The tax credit is different from the deduction in that it reduces the tax owed rather than reducing the amount of taxable income. In other words, under the foreign tax credit method, the tax saving is not dependent on the tax rate that the taxpayer is subject to. It is a dollar-to-dollar reduction. So for the same corporation in the example above, the tax credit produces one full dollar of tax savings, compared to the 35 cents of savings under the deduction method. Thus, even though the foreign tax credit is elective, a credit is preferable to a deduction in almost all cases.

In practice, countries generally grant either an exemption for foreign source income or a credit for foreign taxes paid. In most cases, this is done even in the absence of an income tax treaty. It appears as if a quasi-obligation to prevent double taxation by granting an exemption or a credit has developed and is part of customary international law. Countries would therefore be reluctant to switch to a deduction method.

## B. International tax rules that prevent double nontaxation

*Controlled foreign company rules*—As noted above, resident taxpayers from global jurisdictions could generally avoid tax on foreign source income if the income is earned through a controlled subsidiary. In this case, the tax can be deferred until the income is distributed as a dividend or the taxpayer sells the foreign corporation.

The **United States** was first to put some limits on this phenomenon by enacting the "Foreign Personal Holding Company" (FPHC) rules in 1937, which in some "incorporated pocketbook" cases taxed the U.S. shareholder on a deemed dividend of the FPHC income.

In 1962, the **United States** expanded its antideferral rules significantly by enacting Subpart F, which applied the same deemed dividend approach to passive income and even some types of active income earned through "controlled foreign corporations" (CFCs). The U.S. approach to taxing CFCs was widely followed by many jurisdictions, including pure territorial jurisdictions like for example: Germany (1972), Canada (1975), Japan (1978), France (1980), United Kingdom (1984), New Zealand (1988), Australia (1990), Sweden (1990), Norway (1992), Denmark (1995), Finland (1995), Indonesia (1995), Portugal (1995), Spain (1995), Hungary (1997), Mexico (1997), South Africa (1997), South Korea (1997), Argentina (1999), Brazil (2000), Italy (2000), Estonia (2000), Lithuania (2002) and Israel (2003).[16] The list is likely to expand in the future.

As a result of the wide evolution of the CFC rules, the distinction between global and territorial jurisdictions has lost much of its importance. On one hand, territorial jurisdictions seek to tax passive income earned by their residents from foreign sources through the operation of the CFC rules, and many have endorsed worldwide taxation of individuals. On the other hand, global jurisdictions tend to allow deferral for active income earned by their residents through CFCs, and the recent trend has been to go even further and exempt dividends distributed by CFCs to their parents. This was always the rule in territorial jurisdictions (the so-called "participation exemption"), but it has been

---

[16] For a comparative analysis see BRIAN ARNOLD, THE TAXATION OF CONTROLLED FOREIGN CORPORATIONS: AN INTERNATIONAL COMPARISON, (CTF ACEF: Toronto, 1986) and OECD, CONTROLLED FOREIGN COMPANY LEGISLATION. STUDIES IN TAXATION OF FOREIGN SOURCE INCOME, (OECD 1996).

adopted by global jurisdictions such as the **United Kingdom** and **Japan** and is being considered in the United States.

However, on a more detailed level, significant differences persist even for countries that have adopted CFC rules (and most countries still do not have them). Three major structural variables serve to distinguish between CFC regimes: the level of ownership of a foreign corporation required to designate it a CFC, whether the foreign tax system is relevant to the operation of the CFC rules, and the type of income or activities of the CFC subject to the rule.

On the definition of CFC, most countries (like the United States) require over 50 percent control to designate a foreign corporation as a CFC, but other jurisdictions only require de facto control or even just a substantial interest. France, for example, used to require only ownership of 10 percent or more of the shares, although that was recently changed due to competitive pressure.

On the relevance of the foreign tax system, some countries (like the **United States** and **Canada**) apply their CFC rules to all CFCs wherever they are resident and regardless of the foreign tax rates. However, most countries apply CFC rules only to CFCs resident in low-tax jurisdictions. In defining a low-tax jurisdiction, some countries use a foreign tax rate that is a specified percentage of the domestic rate, but the most common method is a list—either of countries subject to the CFC rules (black list) or of countries exempt from the rules (white list).

On the type of income and activities subject to the rule, **New Zealand** and **Sweden** apply their CFC rules to all income of the CFC, but most countries apply their CFC rules only to specified tainted income or activities.

Under the *transactional approach* (used for example, by the United States, Germany, Canada and Spain), only the tainted income of the CFC is taxable to its shareholders.

Under the *entity or jurisdiction approach* (used, for example, by Japan, France, United Kingdom, New Zealand, Sweden, Finland, Portugal and Italy), either all or none of the CFCs income is taxable. Tainted income typically includes passive income and "base company" income (i.e., active income with no real connection to the jurisdiction in which the CFC is located). Base company income can be limited to income from transactions with the taxing country and/or to income from transactions with related parties (the U.S. approach).

The **Brazilian** example should be mentioned as a hybrid approach, because Brazil is unique in taxing shareholders in all CFCs on all of the CFC's income without regard to either type of income or the foreign tax regime. This policy is under challenge in the Supreme Court.

Finally, countries vary in the way they implement CFC rules. The United States uses a deemed dividend approach, but most countries simply treat the CFC as a pass-through with regard to the income subject to tax (or all income, for countries using the entity approach). Countries generally do not tax the CFC directly because that might violate treaty obligations on taxing a foreign corporation that does not have a permanent establishment in the taxing country.

Overall, the spread of CFC rules presents a remarkable instance of convergence and even direct transplantation. Part of the pressure to converge stems from the fear that tax competition would lead to the establishment of parent corporations in other jurisdictions to avoid the CFC rules (this happened in the United States when public corporations set up new nominal parents in Bermuda, which led to the enactment of Code § 7874 to block such "inversion" transactions and also in the UK where several companies moved to Ireland). However, despite tax competition, countries have not abandoned their CFC rules, which serve an important function in protecting the domestic tax base against shifting income overseas.

*Anti-expatriations rules*—Taxpayers resident in countries adopting the global jurisdiction approach may avoid worldwide taxation by emigrating abroad, formally moving the tax residence to a different country. This can happen both for individuals and for corporations.

For individuals, many jurisdictions provide strict rules regarding the transfer of residence abroad. For example, in **Italy**, Art. 2 of TUIR states that a resident individual who transfers her residence to a tax haven will nevertheless be treated as an Italian resident for tax purposes unless she can prove that the transfer is real (there is an inversion of the burden of proof).

In the **United States,** Code §877 states that expatriating taxpayers have to prove that the expatriation is not tax motivated. Moreover, the expatriation is presumed to be tax motivated if the taxpayer meets a very low asset threshold.

There are rules governing migration of corporations as well. In most of the considered countries, if a corporation transfers its residence to a different country, all of the unrealized capital gains are taxable.

The **United States**, after considering the formal definition of residence, has also adopted anti-inversion rules. A corporate inversion (or corporate expatriation) is a "paper" transaction[17] through which a multinational

---

[17] We refer to a "paper" transaction since it reflects only a formal legal change, which does not involve any change economically relevant (like, for example, a change in the location of the production, an elimination of the U.S. service positions, a relocation of the management headquarters, etc.). Therefore, as it has been correctly underlined, the inversion transaction is neither a "runaway pant" (i.e., a corporation with U.S. manufacturing operations shutting down those operations and shifting production to a foreign location) nor an "outsourcing" (i.e., a corporation eliminating service positions in the United States and hiring service workers in a foreign location). *See* Avi-Yonah, *For Haven's Sake: Reflection on Inversion Transactions, supra,* note 11; R. Avi-Yonah, *Law Professor Testimony on Corporate Inversions, supra,* note 11; Michael S. Kirsch, *The Congressional Response to Corporate Expatriations: the Tension between Symbols and Substance in the Taxation of Multinational Corporations,* 24 Va. Tax Rev. 475, 2005; and Sartori, *supra,* note 11.

group reorganizes its ownership structure in a way so that the parent corporation of the group becomes a foreign corporation (instead of an American one).[18] Usually the new parent corporation is located in a so-called "tax haven" (i.e., a country with low or no tax and/or whose tax authorities do not exchange information with other countries).[19]

The main (presumably only) reason why a corporation may choose to invert is a reduction of the corporate taxes[20] because it would then be easy to bypass the CFC legislation, it would facilitate "earning stripping" and "transfer pricing" practices, and it may facilitate "treaty shopping."

Therefore, with the American Jobs Creation Act of 2004, an anti-inversion legislation was enacted and included in Code § 7874. According to this provision, if, after a corporate inversion, a U.S. corporation's shareholders hold 80 percent or more of a foreign corporation's stock, and if a foreign corporation or its affiliated group does not have substantial business activities in the foreign corporation's country of incorporation, then—for tax purposes—the newly formed foreign corporation is treated as a corporation resident in the United States.[21] By doing so, the three main tax advantages mentioned above are nullified because the corporation will be treated as a foreign corporation following the inversion. This rule has been recently strengthened by reissuing Reg. Section 1.7874-2T.[22] The temporary regulation addresses the various

---

[18] Treasury (2002). Corporate Inversion Transactions: Tax Policy Implications., at 1, *available at* http://www.treas.gov/press/releases/docs/inversion.pdf, defined the inversion transaction as "a transaction through which the corporate structure of a U.S.-based multinational group is altered so that a new foreign corporation, typically located in a low or no-tax country, replaces the existing U.S. parent corporation as the parent of the corporate group."

[19] On the concept of "tax haven," *see* Dammika Dharmapala & James R. Hines, *Which Countries Become Tax Havens?* 2006 *available at* SSRN: http://ssrn.com/abstract=952721.

[20] Nevertheless, it must be noted that American multinationals claim that the new ownership structure would increase operational flexibility, would afford them a better cash management, and would enhance access to international capital markets. *See* Hale E. Sheppard, *Fight or Flight of U.S.-Based Multinationals Businesses: Analyzing the Causes for, Effects of, and Solutions to the Corporate Inversion Trend*, 23 NW. J. Int'l. L. & Bus· 551 (2003), at 554.

[21] Moreover, expatriated entity recognizing gain from the transfer of stock or other property are taxable in full at the maximum corporate tax rate, without any loss, credit, or other tax attributes' offset. Finally, for ten years after the corporate inversion, the expatriated entity is taxed without any offset on the gains on transfers or licenses to a foreign corporation or to a foreign related person.

[22] This is because Treasury, D.o., *Earnings Stripping, Transfer Pricing and U.S. Income Tax Treaties*, 2007, at 4, declared that "*the Treasury Department believes these regulations are an effective implementation of Congressional intent. Nonetheless, there is currently a need for further published guidance under section 7874, and the existing temporary and proposed regulations must be finalized. These*

transactions that involve foreign partnerships as foreign acquirers. The new temporary regulation also removes some of the examples and safe harbors that were previously included.[23]

*Transfer pricing rules*—According to transfer pricing rules, transactions between related parties may be adjusted by the tax authorities to the terms that would have been negotiated had the parties been unrelated to each other. The standard applied in all tax treaties to the transfer pricing problem of determining the proper allocation of profits between related entities is the so-called "arm's-length standard," which has been the governing rule since the 1930s.


## V. INBOUND TRANSACTIONS


Inbound transactions are transactions in which foreigners derive domestic source income. So, if an Italian resident derives income from U.S. sources, this would be a U.S. inbound transaction. From a U.S. perspective, the main issue is whether or not to tax foreigners on their domestic income. For these types of transactions, the concept of source income (explained above) is extremely relevant because it defines the connection that an item of income must have with a specific country in order for it to be characterized as domestic source income, potentially subject to tax in the domestic jurisdiction.

Once established that a foreign person has domestic source income, the source country has to determine how to tax this income. In this regard, the distinction between active and passive income plays a major role in determining how the foreign person is taxed.

For example, in the **United States,** foreign taxpayers are subject to tax on active income, derived from sources within the United States (i.e., business income effectively connected with a U.S. trade or business), on a net basis as if the income was earned by a domestic business.

On the other hand, "fixed or determinable, annual, or periodic" income (FDAP), which includes passive income, is nominally taxed on a gross basis at a relatively high rate (30 percent), but a combination of source rules, statutory exemptions, and tax treaties generally results in such income being taxed only when earned by foreign businesses as part of their active business operations; FDAP income is generally not taxed when earned by portfolio investors.

---

*efforts are in process. Because the guidance process and our study of the effectiveness of this provision are ongoing, the fourth report requested by AJCA will be issued separately".*

[23] For an in depth analysis of the U.S. anti-inversion rule in light of the new temporary regulations, see Lee A. Sheppard, *News analysis: taking the good with the bad in the anti-inversion rule*, 57 TAX NOTES INT'L 627 (2010).

# VI. TAX TREATY MODELS: OECD, UN, AND U.S. MODELS

As noted earlier, there are more than 2500 bilateral income tax treaties around the world. The income tax treaties are extremely similar in their wording because they are based on common models.

Income tax treaties have various goals:

1. Prevention of double taxation (even if, from a practical perspective, domestic laws already prevent international double taxation with the foreign tax credit, exemption, or deduction models);
2. Allocation of taxable income between the residence and source country;
3. Definition of residence, which may be very useful in double residency cases;
4. Imposition of cooperation (exchange of information) between countries in order to avoid tax avoidance and, to a certain extent, double nontaxation.

The most famous tax treaty models are the following:

1. OECD Model: adopted by European countries as a starting point of negotiations;
2. UN Model: adopted by developing countries as a starting point of negotiations;
3. U.S. Model: adopted by the United States as a starting point of negotiations.

Income tax treaties are very similar, and they generally have the same structure: rules defining the scope; definitional and interpretation rules; allocation rules; anti-avoidance rules (foreign tax credit or exemption), nondiscrimination, mutual procedure rule[24]; and exchange of information rule.

Treaties shift the burden of taxation from source to residence country in two ways. The main mechanism for active income is the definition of permanent establishment. Treaties generally bar source based taxation unless an enterprise of the other state has a permanent establishment in the source country. The main mechanism for passive income is a reduction in withholding its source.

Finally, it is worth describing one . . . of the most important provisions of income tax treaties: the tie-breaker rule. In order to avoid double taxation and to facilitate the allocation of income between the source and residence countries, Art. 4, para. 2 of the OECD Model, which is similar to both the UN and the U.S. Models, provides the so called tie-breaker rules, which clarify which of the two contracting States the person concerned is deemed to be a resident in.

---

[24] EHAB FARAH, *Mandatory Arbitration of International Tax Disputes: A Solution in Search of a Problem*, 9 FLA. TAX REV. 703 (2009).

If an individual, according to the domestic laws of the two contracting States, is resident in both of the contracting States, paragraph 2 provides that she will be considered a resident of the State where she has a *permanent home available to her*. According to the OECD Commentary, any form of home may be taken into account (house or apartment belonging to or rented by the individual). The most important factor is that the individual has arranged to have the dwelling available to her at all time, continuously.

What happens if the individual has a permanent home in both the contracting States or in neither? This person is resident in the State where her personal and economic relations are closer (*center of vital interests*). According to the OECD Commentary, center of vital interest means the place where a person has her family and social relations; her occupation; her political, cultural or other activities; her place of business; or the place from which she administers her property. These circumstances must be examined as a whole, even if considerations based on personal acts must receive special attention.

An inevitable question follows: what happens if an individual has a center of vital interests in both of the contracting States or in neither?

In this case, the state of residence would be the contracting State where the individual has a *habitual abode*.

What happens if the individual has a habitual abode in both of the Contracting States or in neither? In this case, preference is given to the State of *nationality*.

Eventually, if the individual is a national of both contracting States or of neither, then the competent authorities of the contracting States will try to settle the question by *mutual agreement*.

Paragraph 3 of Art. 4 of the OECD MC deals with entities (whether legal persons or not). In particular, it deals with cases where an entity is a resident of both Contracting States. The OECD MC follows the "substance-over-form" principle in that if an entity, according to the domestic law of the Contracting States, is resident in both states, then the state of residence, for the purpose of tax treaties, will be the place where the company is *actually managed*. This is the place where the key management is located, and commercial decisions are made. According to the OECD Commentary, it is the place where the most senior persons make the decisions. If the double residence problem cannot be resolved, here, too, the mutual agreement procedures are available.

While the UN Model is similar to the OECD MC with reference to dual income taxation of companies, the U.S. Model is quite different. Under Paragraph 3, Art. 4 of the U.S. Model, a dual resident company is resident under the laws of the country in which it is created or organized. The difference is justified by the fact that under U.S. laws, corporations are residents of the United States only if they are incorporated within the country.

# Conclusion

By providing this brief survey, we have attempted to clarify that while divergence is predominant in individual tax matters, there is some degree of convergence in the corporate tax area and even more noticeable in international tax matters. This is not surprising because it is in these areas that globalization operates most directly, and corporations are more flexible than individuals when it comes to switching jurisdictions.

Nevertheless, the debate between functionalists and culturalists is far from over. Even where convergence does exist, it is frequently superficial and masks a myriad of differences (which are duly exploited to create tax arbitrage opportunities). Moreover, functionalists and culturalists differ fundamentally on the value of harmonization; functionalists see it as a desirable goal (and sometimes even as proof of survival of the fittest and the "end of history"), while culturalists decry it as a disaster. This debate has been going on since Herodotus (a culturalist) and Thucydides (a functionalist), and as we are unlikely to resolve it, you need to form your own opinion.